A Quiet Life

A Quiet Life

Martha Robertson

Whittles Publishing

Typeset by
Whittles Publishing Services

Published by
Whittles Publishing,
Roseleigh House,
Latheronwheel,
Caithness, KW5 6DW,
Scotland, UK

ISBN 1-870325-71-0

The publisher acknowledges subsidy from the Scottish Arts
Council towards the publication of this volume.

Printed in Malta by Interprint Limited

Contents

For my mother and father, and
all like them who dedicated
their lives to the service.

Foreword

Some years ago I had a visit from an old friend of my mother, who in the general conversation revealed a few small but surprising facts about my mother which I had never known. She was a very reticent lady, my late mother.

After her visit I recalled the conversation and realised how little I really knew about my mother's early life. I felt very sad about that. On the spur of the moment I decided I didn't want my two granddaughters to be ignorant of my life so I picked up my pen and started to write all I could remember. I found I had a long, clear, and I hope accurate memory, apart from the first few years.

From that, the book you are about to read evolved. I have never been one to keep a diary. If ever I started one it fizzled out before the end of January, so all I have written is purely as I remember it.

This is not only something to leave for Sarah and Ellen, but a tribute to the many families who chose to pursue a life lived for the most part in places where few would choose to live. Lighthouses are of necessity mostly in the remotest of locations. The womenfolk especially suffered hardships and often had to part with not only their husbands but their children as well. In spite of this, I feel sad when I pass one of these now sightless beacons, all the warmth and humanity removed and controlled by a mindless computer.

Martha Robertson

Inchkeith

I saw Inchkeith again last week. The tiny island humped out of the misty firth, the lighthouse perched precariously on top. Leaning back in my comfortable seat in the air-conditioned, double-glazed high-speed train, I mused on my beginnings as we sped smoothly and almost silently towards the Forth Bridge.

My father, James Scott Petrie, known to all as Jimmy, was born in Arbroath. My grandfather, William, was a lighthouse keeper, and the father of six children. Wee Jimmy led his mother a merry dance, possessing a strong streak of obstinacy along with a healthy curiosity which kept him in constant hot water at school and home. He had a penchant for taking things to pieces to see how they worked and he grew up determined to be the best engineer who ever lived. When he left school at fourteen, he was apprenticed to a firm of engineers in Carnoustie where he became a skilled fitter and turner, with a natural ability to deal with mechanical problems. I have known him to work on a problem, perhaps for days. Eventually he would proceed to put right something that had defied others. I never saw him beaten.

My father in his young days was a thin wiry man with the black hair and eyes characteristic of the Petries, and the slightly bowed legs of which none of us were particularly enamoured. When war broke out in 1914 he was still serving his time in Carnoustie. After his apprenticeship he worked in Beardmore's munition factory at Parkhead in Glasgow, gaining promotion to become foreman of his "shop." He must have been considered of better use in that capacity than as a soldier, as he was never called up, despite being a fit young man.

Inchkeith, about 1924.

It was at Beardmore's, hardly the most romantic of places, that he first saw Cissie, the girl he was eventually to marry. His work mates had been teasing him about getting married to a girl he was courting. To stop it, he had looked at the girls who had been drafted into munitions, picked out a new, rather sad-looking girl and announced, "That's the girl I'm going to marry!" He asked the young lady out and soon realised he really did want her company. He proceeded to court her, and had no compunction about leaving his girl in Carnoustie in the lurch. Once he made up his mind, nothing would stand in his way.

Cissie's real name was Martha Johnson, (her older brother, Jimmie, couldn't get his tongue round "sister") and she was born and bred in the east end of Glasgow. Her childhood had not been entirely happy. Her father was fond of the bottle, never held a job for long, and died at the early age of forty-five. Her mother had worked most of her married life to help keep the family, so Cissie missed a lot of schooling. She was absent a great deal, taking care of her younger sister, Jean, and an adopted wee brother, Davie. As soon as she could, she left school and found work in a milliner's, where she worked long hours, six days a week. During the war, she was directed into munition work, gaining a certificate stating that she was a proficient turner, something she was always proud of.

She became engaged to a fine young man, John Bolling. He was called up to serve in the army and Cissie went into town with his mother and young sister to watch him march proudly through the streets to the railway station. He was killed shortly after arriving in the trenches.

It was some time after John's death that my father set his sights on this quiet, sad girl. He needed all his charm and determination to win her as she was in no mood for romance. It wasn't until the war had been over for some time that he eventually persuaded her to accept his ring, on St. Valentine's Day, 1920.

In the aftermath of war it had soon become evident that there would be a slump, so my father had wisely applied for the secure post of lighthouse keeper. He was readily accepted as his father had been in the service before him, and he served his time as a supernumerary, or "learner" at various stations throughout Scotland before being appointed as assistant keeper at Inchkeith in November, 1920. Only single men were accepted as learners in those days, so it wasn't until March of the following year that the marriage took place in Carntyne Old Parish Church in Shettleston. They spent a few days on honeymoon with my father's brother, Jack and no wedding photographs were taken. It wasn't a romantic start to a marriage, but it lasted for forty-eight years.

My city-bred mother left the old life to embark on an entirely alien life style. She had only been outside Glasgow when she was occasionally sent "doon the watter" to Rothesay where she worked during her holidays at her aunt's boarding house. As she travelled to Edinburgh with her new husband she saw little of the capital because they went from the railway station to Leith docks, where they embarked in a small boat for Inchkeith.

The short voyage across the Firth of Forth on that bright breezy spring day must have made Cissie wonder if she had done the right thing. She was glad when the boat reached the shelter of the island. On the pier stood the welcoming committee of lighthouse keepers and coastguards with their wives, and the soldiers who manned the gun batteries which had been installed in the nineteenth

Inchkeith. This is an unusual lighthouse which resembles a castle. The blinds have been drawn because the tower would have been set on fire if the sun had shone on the lenses. I lived in the house that is in shadow.

century to protect the capital. Hands reached out to help Cissie ashore. Neddy, the island's donkey, stood patiently as Cissie's few belongings were piled on to his cart before the small procession set off up the steep winding road to the lighthouse station. The lighthouse was a grim grey building, looking like a castle with its mock battlements. Perhaps it was built like that in imitation of the castle built by Mary, Queen of Scots which at one time stood on the site.

My mother's house was on the ground floor of this edifice. The house was split in two by a common staircase winding up the tower to the light room, so that anyone could meet my mother on her way from the kitchen to the bedroom. It was small and very basic, having no electricity, gas or piped water, but my mother was unperturbed. What you never have you never miss, she used to say.

As she surveyed the kitchen, she probably thought, "This is mine to do with as I please." The room was already furnished with the essentials that were provided at every station to save on packing and transportation. There was a big deal table with two leaves, a sturdy dresser and several plain wooden chairs. Dominating the room was a big, gleaming black range in which blazed a welcoming fire. No self-respecting lighthouse wife would dream of letting another come to a cold house. Someone always had a fire kindled and a meal ready, even when a family was simply returning from the annual holiday. It was a lovely custom, much appreciated after the long tedious journeys involved in reaching the outlandish places where lighthouses were needed.

Soon the house began to look like home as my mother added her few wedding presents: a couple of sepia prints of country scenes, a big wooden mantelpiece clock and a home-made fireside rug. That evening the newlyweds sat in the comfortable armchairs which were about the only items they had bought before leaving Glasgow, and which were to be with them for the whole of their lighthouse service.

It must have taken my mother some time to adapt to the new way of life. She had been accustomed for years to doing washing with a scrubbing board and the tiresome wringing out of each item by hand. Now she had to learn to peg everything out very firmly if she wanted to avoid losing some article in the North Sea. Shopping lists were planned very carefully. In good weather she could go on a shopping expedition to Edinburgh, courtesy of the supply boat that made weekly trips to the island, but in inclement weather she could only hand her list to the boatman. She had to keep a good store of emergency supplies in case it was too stormy for the boat.

My mother was a good baker and could turn out decent plain meals. However, she blanched one day when my father came in and threw on the table a dead hen, its thrawn neck lolling unpleasantly. Nonchalantly he announced, "That'll do for tomorrow's dinner!" My mother all but screamed in horror. Where previously she had only seen chickens in the windows of the Glasgow butcher's shop, this bird was complete. My father laughed and gave her a lesson in how a lightkeeper's wife dealt with such an everyday chore. Her face screwed up in a grimace of disgust, my mother watched as he plucked and gutted the fowl. Next time he stood watching and guiding as she tackled the job. My mother had a great deal of smeddum, so she soon adapted to this and the other earthier facets of life she found in the lighthouse service.

The newlyweds had scarcely settled down to married life when a new and unexpected problem arose. Three months after the wedding my mother realised she was pregnant. I use the word realised because there was no doctor on hand to discover the great news. The couple were delighted. The problem was, how to cope with a first pregnancy on an island in the middle of the Firth of Forth, with the prospect of bad weather during the waiting months? The baby was due in January. There was no amenity such as an ante-natal clinic and my mother had to hope she wouldn't miscarry or have a premature baby in the middle of a storm. She had kept herself occupied in the long dark evenings, sewing and knitting a layette. Fortunately she was healthy, so she was able to travel to Glasgow to have the baby under the care of her family doctor whom she had known for many years.

I made my appearance at my Uncle Jack's house in No. 343 Wellshot Road, Tollcross, at seven-thirty in the evening of Sunday, 22nd January, 1922, weighing in at ten and a half pounds and almost killing my poor mother. I have wondered on occasion why I wasn't born at my Granny's, who was a qualified midwife. Perhaps it wasn't ethical, perhaps it was to appease the Petrie family, who had not exactly given my mother a warm welcome into their family.

When the statutory three weeks confinement was over and I had been christened,

At Inchkeith in 1924—the author!

I was taken to Inchkeith. It was a novelty for the island inhabitants to have a baby in their midst, so I was fussed over by everyone and grew to take it for granted that I was the centre of the universe. I remained completely unaware that throughout my formative years I was being deprived of something precious and essential to my well-being—playmates. My memory of those first five years is hazy. I remember emotions rather than facts—fear, pride, pain, and wonderment. I don't remember ever feeling lonely!

I was about three years old when I first encountered fear. The lighthouse station, houses, washhouse, gardens and workshops, were encompassed by a high wall broken at intervals by gates leading to the pier, the midden, and the coastguard station. These gates were normally kept closed, due to the proximity of the cliffs. My mother was working indoors and I asked if I could go out and watch my father at work. Reluctant, but knowing how little I had to keep me amused, she said, "Yes, but don't wander about, and come straight back in if your Daddy's too busy!" I went to find my father and the other keepers painting doors. I watched for a minute or two until my father said, "Away you go, back to the house before you get covered in paint." I wandered away and forgot I was supposed to go indoors. I spied a gate standing invitingly open showing a patch of grass covered with daisies.

Some time later, my father went into the house for a cup of tea. My mother, looking up from the pot of soup she was stirring, said "Where's Mattie?" Panic followed when they realised I was missing. They both rushed outside to search for the wanderer. The station wasn't big, so it only took a minute to discover the open gate. There I was, picking daisies on the brink of an almost sheer drop into the North Sea, my back to the frantic pair. Realising that if they called out to me I might lose my balance and fall headlong to doom, my father crept quietly up behind me, grabbed my dress and hauled me to a safer spot. It was some time before they recovered from the fright. I was scared out of my wits, too, but only because I was grabbed suddenly from behind. I have no recollection of the incident, but I do recall the terrible feeling of fear.

Sadly, that episode left me with a fear so deep-rooted that I have never been able to eradicate it from my mind. From that time, it was impressed on me that it was dangerous to go anywhere alone. The lesson was so well taught, that to this day I have a strong aversion to being alone for any length of time. I become overwhelmed by a strong feeling of impending doom and disaster.

The teenage daughter of the Principal Keeper, home for a holiday, kept me amused one day to allow my mother to do her washing in peace. I watched intently as she made a coat for my doll from a tiny piece of fur and scraps from her mother's workbox. The style was copied from her own fashionable coat, with a rolled fur collar sweeping round the neck and down to fasten at the waist with a single huge button. She gave me her mother's button box to rake through for a suitable button, and I almost burst with pride when she said, "I couldn't have chosen a better one myself." I was full of it when my mother came to collect me, and boasted to all and sundry until I was told sharply not to be so prideful. I cherished that wee coat for years until both it and the doll disintegrated.

Pain I remember with great clarity. My mother usually took me to the wash-house with her to keep me safe while she worked. I'd play contentedly with my doll in the warm steamy room while my mother filled the boiler, stoked the fire, and washed and scrubbed, rinsed and wrung out the clothes, before hanging the now spotless sheets and shirts on the line. I loved the smells and the steam that billowed round the stone-walled room, and the sounds of the water gurgling as the white clothes boiled in the great cauldron.

One day, however, I was left alone in the house for a short time. I must have had a cold or I wouldn't have been left unattended. Before she went out, my mother made sure the big fireguard was firmly in place and I had plenty of picture books. I was an unusually quiet, trustworthy child, not given to disobedience. For some time I sat engrossed in my books. Alas, temptation was put my way in the shape of a bowl of oranges. Their bright colour plus the fact they were a rare treat, tempted me to take one. I was only four, so peeling it took a lot of time and effort. It tasted lovely, until I was suddenly smitten with guilt. Looking round for a hiding place for the peel, I concluded that the only way was to burn the evidence. The top of the range had a round cover which I had seen my mother lift off with a short curved implement. By standing on tiptoe I could just reach over the guard and managed to take off the cover. I threw the handful of peel towards the fire when my foot slipped and I lost my balance, my hand landing on the hot hob alongside the bits of peel. My screams brought my mother running. I remember very clearly spending the rest of the day curled up in the big chair, nursing a throbbing hand which was wrapped in bandages soaked in a paste of baking soda. I decided there and then that a life of crime wasn't for me, as the pain of what my mother called God's punishment was too much to bear.

A happier memory is of a party held at the island's coastguard station. The wee community missed no opportunity to hold a ceilidh. One of the coastguards, an Englishman, had visitors from his native land who had more sophisticated ideas. It was announced that there would be a fancy dress party. My father was keen and persuaded my normally shy mother to contrive some kind of inconspicuous costume for them both and to enter into the spirit of the party.

As the entire population apart from the duty keeper would be there, it was necessary for me to attend as well. I was struck dumb by the babble of noise, and the colourful costumes, including the one worn by my normally quietly-dressed mother. I sat entranced, staring wide-eyed at the spectacle before me. I remember the vision of two people dressed as Harlequin and Columbine, and I can still conjure up the feeling of wonder and a misty image of those beautiful costumes in all their delicate shades of lilac, blue and pink.

These are my only true memories of that time; all else is what I gleaned throughout the years from my father as my mother was always too busy to sit down and blether. So I grew, watched constantly by my worried mother and father, and spoiled by the rest of the community. My mother hadn't much time to spare for playing with me. I accepted the fact that I was left to my own resources as I had never known anything different. My mother used to say that she sometimes felt ashamed because I seemed so content. She would put me in the bedroom for an afternoon nap, leaving me with a favourite picture book, and when she looked in later, I'd be sound asleep, the book over my face.

When I was two, my mother sadly miscarried. Fortunately, she was none the worse, as a doctor was able to come over and attend to her. He told her it would have been a boy. Two years later, she successfully gave birth to my wee sister Jean, the last of my mother's babies. The only time I heard my mother expressing regret for things past was when she spoke of "wee Jimmy," the son she never had. I vowed that if I was ever blessed with a son I'd call him Jimmy. Many years later I was able to fulfil that vow.

Jean was born in Glasgow but in my Granny's house in "the back road" as we called Old Shettleston Road. I was four and a bit, but I have absolutely no recollection of the event or the year that followed. Living in a little world of my own, I paid scant attention to other people. My old pram came into use for the new arrival. It was deep and the centre section of the "floor" lifted out, revealing a cavity used for storing extra nappies and other necessities. Later, as the baby grew to be a toddler, this section served as footroom, doing away with the necessity for a pushchair. Jean was fed from a peculiar, banana-shaped bottle with a teat at one end and another at the opposite end. This acted as a valve to prevent a vacuum stopping the flow of milk. The pram and bottles travelled with us until my mother gave up thinking there might be another addition to her wee family.

When Jean was a few months old we all went to Glasgow for the annual holiday. We returned to Inchkeith with an unwanted extra, whooping cough. My cousin Mae, a year younger than me, had been incubating the dreaded germ. Having been reared in almost complete isolation from other children we were particularly vulnerable. There was no vaccine so we both suffered greatly. The next month or two were both frightening and wearing for my mother, who had to cope with us alone most of the time, my father having to sleep during the day to be fit for the night watches. Jean, being so tiny, was in the greatest danger. How she survived was mainly due to her own strong constitution and my mother's ability as a nurse. When Jean started a whooping fit, I came out in sympathy so that while my mother was helping Jean I had to hold on to her skirts for support and hope for the best. Jean would turn almost purple and I wasn't much better. To add to my mother's distress, she was unable to get medical help if things took a turn for the worse. Somehow we all survived and with no lasting after effects.

Jean grew apace after that. She was a much more lively child than her big sister, always smiling and ready for mischief. Unfortunately, she was too young to be a playmate for me. So the winter passed uneventfully, my mother busying herself with her daily chores. Every day the range had to be black-leaded before she could light the fire for breakfast. She swept, dusted, baked, washed and ironed in an interminable round. In the dark evenings my parents sat by the fire, my mother's knitting needles clicking while my father read bits out of old papers. Sometimes they worked on clippy rugs, which were cosy underfoot. The base was a clean coal sack which, opened out, was just the right size for a fireside rug. They cut old coats and dresses into workable lengths to be set into the canvas by a special tool, pushed through the sack, where the clipping was gripped firmly and pulled part of the way back through to the other side. It was hard work and took many evenings to complete. All the dirt and dust imaginable collected in its deep pile and the only way to get rid of it was by vigorous shaking; no easy task, as it seemed to weigh a ton.

Jean being too small, I was virtually still a lone child. I didn't have many toys, mainly my beloved doll and a toy tea set. So I invented some friends. After tea my mother would set up a small card table against one kitchen wall. There I would entertain my "friends," Heely, Keely and Gasty. They were my own three shadows cast on the wall by the three flickering brass paraffin lamps illuminating the room. Apparently I held long conversations with these shadows to which my mother and father listened, often with sadness in their hearts for their lonely daughter.

On another holiday in Glasgow a year after we had whooping cough, my mother was happy to be in the bosom of her family and the hustle and bustle of the city. On the assumption that lightning doesn't strike twice in the same place, she had no qualms about her two little ones catching any germs. She was wrong. Mae had been incubating measles and soon after we went back to the island, Jean and I both began to look peaky and watery-eyed. We had picked up the bug. We were kept in a darkened room with the shutters closed and the lamp shaded at night in the belief that there was a danger of eye damage in strong light. Our unbearably itchy rash was relieved by applications of a lotion made with the old faithful standby, baking soda.

I had one other medical problem which had to be dealt with during my father's spell at Inchkeith. I had to go to Glasgow to have tonsils and adenoids removed. I had driven my mother daft by going about with my mouth open, a habit for which I was constantly checked, some times with a smack. When none of these reprimands cured me, my mother realised I needed to see a doctor. We travelled to Glasgow where Dr. Dunlop diagnosed what my mother had suspected. "I'll do it tomorrow," he said. The operation was performed on my Granny's well-polished front room table. I was laid on a clean sheet, a few drops of chloroform on a wad of gauze was held over my face, and the offending organs were whipped out. A few minutes later I came to, none too happy, but cured.

My father had to fight boredom. Work on maintenance of the station took up a lot of his time, but when he wasn't asleep on off-duty periods he was restless. Like most lighthouse keepers he took up hobbies. His great interest at that time was wireless and he built crystal sets. The wee house was always cluttered with bits of wire, and coils and mysterious pieces of metal.

Photography was his other great love. He had one of those big wooden cameras with a black cloth under which he stuck his head. The plate then had to be developed, so that besides the wireless clutter my mother had to thole developing trays and bottles of fluid, not to mention dark curtains hung over the windows for a makeshift darkroom. Those accoutrements travelled with us until my father lost interest and became enthusiastic about some new hobby.

My mother didn't have time for what she called useless jobs. Her "hobbies" were knitting socks and jerseys for all of us and making simple dresses for me on her sewing machine, not because she enjoyed it, but because it saved money. She was by no means an expert seamstress, but made clothes out of her old frocks. I, being none the wiser, was quite happy to wear them. Even if I had complained, I'd have been told, "You're wearing it anyway."

Sometimes I went shopping with my mother. Weather permitting, she and the other ladies were able to spend a day in Edinburgh. The ladies would set off armed with oilskin coats, warm clothes, and long lists of messages. It was not unusual to see us in brilliant sunshine and warm weather, walking along Princes Street loaded with wet-weather clothes. Five miles across the firth in a small boat could be very unpleasant clad only in a light summer dress.

Most of the shopping was done in Leith where the shops were smaller and prices more in keeping with my mother's purse. If time and finances allowed, we took a tram to the city centre to window shop and have a cup of tea in Crawford's. Before the return trip it was wise to check that nothing had been forgotten, as it might be weeks before another trip was possible.

On rare occasions we went to Burntisland. The little Fife town where King Alexander fell over a cliff to his death, held the coastguard station nearest to Inchkeith, and sometimes "our" coastguards paid a visit there, taking with them my mother (and father, if he was off-duty). It should have been a real treat for the two of them, but on their first trip I ruined their pleasure, albeit unwittingly. We had just sat down to a lovely meal when I started to scream. Nothing would pacify me and I was unable to say what was wrong, my shouted words being unintelligible. My mother was first worried, then furious, as I wrecked the peace of the afternoon. I was eventually banished to the kitchen, where amid subsiding sobs I ate my tea more or less peacefully, while the others ate in the front room. My mother's food tasted like sawdust and her anger smouldered all the way home. I was by then in a more tranquil frame of mind, but that didn't last long. As soon as we were in the privacy of our own house, my mother exploded. Without asking again what was the cause of my upset, she gave me a good and well-deserved walloping. Recovering from my spanking, I was eventually able to reveal that I had taken fright at the appearance of the teenage son of the house, who had come home from a scout meeting in his uniform. I had never seen a boy in a kilt and it had scared the wits out of me. A similar incident occurred on another visit to the same family. Jean, only eighteen months old, took exception to a man sporting a bushy black beard. She screamed hysterically and my mother was so embarrassed she never ventured back to Burntisland.

I saw little of my father during those first few years. The three men kept watch between sunset and sunrise, then from nine until one each day they did maintenance work. In the afternoons two of them were usually in bed, the third standing a daylight watch for fog or incidents at sea. When time allowed, he was a wonderful father, playing the games I invented as though a child himself. I loved him dearly. Sometimes, he entertained me in ways that caused my mother to frown disapprovingly. Like most lighthouse keepers, he kept hens. These lived in a covered run where they were fed and had the shelter of a henhouse, while having access to the island grass by means of a small hole in the wall. My father developed a habit of facing up to a young cockerel while feeding the hens. He'd act like one himself, crowing and flapping his arms like wings, advancing and retiring, incensing the bird until it became angry. I stood outside the netting watching with great interest. My mother found out and was as angry as the cockerel, in forming my father that he was asking for trouble. He just laughed, ignored her warnings and continued to play his daft game at feeding times. The cockerel began to watch for him, advancing towards him ready for action. One day when my father unwarily turned his back to feed the hens, he was set upon from the rear by a feathered fury. He needed all his strength to fend off the angry bird and was lucky to escape with only a few scratches.

It was a chastened man who went into the house to have his wounds dressed by my mother wearing her "I told you so" face and muttering about men who thought they knew best. That night when the hens were roosting, my father crept in and thrawed the neck of the cockerel, which could never again be trusted not to attack. As we ate it for dinner a day or two later, my mother told him, "It's your neck that should have been thrawn!"

After five years at Inchkeith, my mother had become an efficient lightkeeper's

Mattie aged 5 at Inchkeith.

wife, and had lost most of her hankering for the city. She got on with the other wives at the station and came to be accepted as the person to turn to in times of illness or stress. On more than one occasion she was able to save a child after a scalding accident, in each case the child recovering unmarked by burns.

At Inchkeith she never became used to the weekly gun practice by the resident soldiers. The guns were powerful, embedded in rock below the lighthouse. On practice days the women removed pictures and mirrors from walls and took ornaments off the mantelpiece, otherwise these precious things were liable to be shaken from their appointed places by the reverberations. On occasion, taken unawares, my mother had to rush frantically from room to room, rescuing her wee treasures.

In January, 1927, I celebrated my fifth birthday, by which time my parents were becoming increasingly concerned that although I was ready for school there was no sign of a transfer. By all the rules, a keeper was entitled to be sent to a "school station" as soon as his firstborn became eligible to start his or her education. They waited for the official letter, spring and summer passed and they began to worry. At last, in late August, the letter arrived. My father, hoping for a nice mainland station, eagerly opened the letter. He was going to a school station, but it was a rock station in the Isle of Man.

There was no time to wonder why, a "shift" couldn't be refused. It entailed a great deal of planning and hard work. All our personal belongings had to be packed securely in strong, watertight boxes. My father had spent a lot of time and effort constructing suitable crates, so he was well-prepared. The furnishings belonging to the house had to be checked over and left in good clean condition for the incoming tenant. For reasons of hygiene, no papering of walls was allowed. Each wall had to be thoroughly washed down with disinfectant before leaving. During her years in the service my mother used to long for "fancy" wallpaper, yet she realised that paint was much more sensible. We were given three weeks in which to do all this preparation and every minute was needed. My father still had to do the usual watchkeeping until shortly before he left, when a temporary man, known as "the occasional," was brought in until the new man settled in. This man wasn't a lightkeeper, but a local man paid to be ready for such occasions as shifts, illness or holiday periods.

On the day of departure there came into play a pleasant unwritten rule. The family moving out was given breakfast, and lunch too, by the principal keeper's wife so my mother could finish packing down to the last cup the day before. On arrival at the new place the same thing happened.

At departure time everyone helped to move our belongings down to the pier to await the boat. I simply followed where my mother led, and did as I was told. I have no recollection of the journey to the Isle of Man, only vaguely aware that a change was taking place and that my life would be a bit different, and that we seemed to travel forever. Jean was too young to be concerned. My mother was looking forward to her new home because we were going to live in a town, where she could nip out to the shops without having to rely on a boat and the state of the weather. Our destination was Port St. Mary, a quiet seaside resort at the southernmost tip of the Isle of Man.

Chicken Rock

*T*he Chicken's Rock is the kind of lighthouse most people visualise, a tall tower standing on a rock in the middle of the sea. These are in the minority, most lighthouses being on the mainland or on larger islands. My father's new place of work was on a small rock named because it has always been the haunt of the stormy petrel, commonly called Mother Carey's Chickens. The rock wasn't far from Port St. Mary, a wee old-fashioned town of narrow streets and cramped houses where the families of the four keepers who manned the tower lived.

Our new home was one of four flats of basic, unimaginative design. Above the common doorway was the Northern Lighthouse Board logo, a tower in an oval of rope bearing the legend, *In Salutem Omnium*. ("For the safety of all"). We were welcomed by our new neighbours, and given a much appreciated meal before being conducted up a winding stair to the flat awaiting us. My mother was tired after the long tedious journey, but soon unpacked the essentials. In no time at all the beds were made, and Jean and I were tucked up in bed, a bit bewildered but too tired to care.

The next day or two were spent in laying the wax cloth, as my mother called linoleum. Every piece had to be cut and manipulated to fit the rooms, all of which were a different shape and size from those at Inchkeith. Once that was done, the rag rugs laid and my mother's few precious pictures hung on the walls, the house looked more like a home. The whole family went shopping just for the sheer pleasure of being free to do so, Jean in her pram-cum-pushchair, silent for once, as she wondered where all the people had come from.

Port St. Mary. My mother and I lived in this small town when my father was at the Chicken's Rock. My mother thought it was wonderful to be able to go shopping without a boat and to do so without thinking about the weather.

To my mother's delight, the house had an indoor toilet, a luxury after years of having to face the rigours of the weather when the dry outside lavatory at Inchkeith was visited. I was so unused to this that I locked myself in and threw a fit of hysterics until someone climbed a ladder and came in by the window to release me. I got no sympathy from my mother, just a good telling-off for being such an idiot.

Now that my mother could relax and enjoy a more normal life in town, she had to put up with the loss of her husband's presence and support for six weeks out of every eight while he worked his spell of duty on the rock. Three keepers manned the tower, one being exchanged every fortnight to have a two-week break at home. Making the relief, as it was known, was at some rocks performed by one of the four lighthouse ships, but the Chicken's was so close to land it was done by means of a large motor boat. It was often a dangerous task. The area was a danger to shipping, so there was no guarantee that the relief boat would be able to get close enough to effect a landing. A heavy swell was commonplace and in stormy weather the relief had often to be abandoned.

My mother worried every time my father was coming ashore or being taken off. It was only when she heard his footsteps on the stairs and his peculiar whistle through his teeth that she could relax—until the next time. Before each relief day my mother had to pack a "rock box," a strong, watertight wooden box which contained clean shirts and underwear. Inside was also the fortnight's mail, including her own letters to my father, newspapers and magazines, sweets and biscuits. In return, my mother received another box, full of dirty washing and my father's letters. Sheets and heavier items travelled in a canvas bag, the "rock" bag, really a kit bag similar to those used by the army.

Before he went on the rock for the first time, my father had something important to do that affected me. He took me by the hand and led me up the long narrow main street of the town, until we left the town behind. At a crossroads stood my first school, a long single-storey building set in a pleasant grassy area. Great numbers of children ran about apparently at random, screaming and pushing at each other. I was overcome by fear and apprehension, as this was a phenomenon I had never encountered in my young life. It was a traumatic experience for anyone, and I was not yet six. I was put in a class of first infants and abandoned by my father, though I had his solemn promise that he'd come back for me at dinnertime. I have only a few isolated memories of that school. My classroom, though the floorboards were bare and full of potential skelfs, contained a big rocking horse on which I was allowed to play, and an almost life-size toy donkey which reminded me of old Neddy at Inchkeith.

The windows in that first school gave lovely views of the Manx countryside. Just below a long verandah was a strip of cultivated ground, each class being responsible for its own section. The children amicably vied with each other to have the best garden.

None of these happy amenities helped me to adapt. I found difficulty in making friends as I simply didn't know how to play with other children, knowing none of the playground games and shy of learning them. My classmates treated me as an oddity as my speech was as foreign to the Manx children as theirs was to me. One kindly older girl saved me from complete and utter misery by appointing herself as my protector and took me to and from school.

My mother and father at Port St Marys in the 1920s.

In class I was happy, as I was eager to learn, though I was too shy to actually answer questions. I must have been good at drawing, as one episode stands out clearly in my mind. The headmaster made one of his weekly rounds when we were just ending a drawing session. He walked round looking at the work and talking to the children. I was absorbed in drawing in chalk a picture of a yacht in full sail passing an island of high mountains behind which the sun was setting. Seagulls were flying all over the sky and the sea was choppy with "white horses." The headmaster, impressed by my masterpiece, took me by the hand and led me into every room in the school, where he exhibited my picture to the children, telling them that if this was done by an infant he expected greater things in future from older children. It may have given some the incentive to try harder, but I had found it such an ordeal that I never again did my best at drawing lessons, in case the headmaster saw it.

One aspect of the school that terrified me even more than my excursion round the classes was a rather cruel form of punishment which I once fell foul of. The wrong-doer had to hold out his clenched fist, knuckles upward, to receive the appropriate number of raps over the knuckles with a ruler. I don't remember what offence I had committed, but I have never forgotten the punishment. In my terror I held my hand tightly clenched unaware that those in the know only lightly clenched the fist. With the first blow the skin on my taut knuckles split. I went home with a bleeding hand and tears in my eyes. My father, ashore at the time, was incensed at this harsh treatment of his timid wee girl. The next morning he confronted the headmaster. I don't suppose his visit changed anything but I became a paragon of virtue overnight and was never again hit with a ruler.

It was here that I was introduced to Church and Sunday school. I attended both these places of worship regularly and at the end of the school year was awarded two prizes for attendance. I remember my mother taking me to the local bookshop, where I was allowed to choose my prize books. One of them was *Father Tuck's Annual*, which sported a garish purple cover and contained exciting stories, while the other was a smaller volume of little fairy tales much more suited to my age group and temperament. I cherished these until they fell apart from constant perusal.

I was definitely an odd child; timid, painfully shy, unnaturally docile and obedient (most of the time), and withdrawn into a world of my own. Possibly this was just a mechanism to avoid having to cope with the sudden tremendous changes in my life style. Jean, too young to be affected by the isolation of Inchkeith, was happy, cheerful and full of mischief. As a two-year-old, she wandered out on to the landing having discovered how to open the door. She heard someone coming in the entrance door downstairs, so she stuck her head through the railings to get a better view. When she tried to draw back, her ears

— 17 —

prevented her from doing so. The empty high-ceilinged hallway reverberated to her shrieks. My mother came running, as did all the others in the building at the time. Various suggestions were tried with absolutely no success until the keeper ashore managed to prise the railings apart. Jean was unceremoniously turned upside down, given a twist and eased out. She had sore ears for a day or two but was otherwise unharmed.

In an effort to improve my relationships with other children, I was encouraged to attend birthday parties. I was miserable at these functions, refusing to join in the games, mainly because I didn't know how to play them. The hostess would try to make me happy, but invariably my mother had to be sent for. She'd remove me from the festivities and I always went home as reluctantly as I'd gone, knowing that my mother would give vent to her understandable frustration regarding her elder daughter. She wasn't one for showing emotions, keeping a still face in times of pleasure, excitement, sadness or fear, but she certainly couldn't contain her displeasure. Many a spanking I got for, as she put it, "showing her up in front of people." I loved my mother dearly, but life was very difficult.

When my father came home from the rock he wasn't on holiday. The man ashore was responsible for the running and maintenance of the shore station such as the oil supplies and keeping the grass drying greens and concreted frontage spick and span. He had one other important duty. The tower wasn't equipped to communicate with the shore station, so a system of visual signals was used for emergencies. Black metal discs were hoisted on a pole at the top of the tower, different arrangements of the discs meaning different things. At specified times my father would wend his way to a spot where he could read the signs with a telescope. Usually there was nothing to cause alarm, though as it turned out, my father was the cause of one big emergency before he had served his full time at the Chicken's.

These duties apart, he was free to relax, except that my mother used to save up odd jobs for him to do. One was to take me to the dentist's. In those days, there was little stress laid on dental hygiene and tooth cleaning was never stressed in our house. It's not easy to clean teeth using one small cupful of water and nothing to spit in but a basin of water that you have previously washed your face in. I began to suffer from a badly decayed back tooth and for some time my mother doctored it with half an aspirin pressed into the hole—it didn't work for long and tasted horrible. If that failed, the tooth was rubbed with whisky. I had long nights of agony until eventually my mother admitted it would have to come out. She made an appointment neatly timed for my father's shore time.

I, of course, was not told until the time came to set off. We were naturally delayed while I had hysterics and only when I was promised a whole sixpence, a vast sum of money, did I calm down. On arrival in the waiting room I overheard the dentist tell my father he hoped I wouldn't create a rumpus as he had a very nervous patient in the next room. I was duly ushered into the surgery and lifted on to a frighteningly huge chair. The dentist asked me to open my mouth wide, then bent over me with a mirror to examine my teeth. I opened my mouth, but only to scream loudly. Remembering his other patient, the dentist clapped his hand over my mouth, whereupon I bit him. I was immediately ejected from the premises and dragged home by my shocked father. I was doubly outraged when I was denied the promised sixpence, but surprisingly I still had that tooth years later.

During our time at Port St. Mary I became acquainted with some of my father's relatives. Grandfather Petrie had retired from the lighthouse service while stationed at the Point of Ayre at the northern end of the island and, liking the Manx people and their way of life, he and my grannie and two aunts took up residence in an old white-washed farmhouse. My Aunt Chrys, a teacher, had married a Manx farmer and lived nearby. I loved the picturesque cottage with the roses round the porch, its low ceilings and chintzy curtains. My grandparents seemed terribly old and somehow forbidding, though they were kind enough to me and Jean. I felt a kind of coolness in the atmosphere that I didn't understand until many years later, when I learned that the family hadn't accepted my mother as a suitable wife for their youngest son. They had been concerned, too, about her capability of adapting to what they knew from bitter experience wasn't an easy life in the service.

Now they met their daughter-in-law often. My mother felt equally cool towards them. Eventually my grandparents realised that their son was happy, healthy and well-fed. Most of the time Jean and I were clean and tidy, but once or twice at Ballacottier we spoilt that image. Once I fell full length in cow dung from which I emerged stinking. It was a warm summer day so I was stripped off and washed down in a tin bath in the yard. Dressed in a motley assortment of clothes from Aunt Meg's wardrobe, I was mortified as the passengers on the narrow-gauge railway looked sideways at me on the train home.

On another occasion at Ballacottier Jean caused a furore. She had been playing alone that day and all was quiet until suddenly her screams rent the air. The grown-ups rushed out to find Jean running as fast as her wee legs could carry her, followed by several angry geese, necks outstretched and honking loudly. They ran in a wide circle, until my father reached out and swooped the bewildered and frightened Jean off her feet as she flew past him, while the others diverted the furious birds.

My Aunt Meg was the oldest of the family and my favourite. Perhaps I felt an affinity towards her as she was "different." From birth she had been deformed. Her back was humped, one leg was shorter than the other and useless, and she never grew to full stature. She was a lovely person, possessing a sunny nature, a sweet singing voice, and a clever pair of hands. As she crocheted the finest lace, or knitted gossamer shawls, she listened to the troubles of other people. In spite of her disability she was able and willing to do her full share of the housework as long as she didn't have to fetch anything from a high shelf. One day Jean crawled under the table while Aunt Meg was ironing, her useless leg dangling and swinging with the rhythm of the iron. Jean sat in silence, fascinated by the leg movements, until without warning she grabbed the swinging foot and tried to pull it down on the floor, announcing at the same time, "Put that leg on the floor!" Aunt Meg lost her balance and fell, the iron still clutched in her hand. There was a stunned silence, which Aunt Meg broke with a peel of laughter. Everybody joined in and it was several minutes before order was restored and Aunt Meg and her iron were upright again.

Aunt Jean was the youngest of the family. In retrospect she was more like an ant than an aunt, as she always seemed to be scurrying about in a state of anxiety. She had previously given up all thoughts of marriage to a young Manx man in order to look after her ageing parents and Aunt Meg. She was a good housekeeper and, although cheerful, she was too busy to have time to spare for enjoying herself. In later years I felt she became bitter because life had passed her by with nothing to show for her presence.

We settled into a comfortable routine and after a year I was just beginning to acquire some self-confidence when my parents ran into one of the most trying periods of their marriage, a period that lasted a considerable length of time. I was unaware of the trouble. Jean and I were always protected in this way, nothing of any import ever being discussed in our presence, in case we worried.

The day before my father was due back on the rock, we had spent the day at Ballacottier. Shortly after we arrived home, my father began to feel a bit under the weather, and had a restless night. However, he set off for the rock to take up his duties although my mother tried to dissuade him. Her worries were not unfounded.

Soon after he arrived on the rock it became obvious that he was a very sick man. His fellow keepers spent a nail-biting time until the shore keeper trained his telescope on the tower to see the "doctor needed" signal was showing. The shore keeper made his way as quickly as he could to the doctor and the boat's crew. Fortunately the weather was calm; it was difficult to get on and off the rock at the best of times, but more so with a stretcher patient. My father was so ill he couldn't walk. Eventually my anxious mother and helpers waiting at the pier saw the boat approaching. Eager hands lifted the stretcher and soon my father was in hospital.

His illness was diagnosed as ptomaine poisoning, probably caused by eating tainted corned beef. We had all partaken of it at Granddad's, yet no-one else was affected. There being no antibiotics in the twenties, it was some days before my father was pronounced out of danger. My mother, out of her wits with worry, had raved on about his family not trusting her to look after their son properly, when Jimmy had contracted an almost fatal illness after visiting them.

My father was in hospital for some weeks before being allowed home to recuperate. He didn't recover, remaining weak and lethargic and with no appetite. The doctor found that his gums were badly affected by pyorrhoea, which was poisoning his already weakened system. He had to have all his teeth out to cure the condition. It was then even more difficult to eat the nourishing food my mother tempted him with, so he remained under par. False teeth fitted, he should have been recovering, but he woke one morning complaining of a pain in his back every time he drew breath. My mother once more called the doctor, who diagnosed another potentially dangerous illness, pleurisy. He was kept warm in bed, ordered to give up his normal fifty cigarettes a day, and to stay quiet. A few days later he developed an even more dangerous illness, double pneumonia.

It was anybody's guess whether he'd survive or not. All that could be done was to keep him comfortable, sponging him frequently to cool him down, and trying to get him to swallow liquids. My mother, who had given him her undivided attention, waited for the crisis. It was said that the crisis came in the wee small hours, and meant the difference between life and death. The fever suddenly abated in the middle of the night, my father falling into a natural sleep, breathing normally and his skin cool to the touch. My mother slept, too, for the first time in days.

It was obvious that my father would need a long convalescence before he could return to the rock. During the weeks that followed, my mother prayed that there would be no more sickness. Anything more would kill him, she felt. She guarded him like a faithful hound and fed him on the best food she could afford. Her devotion paid off as he put on a little weight and looked less like a walking skeleton.

Now my father had to consider going back to work, though he was still far from fit. The doctor wouldn't sanction it and neither would the lighthouse doctor. Rock conditions required fitness not only of body, but of mind. My father's nerves were such that the authorities dared not send him out to the Chicken's. The only solution was a shift to a mainland station. My parents waited for the official letter which would give them a pleasant station where I could go to school and my father could regain his lost vigour.

He opened the letter eagerly when it arrived. My mother saw his hand begin to shake and his face whiten as he read. The shift was to a mainland station, but to one of the wildest and most inaccessible in Scotland, Cape Wrath. My father couldn't refuse to go as there was no way he could have avoided the shift other than resigning or being sacked for disobeying orders. In either of those circumstances, where else would he get a job in the middle of a depression?

My mother, furious, couldn't understand it. I was only seven, and the nearest school to Cape Wrath was fourteen miles away, and across a ferry in the village of Durness. I'd have to stay in lodgings there with weekends at home—if I was lucky and the weather held good. My mother put her foot down and announced that her puny little daughter was not going to be subjected to such a thing. It was settled that I would be left with my granny in Glasgow, for the time being at any rate. It was not the perfect solution, merely the lesser of two evils.

With heavy hearts the packing was done, my father feeling that the lighthouse board must be peeved with him; otherwise why Cape Wrath of all places? The lighthouse is at the most northwestern point on the mainland, and built on a high cliff which faces the wide unbroken expanse of the North Atlantic, and bears the full brunt of the whole might of the ocean.

Cape Wrath and Cairn Ryan

*W*hen we left the Isle of Man my mother and father parted company, he to go north with all the furniture to the new station, and she to take me to Glasgow to install me in my new home. On arrival in Glasgow, Jean and I were thrilled when we made use of a hitherto unknown means of transport to convey us to Granny's—a taxi! My mother only hired it because we were loaded with enough of my clothes for an extended stay.

While I had been drifting through my first seven years things had been changing in Glasgow. My mother's sister Jean had been married a mere eighteen months when her husband died of pneumonia, leaving her with a tiny baby, Mae, the cousin who passed her germs on to us at Inchkeith. In the same week, Granny's second husband died. The two widows decided to make their home together, Granny looking after wee Mae, while Aunt Jean went back to her old job as dispenser to the family doctor. The arrangement worked well and helped both to cope with their loss. Within a few years they moved to one of the brand new council estates which were springing up all over the city outskirts. The one at Springboig was near Aunt Jean's work and still in the area the family had lived in for as long as they could remember. The "new houses" were constructed of steel. They were mostly in blocks of four flats set in enough ground to give each tenant a modest garden. Granny had two bedrooms, another luxury compared with the old hole-in-the-wall beds, and there was a bathroom. This then, was to be my new home.

I was enrolled in the nearby Budhill School, a dark wooden building. I didn't feel too bad about it as Mae was already a pupil there. I would not be alone to face my new classmates. It wasn't until a week later that the full implication of the situation hit me. I would have to rely on Granny, a comparative stranger. I felt deserted.

My problems were as nothing compared to my mother's. It was on a cold March day that my mother set off with Jean, little more than a toddler, for Cape Wrath. They travelled by train to Inverness and from there another took them to Lairg, a small place in Sutherland which was little more than a cluster of houses round the railway station. From Lairg onwards everything began to deteriorate, as a rickety bus carried the weary travellers across one of the wildest and most desolate areas of the north until they reached Durness. By that time my mother was worn out, Jean was fractious, and the weather had developed into a full-scale blizzard. They lodged for the night in Durness, before setting off on the last lap. The weather having moderated, the ferry was safely negotiated, but to my mother's dismay, she found she was to cover the final and worst fourteen miles in an open trap drawn by a depressed-looking horse.

There was nothing to shelter the travellers from the biting wind, which was driving snow across the bleak moorland. My mother wrapped Jean in a travelling rug and sheltered her as best she could from the worst of the weather. Cold and stiff, the pair at last arrived at the lighthouse. The first thing my mother noticed was that the familiar packing cases containing all her worldly goods were still lying in the courtyard. She knew all was not well, as my father was not one for leaving important work undone. The worried expression on the principal keeper's face confirmed my mother's suspicions. My father looked ghastly—he was a shaking shadow of his former self, with a dull look in his eyes and he didn't even show much interest in his wife's arrival. The sad story soon unfolded over a meal.

My father had arrived looking very ill and unable to take his turn of duty. The principal had sent for the "occasional," the local man who stood in for absentees. My poor father was depressed and had no appetite. Some days later he was found gazing out to sea from the edge of the high cliff on which Cape Wrath stands. He seemed oblivious to the biting wind and was contemplating jumping over to end it all, as he could see no solution to his problems.

The obvious thing to do was send for the doctor, but if the principal reported the situation to the authorities, my father would have been dismissed from the service on health grounds, the essential quality for the job being mental stability. The principal decided to bide awhile before making such a drastic decision and in the meantime everyone kept an eye on him. It took my mother all of ten minutes to decide on the right course of action. The man with the horse and trap was quickly summoned, my father's clothes were packed, and the two of them turned their backs on that desolate place.

The journey back to Glasgow was as wearisome as the upward trip, but now my mother was kept warm by her fury at whoever was responsible for sending a sick man to such an unsuitable station. The big question still remained niggling at the back of their minds. What was to be the outcome of this show of defiance against the authorities?

When I came home from school that day, still feeling as though I had been deserted, I was surprised and overcome to find the family together again. I was too young and excited to notice that my father looked ill and my mother's face drawn. All I knew was that they were back—for good, I hoped.

My father was summoned to Edinburgh to explain why he had abandoned his duties. My mother went with him, and the rest of the family awaited what could only be bad news. Someone must have realised a mistake had been made because, after a thorough medical, my father was sent back to Glasgow on sick leave. There was now some hope that he wouldn't be discharged after all. In due course the familiar letter bearing the "N.L." crest came through the letterbox. It contained good news!

Some less important lighthouses, often situated at the entrance to a harbour and intended only to guide ships into port, needed only one keeper, the light being stationary. It had to be lit at dusk and put out at dawn, but in between those hours the keeper could enjoy a normal night's sleep. Providentially, one of these had just become vacant, so my father was being sent temporarily to Cairn

Wee Granny with Mae on her knee, the author and her mother. Mr Andrews, Granny's second husband, is standing.

Ryan, opposite Stranraer in Wigtownshire. The loch was always bustling with steamers plying between Scotland, Ireland and the Isle of Man.

The lighthouse was just off the main road to the north, and a few minutes walk from the village, a neat wee cluster of houses with a shop or two and a lot of kindly folk. It was well into spring when my father took up his new post and my mother was hopeful that a good summer in peaceful surroundings would restore my father to full health. It was decided I would stay with Granny until the summer holidays, and then see how things were going. I was disappointed. I liked Cairn Ryan and besides, I began to feel I wasn't wanted at home, not fully understanding the reason for my banishment.

Once back at Springboig I soon settled down. My guardians were kind and loving, while Mae was a good healthy influence. We were remarkably good friends despite the difference in our natures. Mae was outgoing and full of joyous energy, while I was quiet and exceedingly solemn. Mae was good-natured, while I had a temper when sufficiently roused. We complemented each other well.

Through the influence of Mae and her chums, I began to take on a more normal outlook on life. There was plenty of room to play in the garden or on the street. Provision vans were still mostly pulled by horses and, as very few people in that area could afford to run a car, it was safe to play on the road. I learned all the street games: games like Peever, the Glasgow version of hopscotch. We marked the "beds" with pipe-clay, the chalky block the tenement wives used to draw intricate patterns down each side of the stairs after they had been washed. The peever could be any flat cylinder, though we usually used an empty shoe-polish tin. I soon became skilled at the natty footwork needed to propel the peever into its desired place. Another favourite game was "Kick the nacket", this object being any old tin can which made a satisfactory noise when it was kicked. It was basically a version of hide and seek, but more noisy and hectic. The air was rent by girlish screams as we played these games and "tig", "ropes" or "girds".

It was during a game of tig that I nearly came to grief. Between the blocks of houses were narrow lanes and on both sides of our lane grew a hedge that reached above the head of a seven-year-old. We ran up and down, in and out of these lanes, chasing each other. On one occasion I was running full tilt along our lane, when I was stopped short by a searing pain in my throat, followed by a sensation of strangulation. I collapsed, unable to breathe or yell, my throat burning. Some idiot had tied a length of string tightly between the hedges just level with my throat. Someone fetched Granny and I was carried, gasping, into the house. I soon recovered, but it was a week before I could speak properly, and the burn marks on my throat stayed there for some time. The culprit was never traced.

Life was quite pleasant at Glen Road; the weeks became months and at Cairn Ryan my father continued to improve. We were all preparing to leave Glasgow to spend the summer holidays at Cairn Ryan when we were wakened one night by a loud crackling sound, and the house seemed filled with a bright flickering light. A house across the street was on fire. It was terrible to watch as the flames reduced it in a frighteningly short time to a mere glowing shell. The occupants escaped with their lives, but not much else.

There had been a spate of fires, which gossip attributed to the construction, the general view being, "This never happened in the old tenements." Whatever the cause, Granny decided she'd had enough. She said she couldn't rest easy in her bed, in case a neighbour was careless with the new-fangled gas cooker. Those "schemes" are still standing, though they have now been modernised. Granny returned to the tenements in Shettleston Road, exactly opposite the one in which she had started her married life. There she stayed until she died aged eighty-eight in the 1950s.

Before the move, we still went to Cairn Ryan where we prepared to enjoy a long holiday although Aunt Jean would have to leave early as she was still working. The weather was glorious, and we spent days exploring the pebbly beach or going for picnics to local beauty spots. We had lots of other visitors that summer. Uncle Jack, Aunt Nan and their two children, Alec and Agnes stayed in an unused house next door. My father loved having a crowd and revelled in organising trips and parties. My mother was delighted to see he had taken a new lease of life, although he still looked unwell and was painfully thin.

One of the trips was to Glen Luce and my mother prepared huge quantities of sandwiches and other goodies, so it was a happy party that set off. Mae, Alec and Agnes, Jean and I, ran ahead of the more sedate adults, impatient to find a good spot for the picnic. Running with my mouth wide open, I collided with a fly going in the opposite direction and inevitably the insect flew to its death down my throat. When I realised what had happened, I screamed blue murder, thinking I was going to choke or be infected by some dread disease. I had been told not to touch flies as they were dirty things. The peace of the afternoon was wrecked. I needed a slap from my mother to stop my hysterics and the party broke up in disarray. For several days I waited in trepidation for the germs to attack, despite my mother's insistence that the fly came off worst.

That holiday was destined not to last very long as the well-known letter arrived with a shift. My father, pronounced fit to take up normal duties, opened it hopefully. He was going to another island, this time in the Orkneys, but although my mother felt she was going far away from her ain folks, I was happy when I heard there was a school on the island. I'd be able to stay at home again. Granny and Aunt Jean returned to Glasgow relieved of the responsibility of taking care of me. There wasn't much packing for my father to do as most of our belongings were still in store. Granny moved about half a mile from Springboig while we set off on the much longer journey north to Graemsay.

Hoy High

*W*e had a long way to travel. It was comfortable enough as we were taken by lighthouse tender most of the way. None of us was seasick, although my mother felt squeamish when crossing the Pentland Firth, notorious for its fierce swirling currents. She recovered enough to enjoy sailing through Scapa Floe where she had her first glimpse of her new abode. The lighthouse was perched on a diminutive cliff, behind it the green expanse of a treeless island with only a few scattered houses. The keepers were already waving handkerchiefs in greeting, before they prepared for our arrival. Meeting us were the principal keeper and the occasional; the assistant keeper, whom my father was replacing, sadly having died. Jean and I were too tired to pay much attention to the house when we reached it. The furnishings were identical to those we had left at Cairn Ryan. My mother and father soon rolled up their sleeves and made the house a home with all our own bits and pieces.

After a good night's rest we arose, ready to become acquainted with our new surroundings. While the grown-ups were getting on with the unpacking, Jean and I explored the grounds, but with my mother's habitual warning, "Mind you don't go outside the gates!" ringing in our ears. The two houses were side by side opposite the tower, which was so tall we had to crane our necks to see the dome which crowned it. To the right of the houses was a walled "park," which contained the two gardens. Our share was neglected, with tall grass and weeds galore, my father's predecessor unable to give it much attention. In the far corner was the henhouse and henrun. As soon as our voices were heard, about twenty birds came

*Hoy High. … the tower,
which was so tall we had to
crane our necks to see the dome
which crowned it…*
Courtesy Northern
Lighthouse Board

through a hen-sized hole in the wall. Outside the wall, the birds were free to roam and they provided us with large, orange-yolked eggs all through the laying months.

That first afternoon we walked the short distance to the farm, where we could buy milk, butter, and the delicious Orkney cheese. There was only one real farm on the island, the other inhabitants making a bare living from crofting. We were welcomed with a cup of tea, and homemade oatcakes before being shown the "shop" a low building attached to one end of the farmhouse. It contained necessities like flour and meal, which were handy for emergencies in stormy weather when the boat from the town of Stromness couldn't make the crossing. It was also the Post Office, and was run by one of the farmer's sisters.

The farm was unimaginatively named "Sandside," situated adjacent to an unspoiled sandy bay, bordered by dunes covered by a prickly grass with blades like swords. The surprisingly good road from the lighthouse wound away to the opposite end of the island where a second lighthouse stood. "Our" one was called Hoy High for obvious reasons, and the other, Hoy Low, for equally obvious reasons. It was the smallest tower I ever saw, only the height of a single storey house with the lightroom perched on top. Halfway between the lighthouses another road led to the other two most important buildings on the island, the church and the school.

The locals were known by the names of their crofts, some of which bore fascinating names like "Quoys," "Garson," and "Quyucks." Danny Sutherland was Danny o' Sandside, Mr. Wilson was Jimmock o' Garson, and so on. My mother fell foul of this practice when she opened the door to the last named gentleman and said hospitably, "Come in, Mr. Garson." She wondered why he gave her a funny look, and squirmed with embarrassment when my father enlightened her. Soon, however, she adopted the habit, after which she was left with the problem of understanding the dialect. The only phrase I can recall is "a peedy gren," (possibly from the French "petit"/small; gren/grain) which turned out to mean a wee bit, or in the case of a cup of tea, a wee drop. In no time, Jean and I were speaking like the rest of the island children.

Before the start of the school term, I made the acquaintance of some of my future school mates. I was still shy and they were even shyer, but at least I saw some kent faces when school opened. My mother took me that first day. The school stood on the summit of the island thus it was exposed to whatever weather the north of Scotland could produce, but at least it was central for the crofters' children. Unfortunately, it was not central for me. I had over a mile to walk come rain, hail or shine. That first day was sunny and warm and I enjoyed the walk with my mother and Jean in a push chair. The school was a small, rather stark building with one classroom, a small cloakroom and a tiny staffroom for the sole teacher. In the middle of the classroom stood a big, black, square "American" stove, its iron chimney disappearing through the ceiling. A strong fireguard surrounded it.

I was placed in a class of three, quite a novelty, as I had been used to large classes. The school was too far away to walk home for dinner, so at first I carried sandwiches. Come winter, my mother arranged for me to go to a nearby croft where I shared the family dinner for a few pence a day. I did this reluctantly, because I hated the homemade butter on the bread which came with my soup.

The school group at Graemsay (Hoy High). The author is at the far left.

Once the colder weather arrived, the big stove was used. When it rained, the classroom was redolent of wet clothes drying and damp wellingtons ranged round the stove. The wind and rain whipped over the treeless island, making my walk very exposed. I was often soaked and frozen until my mother devised a bad-weather outfit. I wore the normal garb of woolly jumper and skirt with long woollen stockings. On top of this was an enormous warm scarf wrapped round my neck, then folded across my chest, under my arms and round to the back, where it was secured by a safety pin. On top of all that I wore an oilskin coat. On my head, on top of a woolly hat, perched a sou'wester, while my hands were protected not only by gloves, but homemade oilskin mitts. My feet were encased in wellington boots, with an additional length of oilskin attached to the top, like fisherman's waders. These were held up by a contraption like a suspender belt, invented by my mother. The entire ensemble was so stiff that I must have walked like a robot. On arrival at school I had to be helped out of it by the teacher. I was still a skinny little thing, so it's a wonder I ever reached school before collapsing from sheer exhaustion.

At first I had to walk the long road to school alone. Once the winter had passed, I could run and skip and enjoy the small pleasures of the route, looking for wild flowers and insects, and keeping an eye open for birds' nests. I once had the joy of finding a peewit's nest. The mother bird startled me by flying up suddenly from near my feet, screeching frantically, and then trying to entice me away from the spot by pretending the nest was some distance away. I really couldn't be deceived by her antics as I almost stood on the eggs. Thereafter I followed the same route to school, watching the progress of the family, until I was rewarded by seeing four little ones hatch out, and the babies turn into fully fledged peewits. One day the nest was deserted and I felt bereft.

Soon however, I found a new interest. On my way home I often left the road to traverse the beach, where the dunes were pockmarked by hundreds of rabbit burrows. One fine day I decided to investigate further. Lying down on the warm sand, I carefully inserted my arm into one of the burrows. At first I found nothing, but then suddenly I had the thrill of making contact with a bundle of warm furry wee bodies. At first I just felt them gently, but it wasn't long before I was tempted to lift one out. Once in my hand I couldn't bear to part with it, so I tucked the quivering rabbit inside my coat and carried it home. My mother gave me a lecture on the crime of taking a baby from its mother. My father, realising it was impossible to return the creature to its rightful home, set about making a hutch for it. I had acquired my first pet.

Telling myself that my wee bunny would be lonely, I eventually added six more rabbits to my collection. The last one was unusual; it was a beautiful golden colour, similar to a pale ginger cat, and with eyes to match. My father said the hutch would hold no more, but like Oliver Twist, I wanted more. One day, I

A recent photograph of Graemsay. This is the road to the school and the sandy bay where I caught the rabbits.

thrust my arm down a burrow to find, not the furry bundles I had expected, but an irate mother rabbit. She promptly sank her sharp teeth into my finger. I yelped, withdrew my hand far more quickly than I had inserted it, and ran home in tears. As my mother cleaned and dressed my finger she scolded, "Don't expect any sympathy from me. It serves you right. Now maybe you'll leave them alone!" From then on the rabbits were left in peace, except for my own little brood which I still loved and cared for. They all grew quickly and became tame, coming to my call when I allowed them to run free in the garden. The only problem was that they began to decimate the lettuce and cabbages my father had so carefully nurtured.

One morning I was shattered to find the hutch empty. I wept while my father told me my pets had all died overnight from the autumnal cold. It was years later before I began to suspect that my father had told me a lie. Realising they were fully grown and ready to breed, he had released them into the wild while I slept. In a time when children were not taught the facts of life my father's lie was his way of avoiding the embarrassment of trying to explain the truth to me.

My father steered my attention away from pets by designing a flower garden for Jean and me. That winter he constructed neat beds and paths with a low fence which separated our garden from the main one. In the spring he showed us how to sow and weed. I was very proud of the sweet peas which grew right over the six foot wall that sheltered the garden from the northerly winds.

When we first came to Hoy High, my father was still not completely fit. In my childish ignorance I didn't notice how his health improved as the months passed. We had only been there a few days when Danny o'Sandside and his sisters started

The boat which took us to Stromness. Here it is being met by my mother.

to send along presents of cream, a leg of lamb and other home produced delicacies. Months later, when we were better acquainted, the Sutherlands confessed that when they saw how ill my father looked, they thought, "Here's another poor soul come here to die," and decided to do all in their power to prevent such a tragedy, hence all the nourishing foods. My father didn't disappoint them. By the time he started to construct our flower garden his health was completely restored.

My mother adapted quickly to the new place. A motor boat took us across the two miles of water to Stromness, which, though old-fashioned and picturesque, was a good shopping centre. The narrow streets held enough shops to cope with all but the more uncommon purchases. On a few occasions we ventured further afield to Kirkwall, a lovely peaceful town full of historic buildings, the most famous being the magnificent St. Magnus Cathedral.

It was from Kirkwall that our wee family once embarked on a holiday which almost culminated in our demise. We set off to spend a weekend at yet another island lighthouse as guests of the principal keeper, whom my father had known for some years. It was on the way back from Helyar Holm that we ran into trouble.

Going on holiday from Hoy High. This is a street in Stromness.

Haymaking at Sandside, Graemsay (Hoy High), around 1930.

As the motor boat crossed the strip of water leading to Kirkwall, the steamer *St. Magnus* passed on her way into the harbour. Our boatman was late in turning his boat to meet the wash from the ship, the boat rocked madly and almost capsized. My mother screamed and grabbed hold of Jean and me, sure that our last hour had come. None of us had ever learned to swim, so we had little chance if thrown into the sea. Thankfully the boatman kept control, so we reached the harbour safe though shaken, my mother white-faced and my father muttering angrily about incompetent seamen.

On Graemsay our family had a good social life, even in the dark days of winter. The islanders were a hospitable, friendly lot and fond of a good ceilidh. It was cosy in the cottages, the glowing fire filling the room with warmth and the inimitable scent of burning peat. As far as possible these informal get-togethers were held on moonlit nights, but when the sky clouded over, flashlights and lanterns could be seen bobbing converging on the host croft. Moonlit nights were best. There was magic on a cold clear evening, every silvered blade of grass as clearly visible as in broad daylight. We often chose this kind of weather to visit the keepers at our sister light, Hoy Low, walking home with the moonlight glittering on the frosty road. We sang as we went, my father carrying Jean on his shoulders, my mother and I close behind. Sometimes we were privileged to see the Merry Dancers, sweeping and flashing across the skies. I took it all for granted, not realising I was seeing a wonder of nature that most people would only read about.

Life was pleasant, and we were happy. In summer we helped with hay on top of the stack, my mother helping with the raking and providing her share of food for the workers. Jean and I romped in the loose hay, no doubt getting in the way of the men, but they were tolerant, remembering their own childish pleasure in the same capers. The sweating men quaffed copious draughts of meallie water, a beverage made by shaking up a handful of oatmeal in a bottle of water. It was very refreshing and apparently wasn't likely to cause a chill on the stomach of anyone overheated. It was economical, too, the same meal being used again by simply refilling the bottle with water.

We learned a lot of practical things from the Orcadians. My mother and father learned about spinning, though they were unable to afford their own spinning wheel. They became proficient in carding (teasing out the fibres of wool preparatory to spinning), and twining (twisting the single strands of wool into two or three ply). My mother made some lovely mixtures from which she knitted all our socks and jerseys and learned some of the simpler Fair Isle patterns. I learned how to knit too and my first memories were of sitting by the fire with Jean on a low stool in front of me as I guided her hands and taught her to knit.

At Graemsay I was introduced to another love of mine, embroidery, or as it was then called, "fancywork." The wife of the resident missionary taught me and the first thing I decorated was a tray cloth, working straight stitches round the edge in the somewhat garish colours of my own choice.

My father learned to "cure" sheepskins, and make them into cosy rugs, a far cry from the clootie ones we were used to. Occasionally a sheep would die at lambing time, leaving a motherless lamb. If there was no convenient sheep available, the orphan lamb had to be hand-reared. Somehow these "caddy lambs" never grew to full size, so were not profitable and were usually killed for the farmer's own table. My father was given a few of these smaller fleeces, the curing of which he undertook with his usual enthusiasm. The process was long and smelly and my mother complained bitterly, insisting that my father keep it away from her house. "And don't come in here until you've washed the stink off you!" she'd demand. She changed her tune when presented with a luxurious silky rug. Several of these adorned our parlour for many years, until the cats discovered the delights of kneading and sucking at the wool. They were constantly chased out, but cats are persistent and eventually they kneaded big holes in the rugs. My mother, admitting defeat, gave them to the cats for a bed.

Occasionally the peaceful, relaxing life on Graemsay was interrupted by an unusual event. One bright summer day the stillness was broken by the sound of a motor although there was no motor vehicle on the island. My mother rushed outside to find my father and the principal keeper, paint brushes in hand, gazing skywards. Floating in the air, slowly and majestically, seemingly not much higher than the tower dome, was an airship. It was a sight to remember, silhouetted against the brilliant blue sky, the legend R100 emblazoned in huge letters on its side. We waved to the passengers, who waved back. Only then did my father suddenly realise that this should be recorded. He rushed into the house for the Box Brownie camera, but by the time he found it the airship was gliding off into the distance. He spent the rest of the day fretting and fuming until eventually my mother told him to stop making a fuss. Not long afterwards we heard that her sister ship R101 had caught fire in France with great loss of life

Not all happenings were pleasant. There was the dreadful thunderstorm, for example. By the time I was ready to leave for my long walk to school, black clouds had gathered on the horizon and my mother kept glancing anxiously out of the window, wondering whether to let me set off or not. In the end she decided I should go, but dressed in my oilskin coat just in case.

I was about halfway along the road to a croft where I was to pick up a wee girl, when I felt the first big spots of rain. A minute later came the first rumble of thunder. I thought of turning for the safety of home, but the lighthouse looked terribly far away. The croft seemed nearer, although a long way off across a wide open field. By now the thunder was almost overhead, the lightning was scaring me stiff, and the heavy rain was soaking what bits of me were still exposed. I ran full tilt across the field, my feet seeming not to touch the ground. The people at Quoys saw me coming and opened the door. I almost fell in, breathless and shaking. I was comforted and put in the box bed out of sight of the lightning.

My mother had watched my progress from a bedroom window from where she could just see over the high wall that surrounded the station. She was helpless as she watched the lightning strike all around me as I ran. As soon as the storm abated, my parents came to the croft to see how I was. I was asleep and none the worse, but there was no school for me that day. I think that was the summer of 1930 when many parts of the country suffered the worst thunderstorm in living memory.

I seemed prone to frightening experiences in those days. One evening while my father filled a wheelbarrow with seaweed to use as manure, I wandered happily on the shore nearby. I spotted what looked like a wee cave, halfway up

The author, her father and sister Jean at Hoy High....I loved my demonstrative father...

a shallow cliff. I climbed up and something inside emitted a loud hissing, snarling sound. All I could see were two shining eyes and a lot of sharp teeth. I didn't wait to see more, almost falling back down the cliff in my hurry to escape. When my father had calmed me down we went home white-faced. When my mother heard the tale we got a row, me for climbing where I shouldn't and my father for letting me. I had stumbled on a wildcat's lair, the mother cat naturally defending her young. Like most children, I learned my lessons the hard way.

Jean was only four and therefore still not able to be a real companion to me. I was eight, but not old enough to be entrusted with the safety of a four-year-old. I was therefore still something of a loner, there being no children at Sandside. Thanks to the influence of the two big schools I had attended, I had come out of my shell quite a bit. I spent a lot of time with my father, though not as much as I'd have liked. In spring and summer when there was almost no darkness in those northern isles, he had more time to spare to take both of us for walks, during which he taught us the names of all the wild flowers and birds. I doted on my father. It was he who taught us how to play Ludo, Snakes and Ladders and card games which kept us occupied in the long winter evenings.

My mother had little time for playing silly games. I rather took her for granted as the person who fed us and saw that we were warm and well clad. She was always there when needed, to minister to our wounds and cure our ailments. It was partly her own fault, as she was an undemonstrative woman. I don't remember her using a term of endearment, or giving us a spontaneous cuddle. I never saw her give my father a quick kiss. She'd have said, that she had "no time for that sort of thing." We all trusted her implicitly, though, accepting anything she said as Gospel truth.

Thus it was that I loved my demonstrative father and sought his company. Occasionally he'd take me up the tower with him while he "lit up." I loved the oily smells in the circular lightroom, in the middle of which stood the all-important clockwork mechanism that kept the light turning at exactly the right speed to conform to its own particular "character". No two characters are alike, so that passing ships in the darkness cannot be confused as to their position. A steep iron ladder led to the upper section of the lightroom which held the light itself. There an iron catwalk enabled the keeper to walk round pulling up the yellow linen blinds which were vital tp keep out strong sunlight. The light was merely a small incandescent lamp which was given the necessary magnification by a series of powerful prismatic lenses. By the same token the sun shining through the lenses could have set fire to the tower, with drastic results. Hence the blinds. I loved it when I was allowed to pull up the blinds while my father ducked underneath the lenses and set about warming up the light apparatus. The lenses fascinated me with their myriad colours as I very cautiously walked round the catwalk in case I fell through the open entrance hole. My father and

I laughed at each other as seen through the lens. It was like the hall of mirrors, our features were so distorted.

My father clipped a little container of methylated spirit round the narrow pipe below the mantle and set it alight with a wax taper. For a few minutes it burned with a soft bluish flame, then just as it was dying down he would turn a little knob and the miracle happened. There was a hissing sound and the mantle filled with a bright light. The lens took up its function and for yet another night ships could sail safely up the Sound of Hoy. The machinery ticked over quietly except for a pinging bell which told the watchkeeper it was revolving at the right speed. My father would go down to the lower room and write on a slate. He was recording the log, which would then be written in the Book later. After that, as I went down the spiral staircase to the house, I'd hear his footsteps as he began the "lightkeeper's walk." On no account was a keeper allowed to leave the lightroom when on watch. Anyone caught doing so would have been instantly dismissed.

After the light was lit and the main work completed, there was nothing to do for at least half an hour until it was time to wind up the clockwork mechanism. It was therefore necessary to devise a method of passing the time that would prevent him from falling asleep under the soporific influence of the pinging bell and the quiet turning of the mechanism. Thus was born the lightkeeper's walk, a slow pacing, following the shape of the room, turning automatically just before the hole where a ladder led down to the spiral staircase. My father continued this habit far into his retirement, pacing up and down the kitchen in a steady rhythm, hands in pockets, and whistling softly through his teeth.

Fifteen minutes before his watch ended, my father pressed the bell to rouse the next watchkeeper. The bell, strategically situated near the keeper's bed, would have wakened the heaviest sleeper, and the man had to press an answering bell before my father stopped ringing. In all their married life, my mother and father seldom achieved an unbroken sleep because of this. Even after they retired they still woke up twice nightly.

Our happy life on Graemsay continued, interrupted only by an annual holiday spent in Glasgow. My father's health fully restored, he could have stayed there forever. My mother, too, was content and Jean was ready to join me on my long trek to school when, almost two years after we arrived, the event of the year was announced. Danny o'Sandside was to be married.

An island wedding was really something. My mother was thrilled when the invitation was sent to us, although she didn't show it by jumping for joy. She immediately wondered what she could wear and whether she could manage a trip to Kirkwall to find something suitable within her means. She had little need for fancy clothes in her isolated homes and hadn't been to a big function for years. The same state of excitement prevailed in every home on the island.

Long discussions took place among the womenfolk about wedding presents. Danny wasn't only one of the most important men on the island, but he was also well-liked. At Sandside preparations went on for a week before the great day. The barn to be used for the wedding feast was cleared and scrubbed out. Sheep and chickens were earmarked for the chop to provide the main course, and the farm kitchen was filled with the scent of baking every time we called in for our milk.

About the beginning of that week my father had an odd dream. It was so vivid he recounted it at breakfast, making a joke of it by saying he must have the wedding on his brain as the dream was all about the preparations. In the dream he was walking from the lighthouse to the farm carrying two chairs. He saw one of the farm hands leading two horses who seemed to be pulling a kind of sledge. Suddenly one of the horses reared up, throwing itself over a fence, while the man struggled to control it. Next my father saw the man leading the beasts again, one of them had a long jagged scratch on its flank, while the man seemed to be nursing a broken arm. That was when he woke up.

Later that day Frankie, the farmhand, came to ask if we could lend some kitchen chairs to help with the seating. My father said, "That's funny. I was dreaming about you last night," and recounted the tale again. He was astonished when Frankie paled and looked decidedly shaken. My mother plied him with a cup of tea while he explained his reaction. A few weeks previously he had visited a fair in Kirkwall, and a fortune-teller had told him to beware of horses as he could be involved in an accident. It was quite the kind of thing a fortune-teller would tell a countryman, but Frankie announced he was going to steer clear of horses, as he had no intention of missing the wedding.

A few days after the event, the dream forgotten, my father was walking to the lighthouse, carrying two of the chairs he had loaned out. Hearing a whinnying sound, he looked around and saw Frankie struggling with a rearing horse on the road he had seen in his dream. My father stood stunned, watching Frankie extricate the animal from a barbed wire fence and lead it down the road past my father. On the horse's flank was a long deep tear and Frankie's arm hung limply by his side, broken. The sledge of my father's dream was actually a bogey laden with planks that had been borrowed as seating for the guests.

The last couple of days before the wedding were hectic. Feathers flew as innumerable hens were plucked and dressed and an aroma of roast lamb and pork hung appetisingly in the air. The men set up trestle tables in the barn and covered them with spotless white sheets. The planks of my father's dream, set on bales of straw as seating, were augmented by the long schoolroom benches. Only the top table was provided with real chairs as befitted the principal guests.

The wedding day dawned bright and warm. Everyone walked in procession to the church, traditionally led by the last couple to be married there, followed by the bride and her attendants and the guests in order of precedence. I can't remember where the bridegroom came in. As the cavalcade progressed, families joined on at various road ends. After the ceremony the procession reformed, led now by the bride and groom.

We had been told that an island reception could last for several days depending on how long the food and drink and the stamina of the guests held out. By the look of the tables, my mother said, this one should last a long time. When everyone was replete the tables were cleared away for dancing, the excess food being stowed away for later consumption. Now another traditional ceremony took place. The bride and groom moved among the company carrying the cog, a small wooden tub, full of ale. Everyone had to drink from it to ensure good health and happiness for the young couple.

Then the fun began. Many of the islanders were self-taught fiddle players, the skill handed down from father to son, and there was always somebody who could knock a tune out of a melodeon or a mouth organ, so a band was readily available. My father who could play the fiddle and the concertina reasonably well was delighted to join the band. The dancers went through the entire range of country dances several times, remaining untired in spite of dancing on a rough stone floor. Soon the atmosphere was like a thick fog from the heat and the dust.

We children were allocated our own section of the barn, a raised area at one end separated by a couple of steps from the main dancing area. Here we could watch the dancers from our elevated position and perform our own version of the eightsome reel and quadrilles. It kept us out of the way of the adults, many of whom wore heavy boots and threw themselves about energetically, arms and legs flailing. Every so often someone regaled us with lemonade and titbits which we munched happily until eventually we lay on the sweet-smelling hay and fell asleep.

My father and the principal keeper had to take turns at the reception, because the light still had to be watched. As it was summer, the light was only lit for an hour or two, our wee island being almost in the land of the midnight sun.

Jean had celebrated her fifth birthday in March, so the next excitement in our family was when she started school. Winter came quickly in the northern isles, so my mother looked forward with some trepidation to a difficult winter. Her worries turned out to be unfounded, however, because at the beginning of November, the familiar letter came with a shift.

Shifts were never an absolute surprise. There was a grapevine by which every lighthouse heard who was due to retire, or which keeper had died. These events meant a series of shifts would follow, with perhaps as many as a dozen being moved around at a time. My father didn't expect to be on the receiving end of the latest batch, as he had only been two years at Hoy High, the average spell being four years. It came as something of a shock therefore, when the letter arrived. My mother held her breath. Although she had been happy there, she did hope for a mainland station where Jean and I could go to a nearby school, and where she could go shopping without a boat. Sadly, my father broke the news. We were going to another rock station. My mother wouldn't have felt so bad if she could have lived in lighthouse buildings in a town, but the shore station for Skerryvore was on yet another wee island separated from the large island of Mull by a narrow stretch of water. Once again the scrubbing and packing was tackled, and we had to say farewell to the many good friends on Graemsay. Jean and I were not happy to leave until we heard that we wouldn't have far to walk to our new school.

We travelled on a brand new ship, the *Pole Star*. She was based in Stromness to attend all the lighthouses in the north of Scotland area, her main job being to make the relief at the rock stations there every two weeks. On this occasion, she was sailing to the Clyde to be fitted with stabilisers. When my mother heard that piece of information, she immediately prayed for calm weather. My father, who was never seasick, forgot his reluctance to leave Graemsay in his eagerness to see the new ship, especially the engine room. Even my mother showed an interest in seeing the modern cabins, so it was with a modicum of pleasure that we embarked on yet another adventure.

As soon as my father could leave us in our gleaming new cabin, he disappeared into the bowels of the ship. My mother tried to calm her two offspring down as we were getting overexcited at the prospect of a sea voyage. I liked the rhythm of the vibrations as the ship's engines got under way, and Jean and I climbed on the top bunk to look out at the green water rushing by. Once out of the shelter of the islands we were in the open Atlantic and the ship, devoid of stabilisers, began to rock and roll, climbing up one side of the great rollers, hesitating, then lurching sickeningly down into the deep troughs.

We took to our bunks, finding it difficult if not downright dangerous to stay on our feet. It wasn't long before Jean began to wail. My mother was just too late. Jean was sick and I promptly threw up as well. My mother rose to the occasion as always, though her own stomach wasn't too happy. As she ministered to us and cleaned up the mess she muttered imprecations about my father under her breath. "He's never here when he's needed," was one of the milder ones. Jean and I were miserable for some time before mercifully dozing off.

When my father returned from his happy explorations below decks, my mother was feeling too much under the weather to tell him her true thoughts. My father, unaware of any coolness in the atmosphere, cheerfully announced she would feel a lot better with some food in her stomach and as Jean and I seemed to be over the worst, he talked her into going to the saloon for dinner. She walked with difficulty, rolling about and bumping off walls as she went.

Once seated in the saloon, the first food set before her was a plate of thick green pea soup, which slid gently about with the motion of the ship. That was enough. My mother staggered back to the cabin and fell on her bunk, from which she didn't arise until the ship dropped anchor for the night.

My father's lack of understanding was not finished with the disastrous meal. The voyage took us past the dreaded Cape Wrath. As we approached it he rushed into the cabin and said, "Come on up on deck and look at Cape Wrath!" It was the wrong thing to say. He left the cabin quicker than he had come in and my mother didn't speak to him for hours. Leaving it behind, we crossed the top end of the Minch, passing the Butt of Lewis, another exposed point guarded by a lighthouse, before sailing down the west coast of Lewis to drop anchor in a small bay round which lay the tiny village of Breasclete.

Much to my mother's relief we were put ashore there to spend the night as guests of the keepers of the Flannan Isles light. We watched apprehensively as the boat bobbed up and down on the choppy sea. My father jumped into the boat with Jean in his arms, then I leaped into the arms of a seaman. My mother managed to keep her dignity and we were soon ashore. As I walked up to the lighthouse buildings I had the odd sensation that I was still going up and down with the motion of the ship. Thank goodness I was back to normal by morning. In the morning I became more aware of my surroundings. The womenfolk who lived there were thankful that at least they were on Lewis, and could occasionally have a trip to Stornoway. They could so easily have been on the Flannan Isles, which was extremely difficult to land on, so it was destined to be a rock station.

Wild and desolate, surrounded by the Atlantic Ocean, it nevertheless achieved world fame in the most tragic and strange way. Some time after it had been put into service, a passing ship noticed that the light was not lit and reported the fact. A ship was immediately sent to investigate. The captain saw no sign of life, unusual in itself, as the coming of an unexpected vessel would have sent the three keepers scurrying down to the landing place. A small landing party was sent ashore where they found a "Marie Celeste" situation. The lighthouse was silent and deserted. In the house was a half-eaten meal, an overturned chair, and nothing to show what had happened. Many theories have been put forward, but the missing men were never found, and the mystery has never been solved. The lighthouse was re-manned, not without some qualms, but since then everything has gone as smoothly as possible in such an outlandish place.

We had been put ashore to save us an extra day at sea, as the *Pole Star* was going to make the relief at the Flannans, while we enjoyed the comfort of a night free from rock and roll. We were to travel by bus to Stornoway to rejoin the ship for the final stage of our journey. The principal's wife made us welcome and we rose next morning to the smell of fried bacon. We were introduced to a gentleman who seemed also to be a guest, though from his lilting accent he was a local man. This man started to talk in Gaelic as we sat down and seemed to hold the company enthralled as no one began to eat. After almost ten minutes, Jean slipped out of her seat and out of the room unnoticed. A minute later, while the speech was still in progress, my mother asked somewhat anxiously, "Where's Jean?" The man stopped talking and all heads were turned towards my mother. The old chap had been saying Grace! I've often wondered how long he would have continued without the interruption. My mother left the room in embarrassment when she realised her terrible faux pas, saying she had to find Jean. Her lovely breakfast was spoiled as she had no appetite left by the time she plucked up courage to come back.

After breakfast, we set off on the next leg of our journey. The bus was ancient and rickety, with wooden seats and a driver who took off over the narrow twisting roads. My mother began to wish we were still on board the *Pole Star*, as we bumped and rattled along, the driver carrying on a constant conversation in Gaelic with his other passengers, turning round occasionally to emphasise some point. Jean and I enjoyed this. It was like being on a roller coaster. We arrived safe and sound, though not without a few bruises, in Stornoway, to rejoin the ship for the last leg across the Minch.

The weather had moderated so the remainder of that eventful voyage was dull by comparison. The *Pole Star* dropped anchor close by the island of Earraid, which was to be our new home, though for how long we had no idea.

Skerryvore

Skerryvore was built with a great deal of difficulty and surprisingly few accidents, on a slippery slice of rock at the northern end of a reef which stretches for fourteen miles off the west coast of Scotland. It is ten miles from the island of Tiree and about twenty-seven miles west of Mull. I never saw the tower close-to, but from photographs it seems incomparably beautiful and graceful. It was built by Alan Stevenson, a close relative of Robert Louis Stevenson. At the other end of the reef stands Dhuheartach Lighthouse, of equal importance though not so imposing as Skerryvore.

The families of both lights lived on Earraid, which I saw first from the deck of the *Pole Star*, waiting for the launch to be lowered, the water being too shallow to allow the ship alongside the pier. One of the crew pointed out St. Columba's holy island of Iona, lying a couple of miles or so behind us. To the left was the mainland of Mull, and we could see only a solitary farmhouse about half a mile from the narrow sound that separated Earraid from the bigger island. My mother thought it didn't look too promising.

As we approached the pier we could see the welcoming committee waiting. The pier was constructed of great blocks of stone, rounded off at the corners by many years of weathering. I never wondered how such a wee place warranted such a big pier and, as I soon discovered, a huge granite quarry. It was only later that I learned most of the quarrying for the building of the Dhuheartach tower had been done at Earraid, hence the need for a substantial pier.

As we drew alongside, the low tide exposed the long slimy green seaweed that hung in fronds from the high-water mark. The steps were covered by the slippery stuff so we had to pick our way with care. I saw what looked like a great concourse of people, but which proved to be less than thirty souls, the entire population of the island, plus one dog. After much shaking of hands and chatter we all moved up to see our new abode, leaving the crewmen and the resident keepers to unload our belongings. We passed a number of granite buildings on the way along what was little more than a cart-track in which jagged pieces of granite were embedded, until we came to "The Street." The houses for the eight families, four attached to Skerryvore and four to Dhuheartach, stood in a row of four blocks of semi-detached single-storeyed cottages on one side of the street, the opposite side bounded by a low wall leading to the gardens.

After the welcome meal in the Principal Keeper's house we were shown our new quarters. My mother was disappointed to find we had

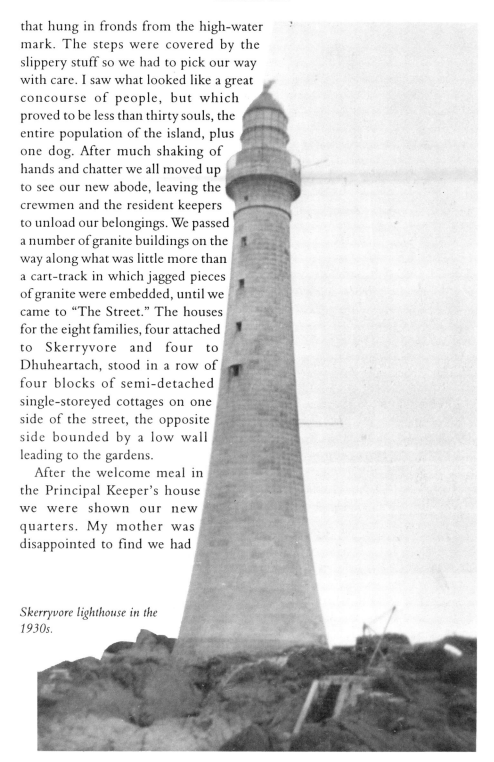

Skerryvore lighthouse in the 1930s.

The view from the balcony. The pole jutting out fom the tower is the aerial and the two holes on the left are the coal bunkers.

to live in what was known as "the wee house." While seven of the houses were identical, the eighth one was small and inconvenient, had no scullery and no back door. The kitchen was smaller than we had been used to, and an even smaller bedroom led directly off it. A short lobby led to the parlour, which in turn gave access to another small bedroom.

Jean and I were ecstatic to find that the school was right next door. The school had its own teacher solely for the Earraid children, though three other children attended it, two girls from a farm across the water and Hughie the postman's nephew. The teacher lived halfway between the street and the pier. Jean and I joined the school right away although it was only a few weeks before the Christmas holidays. I had a warm kind of feeling when I thought of my mother being virtually through the wall from where I sat on the middle bench of the three that comprised the main furniture of the classroom. Jean sat on the front and lowest bench, while the two or three older pupils in the "qualifying" class sat at the back on a higher bench. My pleasure turned to misery when one

Where daily walks were taken, weather permitting!

Earraid. We had no water in the house, or electricity for lights. We used paraffin lamps for lighting, coal for cooking and carried water in pails for washing up. Here you see my mother washing the dishes outside in the summer.

of the big boys persisted in whacking me over the head with his ruler every time the teacher's back was turned but he soon tired of this game, possibly because of my lack of response.

The schoolroom was light and airy and dominating the wall opposite the benches was a fireplace exactly like the one in our parlour, in which at that time of year a roaring coal fire was burning. The first thing I noticed was a big whisky bottle on the mantelpiece containing a golden liquid in which was coiled a snake. I wasn't too happy about it as it looked very much alive and I was afraid it would slither out. It was an adder preserved in whisky, presumably by some teetotaller. The reason for its existence was that Earraid had no snake population of its own, while they were rife on Mull, a mere hundred yards or so distant.

At Earraid and the other wee schools I was given an excellent education. Most of the day-to-day work was done on slates, jotters only being brought out once a week for tests. I hated the feel of the dry slate under my hand, and the sound of the slate pencil squeaking sent shivers running up and down my spine. We had to provide ourselves with a slate cleaner: a piece of sponge or, less opulently, a wet rag. There arose among us a sort of rivalry as to who had the best cleaner or the best tin to keep it in. In practice the tins quickly became rusty and the damp sponges sour and smelly, especially if we forgot and left them closed in the tin over the weekend. Slate pencils squeaked, and if they were dropped they snapped into several pieces far too short to allow of our best writing. They quickly became blunt, too, and the outside wall of the schoolroom was scored and smoothed by the sharpening of slate pencils by many generations of lighthouse children.

When I first joined we were busy practising for the Christmas Treat, learning carols and preparing party pieces. I was excused a party piece for that year, on the grounds that I hadn't time to learn anything new. I was thankful to escape having to make a fool of myself in front of virtual strangers. The following Christmas I suffered agonies as I and another girl, wearing old ragged clothes and bearing trays on which were bunches of artificial flowers, sang a pathetic melodramatic Victorian song, entitled, "Won't you buy my pretty flowers?" Our rendition was even more pathetic than the song.

The only sad note in our first Christmas at Earraid was that my father was not at home. He had to do his spell on the rock. We didn't keep Christmas with as much enthusiasm as the English, but Jean and I always hung up a pillow slip, hopeful of finding it full on Christmas morning. Miraculously it always was. Our far-flung relatives sent gifts. My mother and father managed to give us one present each and the inevitable Annual. In the spring with the advent of longer daylight and better weather we discovered that we were residents of a huge natural adventure playground. Near the station was a beautiful unspoiled sandy beach where all of us spent long hours on non-school days. We did all the usual things, building sand castles, paddling and collecting shells so delicate and translucent that they looked unreal. These we kept for wet weather ploys like decorating wee boxes to give as Christmas presents. A bit further on was the Full Vake. That is a phonetic spelling as I have no idea of the correct Gaelic spelling or its meaning. As the tide ebbed it revealed a sandy floor which transformed our island into an isthmus, enabling us to walk dry-footed to Mull. It was comforting to my mother to know that we were not cut off for long and a doctor could be summoned in emergencies. For the children, it was another wonderful place to play. Its particular attraction was a natural bathing pool left

The School group at Earraid, 1932–33.

full of water even at low tide. The sandy bottom of the pool sloped gently towards the rocks at the far side, where it was deep enough for swimming and diving. I was a non-swimmer, but had great fun splashing about in the shallows, in water warmed by the sun. The first time I ventured in I was enjoying the feel of the sand when I suddenly felt a wriggly movement under my feet. To the amusement of the other children I leaped out of the water. The pool was full of baby flounders which lay buried just below the surface of the sand. Once I was convinced they would do me no harm, I joined in a game of "who can find the most flounders?" We trod gently over the sand getting a little thrill out of the wriggling movements as the fish moved to a safer area.

At the back of our houses was a steep hill, sparsely covered by coarse grass and heather and dotted about with outcrops of grey granite. This provided us with another source of amusement and healthy exercise. We held competitions to see who could climb up and down the hill most often before giving up through sheer exhaustion.

Winding round that hill was a 'granity' road which led to a disused quarry that had provided the blocks of granite for Dhuheartach, and our houses. We knew better than to try climbing the perpendicular walls of the quarry, but on the other side of the narrow road was a huge heap of unwanted blocks of stone. We played among these monstrous stones, climbing on and under them unaware of any potential danger. I don't think the grown-ups knew, or our play would have been stopped abruptly.

Further up that road stood two abandoned houses, the interiors carpeted with grass and wild flowers. They made wonderful playrooms in the warm summer days as they were everything we wanted them to be: houses, forts, pirate ships, castles and anything else our fertile imaginations dreamed up. I have heard that it was in one of them that Robert Louis Stevenson started to write the story of

View of 'The Street' at Earraid from the hill behind.

Kidnapped. It is highly probable, as his uncle was the engineer responsible for the building project. Certainly that fascinating tale of the young David Balfour revolves around the Torran Rocks on which the lighthouses now stand, the young hero being shipwrecked and washed up on Earraid, almost starving before he discovered he could walk ashore at low tide.

Beyond these ruined houses the road petered out into a path which wound steeply up to the highest point of the island. Perched on the very top was the "lookout," a small octagonal building like a summerhouse made of iron and glass. It housed a powerful telescope which in days gone by had been the only means of communication between the towers and civilisation. By the time we reached Earraid, however, wireless had replaced the outdated black discs. If the wireless broke down, the shore keeper reverted to the telescope. The lookout was never locked. We children often made use of the telescope to scour the horizon, focusing on the towers hoping that we would see the keepers. Our hopes were never rewarded as the men seldom went out on the balcony.

Tiring of that, we'd turn the telescope on closer views. From our vantage point we had a panoramic view encompassing the innumerable nearby islets. Further away was Iona with its sparkling white houses but the Abbey wasn't so easy to spot, its ancient brown walls blended too well with the scenery. Beyond Iona was the island known as the Dutchman's Cap. Near it lay Staffa, the best known and most spectacular island of all, famed for its cathedral-like cave formed from the strange basaltic columns that look as though carved by hand.

At ten I wasn't interested in either the history or geography of my surroundings. There was too much to amuse us close at hand. When we tired of spying we'd race down to The Street where we soon found other exciting things to do, like raking the middens. At Earraid, there was no such amenity as a refuse collection. We had middens instead of dustbins, sited for obvious reasons near the sea. This primitive method of rubbish disposal was not a health hazard as none of us ever caught any disease and I never heard of a midden starting an epidemic. Any rotting vegetation was recycled. What wasn't fed to the hens was used as manure for the gardens. The middens contained mostly broken dishes or other household items, with a sprinkling of empty tins which were soon washed clean by the sea. The midden, therefore, gave us another source of pleasure, as we raked for treasures with which to furnish our "hoosies" among the rocks. Our "kitchen" held chipped plates, cups minus handles, cooking pots with irreparable holes, boxes and old sweetie tins. We "cooked" soup made from weeds and flowers, and generally had a whale of a time.

During one of our midden rakings Jean and her best friend came to blows over an alarm clock, the alarm still working if you twisted the winder. Jean had found it, but her chum claimed prior rights to it as it had been her mother's. The screaming brought every mother running. The two mothers defended their

*The author's father at
Earraid in the 1930s.*

own child and it was many months before they made up the quarrel, while the
girls were playing happily together the next day. My mother said later she learned
a lesson; never quarrel over children's squabbles, as they soon forget their
disagreements and sort it out for themselves.

On one of my father's spells ashore he constructed two swings for us and we
had a seesaw, too, simply a plank inserted between the bars on the gate at the
bottom of The Street. We had hours of fun with our mini play park. At the end
of summer my father dismantled the swings and returned the ropes and ladders
to their normal use. At every subsequent station, until we were too old for such
delights, my father constructed swings. No wonder we loved him so much. He
was always willing to put himself out for us, and he enjoyed a turn on the
swings himself.

All of us children were as agile as young goats and just about as sure-footed.
We raced over the huge rocks that littered the foreshore, bounding from one
boulder to another. The station was surrounded by the inevitable high wall
broken at intervals by gates at the foot of each garden. We'd run along the
rounded top of this wall leaping the gate spaces and land unerringly on the next
section of wall. To my knowledge none of us ever fell, but my mother and the
other ladies had many a heart-stopping moment when they caught us at it. We'd
be ordered down with dire threats if we ever did it again, but it was such an
exhilarating game we'd be back at it as soon as the coast was clear. Earraid
removed a lot of my fears and shyness and gave me much more joy in my life.

Some of our excursions were shared by the adults. At the back of the island
was a secluded sandy beach named Balfour's Bay, but which we simply called
Sandy Beach. On sunny summer days several families would plan a grand picnic
to Sandy Beach. We set off wearing big straw hats and carrying vast amounts of

equipment. We carried biscuit tins filled with home-made goodies, and innumerable sandwiches. Some of the party were weighed down by deck chairs, travelling rugs, a primus stove, and other impedimenta. Then there was The Tent. My mother had bought it by mail order from either J. D. Williams or Oxendale's as she did any other large item. The Tent was not strictly speaking, a tent; more of a contraption. The framework opened out like a trellis to form a three-sided box shape, standing about five feet high. A striped canvas awning was stretched over this, tied at strategic points by tapes, and pegged to the ground. The fourth side was open. My mother took no hand in the erection of this shelter, but installed herself inside, from where she presided over the food. She said direct sunshine gave her a headache, so The Tent was a boon to her although my father had to carry it.

The route to Sandy Beach led over a rise and below us lay a little plain with a wee burn, and beyond that the bay itself with silvery sand untouched by human feet except our own. Beyond that was the vast expanse of the Atlantic, on such days looking like a millpond, its treachery well hidden.

We set off downhill, through the tall cool bracken, at which point my father started to complain about The Tent, as the long trellis tangled in the fronds of bracken. Jean didn't like walking through the bracken either and she hated the spiders that wove strands of cobweb between the stalks on a level with her face. She soon learned to walk behind some taller person, who obligingly broke the hated strands for her.

Once out of the bracken we traversed the plain, went round a bluff and then we had arrived. The Tent was erected and filled with my mother and the comestibles. Everybody – except my mother – rushed to paddle in the clear greeny-blue water, the men with their trouser legs rolled up and knotted hankies on their heads, the ladies holding up their skirts, and the girls with their skirts tucked inside their knickers. We paddled and ate and ate and paddled, or climbed the slopes to pick wild flowers. The men and boys had the inevitable game of football. My mother usually decided when it was time to pack up, saying in her no-arguing voice, "Right! That's enough! Time to go home."

Favourite of all my diversions was fishing. It was a pleasure that was rationed by two things, the weather and my father's shore time. On our first fishing expedition, Jean and I rowed with my father among the islets which abounded at the north side of Earraid. We sat in the boat in complete silence, the only sound the burbling of the water against the gunwale as we glided through the glassy stillness. These wee islets were the strangest I've ever seen. They ranged from only a few square feet in area to about twenty, standing high out of the water at low tide, each one a miniature plateau on top of miniature cliffs. The tops were covered by a layer of fertile soil which on that spring evening were thickly covered by the tallest, bluest wild hyacinths it has ever been my pleasure to look on. Fishing was forgotten as we rowed slowly in and out, abandoning ourselves to the sheer magic of the moment. Leaning over the gunwale we could see as clearly as through a glass-bottomed, boat the long fronds of seaweed moving in slow motion in the eddies, fish gliding among them. My father christened the place the "Dardanelles" and we returned often, but that evening we fished elsewhere. It would have been sacrilege to disturb the peace.

We fished not with a rod but a line, on the business end of which was tied a red rubber eel which hid the hook. The eel spun in the water, attracting the unsuspecting fish. There is a strange thrill when the fish takes the hook, the little jerking movements transferred through the line to the hand that holds it. I felt no qualms about hauling in the protesting fish, as we needed them for food. Fish were plentiful and we never went home empty-handed.

That same lack of conscience applied to the hens. When we needed one to eat, my father chose one past the laying stage and wrung its neck. It was hung upside down for twenty-four hours before my mother prepared it for the table. Jean and I always pleaded for the feet to play with. When we pulled a certain protruding sinew, the claws opened and closed in a fascinating way.

In wet weather we were still not deprived of freedom to use up excess energy. We were allowed to play in the Skerryvore store, a commodious building down by the pier. It was originally used by the workers on the building project but when we played there it contained little but some ropes, battens of wood and unidentifiable bits and pieces. Against one wall lay a biggish boat which appeared abandoned, but it provided us with hours of fun as a pirate ship or as a vessel taking explorers to unknown lands. The store seemed as big as a church with its high ceiling and vast floor of rough flags. It was dark, the only light coming from narrow slits in the thick walls. We had to leave the great double doors open for both light and air. Someone had hung a strong rope from the rafters ending in a loop about two feet from the floor. We took it in turns to stand on the gunwale of the boat, placing one foot in the loop and taking off, swinging back and forth in a great arc, turning in dizzy circles at the same time. None of the adults knew of that ploy or the doors would have been firmly locked against us for all time.

Summer over and the nights closing in, we had to devise other entertainments. On frosty moonlit nights we'd congregate in The Street to play a variation of hide and seek. We borrowed sheets and dressed up as ghosts, pouncing out from hiding places to scare each other. It was all great fun, especially as Hallowe'en approached and ghost stories abounded. I was the means of having this super game forbidden and had my bottom heated into the bargain.

For some reason I thought I'd play a trick on one of the girls who hadn't joined us that night. Wrapped in my shroud, I knocked loudly on her door, then lay down on the doormat to await results. As often happens with practical jokes, it didn't work the way I'd planned. It wasn't my chum who answered the door, but her three-year-old sister. When the door opened, I rose up, raised my hands slowly above my head, and moaned and groaned horribly. The poor lass had hysterics, she had nightmares for weeks and wouldn't go near the front door for many months. I earned a sore bottom and the disgust of the others when the game was banned as a result.

Earraid may have been a wonderful place for children, but my mother still had no amenities like electricity or running water and shopping was difficult. Although it was possible to walk ashore, the quickest way to the nearest village was to row across the "ferry" to a slipway and walk a couple of miles to Fionphort (pronounced Finifort). A large motor boat made regular crossings to Iona, carrying passengers and animals together. Fionphort consisted of a handful of houses and two shops, the Post Office-cum-general store and Miss Mackie's. My mother preferred Miss Mackie's couthy wee Jenny-a'things shop to the slightly more opulent Post Office. Miss Mackie seemed aged to me, but then everybody over thirty was old to a child of nine. I loved that shop! It smelled of a delicious mixture of sweeties, apples, oatmeal and paraffin.

Normally the island ladies made the trip in twos or threes, as it was more pleasant and noticeably shorter to have company. The road back carrying a load of messages was downhill, and was usually broken by calling in at the farm cottage for a cup of tea. The bulk of our supplies came from Oban. Once a month a big box of groceries was dispatched from Lipton's by freight on the *Lochinvar*, the steamer which formed the vital link between Mull and the mainland. Put ashore at Craignure, the box came to Fionphort and down to the ferry by road before being manhandled into the rowing boat and across the ferry.

We had been less than a year at Earraid when we moved to a bigger house further up The Street. The "wee house" that we had been in was always reserved for the newest arrival. When the next batch of shifts involving Skerryvore came round we flitted, leaving the wee house to the next unfortunate. Everyone available helped to carry our belongings. Jean and I hated upheaval, but on this occasion we were spared the worst of it as it took place on a school day. We came home for dinner that day to an unfamiliar but tidy house.

My mother was charmed as the new house had a big entrance hall, a parlour and beyond that a small bedroom, which Jean and I were to share. Another door led to what would now be called the master

The Street at Earraid.

bedroom, while another opened into a big kitchen-cum-living room with a bed recess. There was a scullery and back door opening out on to a paved area with a drain in the middle. Beyond that there was a gravel path and the drying green. This house would be much easier to keep clean. Although a vast improvement on the wee house, this one still had a lot of work to keep my mother busy. Jean and I carried half a bucket of coal at a time, or fetched half a pail of water from the well about a quarter of a mile away. Only when my father was at home did my mother find her chores eased as he carried buckets, cleaned the brass lamps and brought in coal and paraffin.

It was at Earraid that I realised the big part in our lives played by buckets. Two or three times a day coal had to brought and this pail sat beside the range. Ashes had to be carried out in another bucket and taken to the midden down near the sea. We used rainwater for all washing; it collected in a big tank by the back door, but still had to be humped into the house in a pail. In the scullery was another into which slops were poured, when we, the dishes or the vegetables had been washed. This in turn had to be carried outside and emptied down the drain. Drinking water from the spring well was kept in a peculiarly-shaped pail. Black and shiny, it was a king among buckets. With a lip for pouring and a tight-fitting lid to keep out dust and insects, it had a place of honour in the scullery, on top of the table.

The final bucket was perhaps the most important of them all. At the foot of each garden stood the edifice known to us as the Shunky. Officially it was the lavatory. Each family had its own, unlike the city tenements where sometimes three families had to share. Our wee building housed a contraption. This was made of wood with the essential hole in the middle of the seat and a door underneath for the insertion of a specially wide bucket. The back portion had a hinged lid. This part was supposed to be filled with sand or earth, then when the occupant arose a hidden device would release a quantity of sand into the bucket below. The idea was one of Victorian ingenuity, but as it didn't work we were issued with a plentiful supply of a disinfectant called Jeyes Fluid, which was poured liberally into the bucket. In later years the contraption was supplanted by an Elsan toilet. The obnoxious lavvy bucket had to be emptied daily, probably at dead of night by the shore keepers.

Answering the call of nature was an expedition. In winter or wet weather it necessitated dressing in welly boots, and slinging a big oilskin over the head and shoulders before sprinting the length of the garden. The lavatory was well ventilated and was not a place to dally in even though the squares of newspaper that did duty for toilet paper made interesting reading. The provision of this became a duty for Jean and me. We cut the newspaper into squares which were threaded onto string by a villainous-looking curved sacking needle. It was a source of irritation when passing the time in good weather reading the toilet paper to find that the print had been cut at the most interesting bit. The reader then searched through the rest of the squares to find the bit that matched.

In the long winter months we made our own entertainment indoors. We had the wireless my father made and I remember the strange pungent smell of the ebonite that he used for the front of the set, as he burned holes in it for the knobs. I was fascinated by the tangle of coloured wires he carefully soldered into place which resulted in good reception of our favourite programmes. One thing that puzzled me was why it was called a wireless when it was full of wires.

Jean and I had several hobbies. One was decorating glassware with silver paper. On our Saturday forays to Fionphort we bought sweets from Miss Mackie who sold assorted caramels in a big tin which gave off a lovely aroma of sweetness. She'd let us pick the ones we fancied which were those wrapped in silver paper. It came in a variety of colours and patterns: tiny flowers, fruit, spots and stripes.

We carried our spoils home arguing happily about who had the best selection. We carefully unwrapped them all, our priority being to smooth out the silver paper carefully and add to the collection already saved in a special box. My mother supplied us with wee glass ashtrays, redundant since my father gave up smoking. Sometimes she'd find a glass butter dish or an old vase, but a jam jar would do. We were absorbed for hours cutting out shapes and gluing them onto the glass. Butter dishes and ashtrays had the paper on the underside, vases on the inside with the patterns nicely displayed. A coat of varnish fixed the paper firmly and made it waterproof. We gave the resultant pieces away for Christmas presents to our unsuspecting, but suitably grateful relatives until my mother ran out of dishes and we ran out of enthusiasm.

Autumn gave us a new use for silver paper. Just before the harvest we'd scrounge a bunch of oats from the nearest farmer, each ear of which was painstakingly covered by a tiny square of coloured tinfoil. Frustration arose when the ears fell off under a too heavy-handed approach. Mostly we were successful and the house was filled with vases full of shimmering multi-coloured corn to brighten up the winter.

In winter we seldom had visitors from across the water, except for Christmas dances in the school and the occasional wee concert. Sometimes for weeks the only visitor was Hughie the postman. Hughie lived on the island with his aged mother, his sister and his nephew, wee Hughie, who also attended our school. The island's only other inhabitants apart from the teacher, they lived in a wee cottage like a black house, the ancient abode of the highland peasantry: low, thatched and built of rough stone blocks. Hughie's cottage was just off the foreshore, so near to the beach that a wall had been built to keep out the highest spring tides or an exceptionally wicked storm. Hughie only paid a nominal rent of 5/- a year because of the proximity of the house to the sea.

Hughie was our private postie. He had no uniform except for the official skipped hat. Every day he emptied the official letterbox which was set into the wall exactly halfway up The Street. He carried the mail down to the pier, rowed across the ferry and walked to a grassy mound whereon he sat, smoking his pipe and awaiting the Fionphort postie. The two men sat awhile exchanging mail and gossip. Sometimes he took some children with him. I'd sit listening without understanding the Gaelic, but it wasn't hard to guess at the topic, as they read every postcard and examined every postmark on the letters to find a clue to the sender. Each parcel was gently shaken or sniffed at for an inkling of its contents. When every item had been dealt with and the pipes extinguished the two parted, Lachie to continue on his round to the outlying farms, and Hughie to amble back to the boat to finish his daily darg. Once back in The Street he'd knock at every door before opening it and call out in his soft highland lilt, "There's a letter from your mother today. I hope she is well." Or, "You'll be well off this week; I've just given the Principal the pay envelope." Or, "I see your aunt has been to Dunoon for her holidays. She'd have good weather," as he handed in a postcard. The rest of the day was his own.

Hughie was a character much in demand as a purveyor of local news. He announced births, deaths and marriages, bits of scandal, and the occasional tragedy. He was a kindly man too, often bringing little gifts. During one of Wee Granny's visits, he opened the door and threw in a pair of live lobsters, their huge blue pincers snapping. Granny nearly had a fit. "That's for your tea," said Hughie unperturbed, and withdrew rapidly in case anybody tried to thank him. He was a shy man and would have been terribly embarrassed.

I wasn't often deliberately naughty, as I knew from experience that my mother had a hard hand. On one occasion however, I earned a skelped bottom when Jean and I and another older girl were taken to visit Hughie's old mother. These people were poor, barely scratching a living from Hughie's post office pay and a wee bit of fishing, but they had the pride and courtesy of the highlander. What followed was unforgivable. At the best of times very little daylight got into the house through the small windows, but that day the weather was dull, making the room murky. The lamps were never lit until it was dark, to conserve paraffin. I had to peer to make out the old lady as she sat beside the peat fire which wasn't bright enough to relieve the gloom. We three children were ensconced on a high-backed settle behind the table. In those days the rule was that children should be seen and not heard so we soon became bored. When we were handed something to eat, my wayward friend whispered, "What is this we're eating?" because it was so gloomy we couldn't see the food. I started to giggle which started off the other two, as we examined the fruit cake, vying with each other in ever more ridiculous guesses as to its origin.

It was soon obvious to all present what we were up to. My mother shot us a look that should have stopped the nonsense, but we were too far gone in mirth to heed the warning, and couldn't see her properly anyway. We were speedily removed from the premises with apologies from my mother to our affronted hostesses. I had a good walloping as soon as we were back home.

I seemed to earn my mother's wrath without even trying. One such time was when Jean accidentally knocked over the sugar bowl scattering sticky grains everywhere and smashing the bowl. I was sure my mother was going to be angry with Jean, so I started to cry. Jean escaped the wrath and stared unconcernedly as I was smacked instead for making a fuss about nothing.

My cousin Mae spent most of her summer holidays with us, becoming more of a sister than a cousin. It was on her behalf that I gained another skelping from my mother. Mae and I had been sent to the well for a bucket of drinking water. We decided we could manage a full pail, but it was a struggle to carry it. On the way Mae stumbled and fell, skinning her knee on the granite. She examined her bleeding knee in silence while I, however, burst into tears thinking she was badly hurt. My mother came to see what the noise was about and smacked me for making a fuss, while Mae, her wounds bathed and plastered, went to play and show off her bandages to an admiring throng of children.

I didn't seem to learn from these experiences. Behind our lavatory was a secluded space which originally held the coal supply. In our second year at Earraid, a thrush decided to build her nest in a handy wee hole in the wall there. Jean and I monitored the proceedings, seeing four babies hatch and grow to be fledglings. We kept it secret in case the birds were disturbed and, to our great delight, a week later we found another clutch of eggs in the same nest. Thrilled to bits by this extension of our pleasure, we again kept watch. The new family duly hatched and were almost fully fledged when tragedy struck. One of the small boys had nipped down to see what was interesting us. Unfortunately, he was not only curious but spiteful, taking all the babies out of the nest and killing them one by one, tossing them over the wall when he had finished. Arriving just too late I saw red but he was too quick for me. I gave up the chase and ran home in distress to tell my mother. She was entertaining two of the other wives when I burst into the kitchen breathless, gasping out incoherently, "Johnny's killed... Johnny's killed...." The three women turned white and rushed out, fully expecting to find Johnny lying dead. When they found no trace of Johnny, either alive or dead, I was ordered to calm down and tell the story properly. I felt it was most unfair that I was given a hot bottom for giving everybody apoplexy whereas Johnny deserved dire punishment for committing murder.

At least I could hold my own in school. Towards the end of summer term that year I was remarkably unconcerned when the teacher told me the time had come to sit my "qualifying" exam, which would allow me to go on to higher education. I was the only candidate at Earraid. I ran happily down The Street that Saturday morning of the exam, Saturday being the only day the teacher could invigilate. I mightn't have been so happy if I had realised that my life was about to change and would never be quite the same again. My idyllic island existence was about to come to an abrupt end.

The lighthouse authorities were obliged by law to provide a full education and if it wasn't possible at a particular lighthouse, they had to pay the expenses at a suitable school elsewhere. The nearest to Earraid was in Oban, where I would have to live in a hostel. I had jumped a whole year during my numerous changes of school. I was almost six when I started school, yet here I was, only eleven, ready to start secondary school. My mother and father felt I was far too young to live with strangers in a strange place. Many discussions took place in which I, whose future was at stake, was never consulted. The alternative to Oban was for me to go to Glasgow to live with my relatives, in which case the lighthouse authorities took no responsibility and my father would have to bear the full cost. Letters, of which I was blissfully unaware, passed back and forth. I knew nothing of this intrigue or I might have been tempted to make a mess of the exam and gain another year at home. As it was, I passed!

I was almost as familiar with Wee Granny by this time as with my mother, as she and Aunt Jean and Mae spent most of the summer with us and we in turn spent holidays with them, so when the news was eventually broken to me that I was to go to school in Glasgow, I was sure I'd be staying with them in Shettleston and wasn't too upset. However, this was not to be the case.

Some years earlier an accident had befallen my grandfather Petrie in the Isle of Man. He injured his eye badly which meant he had to attend hospital in Glasgow and suffer the eventual removal of his eye. For months he made the journey back and forth to Glasgow, as the specialists were worried about the remaining eye. This had proved a tedious waste of time and money, so to save any further expense my grandparents, with Aunt Jean and Aunt Meg, moved to Glasgow, to a tenement in Tollcross near my Uncle Jack. For some reason it was decided I'd stay with them instead of my beloved Wee Granny. I was bitterly disappointed, but was not allowed any say in the matter.

Glasgow

My father arranged his annual holiday so that we could all go to Glasgow to see me settled. In the bustle of preparation I had no time to think too much, and, childlike, I enjoyed the sensation of excitement that prevailed. I felt a bit sad as we crossed the ferry in the early morning, to travel all day to my new life. None of us had seen my father's folks since we left the Isle of Man, so for me and Jean it was almost like meeting strangers. Adult tongues wagged as they caught up with all the family news and all the other relatives had to be visited. We went shopping in town and I was fitted out with a school uniform of two navy blue gym tunics and thick black stockings, black elastic-legged knickers and serviceable black shoes, all bought at a wholesale warehouse in the city centre, by means of a "line" from one of Wee Granny's neighbours who ran an agency; the goods to be paid for later. The outfit was completed at a local outfitters who had the monopoly on the Eastbank uniform. There I was equipped with two bright yellow blouses, a blue and gold striped tie and badges bearing the school motto in Latin round a gold star.

The holiday passed quickly and I had to be enrolled at Eastbank Academy. My father was delegated the job of escort. I was puzzled that immediately opposite where my grandparents lived, was a big sandstone school, yet I was being taken on a long walk to another. My father explained that Wellshot School provided only a three year course and I was expected to do five years. The thought of five years in Glasgow depressed me before I'd even started school, so it was with a heavy heart I followed my father.

In fear and trembling I climbed the stair of the old building to the headmaster's room. In the playground the rest of the newcomers lined up, secure in familiar surroundings, as the primary department of Eastbank was just across the street from the "big" school. I was struck dumb in the presence of the headmaster, who was resplendent in something I had never seen before, a flowing black gown, into which he hooked his thumbs as he spoke to my father. He looked like a big fearsome bat and studied me as if I was a specimen in a lab. After a lot of form filling, I was taken to join my new class, escorted by the school secretary. As I walked in, thirty odd pairs of eyes turned to stare at the newcomer. I know I blushed, but it must have been covered by the deep tan I had acquired in the clean highland air. Some of the children had never been out of Glasgow and looked ill with pale faces. Sunlight reached through the sooty air, but the tanning rays couldn't penetrate it.

I did have one thing in common with my classmates. We were confused by the routine of constantly moving from one classroom to another every time the bell rang at the end of a period, remembering to keep always to the left in the corridors. During that week, the rest of the family went home to Earraid. I felt completely bereft coming home from school to find only comparative strangers to greet me. I hated Trainard Avenue which was an ordinary side street in the east end of Glasgow. The flat was on the top storey of a grey tenement, and the occupants of the other flats were either elderly or childless. I found no one I could make friends with.

That first evening I stood for a while looking out of the kitchen window. I had a panoramic view of the back yards of a dreary rectangle of identical tall tenements, their stark grey dusty walls dotted with innumerable dead-looking windows clothed in dingy curtains. The housewives fought a losing battle against the grime from the factory chimneys all around. At intervals the back entrances to the closes gave access to the equally grey concrete drying "greens", a misnomer if ever I heard one, fenced off by high spiked railings and each containing a dank-looking washhouse and several square dustbins, the contents of which were scattered around by scavenging cats and dogs. Only a tiny patch of grass here and there indicated that at one time the "greens" had really been green. After my beautiful open colourful landscape at Earraid, this was dreadful to behold.

The front windows gave a fractionally better outlook. If I leaned my cheek on the window pane and squinted, I could catch a glimpse of the trees in Tollcross Park, the main gates of which were opposite the end of our street. It was some solace to know that I could walk along its winding paths and feed the ducks by the burn, to recapture some of the feeling of freedom I had lost.

My new guardians were kindness itself and took good care of me. It's a pity I didn't appreciate it. I couldn't take to Aunt Jean at all. She was brusque and had

At the museum in Tollcross Park.

little patience with her niece. It was only when I grew older and understood her better that I grew fond of her. Granny Petrie was as deaf as a post. I was both scared of her and shy of shouting directly into her ear, which was the only means of communicating with her. As for Grandpa, I was unnerved by his glass eye. Whenever I looked at him I found myself staring at the false eye, not noticing that his good eye had a twinkle in it like my father's. In time I grew accustomed to him but in the meantime I was scared of him. He treated his false eye as many people treat dentures. When it irritated him, he put it in a glass of water. It was disconcerting to go into the scullery for a drink and find that eye staring up at you. Worse still, Grandpa looked even more fearsome with an empty socket.

If it hadn't been for Aunt Meg I'd have been very unhappy indeed. Her small stature and twisted body didn't frighten me at all. She cheered me up by regaling me with hilarious tales of her childhood in the lighthouse service, like the occasion when her school was taking part in a parade in celebration of some royal event. The children marched three abreast. Aunt Meg, disabled but refusing to be left out, was placed right in the middle so that the children on either side could hold her hand and help her along. She could see nothing but legs and feet moving in hypnotic unison. Feeling sick and dizzy, she had to be held up by her companions, and trailed along for the rest of the march.

Another of her stories was of the time when she and her two sisters, all in their teens, were enjoying a quiet stroll near the lighthouse. Some local lads decided to play a trick on them. They crept among some bushes, rustling the leaves and making strange sounds as the girls passed. The young ladies were satisfactorily scared. They took to their heels, Aunt Chrys and Aunt Jean each taking Aunt Meg's hand to help her. They ran so fast that her feet hardly touched the ground. I loved Aunt Meg and came to admire her for her attitude towards her disability.

At school, I enjoyed most lessons. I heartily disliked history, feeling that there was no point in knowing when kings had reigned, or when the battle of

Bannockburn had been fought. I daydreamed through those lessons with disastrous repercussions some years on.

Life in the playground was difficult. The hundreds of girls all seemed more worldly-wise than I was and I was alien to them. My speech was different, a mixture of Manx, Orcadian and East Coast Scots with a highland lilt I had acquired in Mull. I was very shy and left more or less to my own resources. I found it hard to understand the general habit of tearing around the playground screaming and I was ignorant of the ways of the older girls. At playtime I took refuge in the shelter, trying to look inconspicuous behind a comic.

I avoided the school toilets, finding them more unpleasant than the dry lavatory at Earraid, despite they were the so-called hygienic water closets. They were, of course, mistreated by some pupils. Thus I often arrived home at dinner time in great distress. A sensible arrangement was made whereby I went to my other granny's for dinner, as she lived just a couple of minutes walk from the school. This alleviated my discomfort, and I was happier and more relaxed in her wee house.

The first term wore on and I didn't settle as I should. Aunt Jean unwittingly made me unhappy by treating me as a three-year-old at bath time. She insisted on washing me from head to toe. I felt an unnecessary sense of shame and humiliation, but suffered in silence as I'd only have been told not to be cheeky if I had complained.

My father's people were very God-fearing and strict. I wasn't allowed to go to the pictures or listen to the wireless. On Sunday we went to the Methodist Church both morning and evening. The rest of the day was spent in quiet pursuits like reading. I couldn't even do my beloved "fancywork" on the day of rest. I found it all very monotonous and thought even more of home.

As November approached, Glasgow seemed more and more unattractive. I grew listless and withdrawn, lost my appetite and interest in everything. When not at school I complained of not feeling well. My guardians, thinking it was just homesickness, waited for it to wear off. Wee Granny eventually wrote home advising my mother to come and see for herself. Christmas was approaching and my father was on the rock when my mother and Jean came to stay at Wee Granny's. My mother saw at once that all was not well. Visiting the school, it was confirmed that my work had deteriorated. The doctor could find nothing vital wrong, coming to the conclusion I was a bit run-down, and perhaps a holiday at Earraid would put me back on my feet. As I seemed much happier with my mother close by, it was decided she would spend Christmas and New Year in Glasgow, instead of at home without my father. Shortly after the New Year we set off for Earraid. I was overjoyed at the prospect of seeing my real home again, putting at the back of my mind the knowledge that in a week or two I'd have to return to the hated city.

The journey was uneventful apart from there being quite a strong wind blowing at Oban. My mother wasn't worried about the crossing in the *Lochinvar*, but my father was due off Skerryvore that day, and the *Hesperus* might not be able to make the relief. Reaching Fionphort we turned down the rough road for the final mile or two towards the ferry. I could hardly wait to get home and I was impatient when the driver of the hired car had to slow down to avoid damage to his back axle. Halfway to the ferry we met Miss McKinnon, the teacher, hurrying white-faced and anxious-looking towards Fionphort. Waving frantically, she flagged us down. Something must be wrong at the rock! My mother wasn't surprised when Miss McKinnon gasped out that there had indeed been an accident during the relief, though she couldn't say which of the two rocks was involved.

My mother said, "My God!" and sat silent while the driver covered that last bit of the journey unheeding of possible damage to his car. On relief day Hughie the postman did standby duty as boatman. He, like everyone else, had been "listening in" on the lighthouse shortwave band to the conversations between the lighthouses and the *Hesperus*. He knew no more than the teacher, as he had waited for us after ferrying her across. My mother looked more and more drawn by the time we reached the pier after a choppy trip in the wee boat. She headed

A more recent picture of Skerryvore showing the dangerous narrow metal pier used for the landing and taking off the keepers. To the left is the helipad which is used nowadays.
Even in calm weather the sea always seems to move over the rocks.

straight for the wireless room where several wives were already waiting anxiously for news.

Everyone was solemn. Only oddments crackled over the air, then came the news that no-one was badly or fatally injured. The tense faces relaxed. One of the Dhuheartach keepers had escaped with a badly twisted ankle. It wasn't until the *Hesperus* dropped anchor and landed my father safely ashore that the whole story unfolded.

The relief at Skerryvore completed, the ship had steamed to Dhuheartach and lowered the launch in reasonable conditions for the time of year. It is seldom really calm, but all involved were skilled and used to the constant surge of the waves. The on-going keeper had been safely if wetly landed by the breeches buoy, and the shore-going man was preparing to be taken off the same way, when an extra big wave was seen to be approaching the landing stage. Someone called out a warning which most heard, except one keeper who was taken by surprise. He was swept off the catwalk, disappearing in a welter of water and foam, falling about twenty feet into the sea. The onlookers were unable to help, but when the water subsided, the unfortunate man could be seen dangling at the end of a rope in which his foot had become entangled. The rope undoubtedly saved his life as he would have been swept away and battered to death on the jagged rocks. He was hauled up by his fellow keepers but it was a day or two before he could be taken off the rock.

When the excitement was over and everyone had time to think straight, the men realised that all through the rescue the sea had remained calm, not one wave breaking to hinder the rescue. The event made headline news. The next day we were intrigued and entertained by planes full of photographers and reporters buzzing above our peaceful wee island. We seldom saw a plane, so when we heard the sound of one approaching we'd all rush out and wave frantically at the occupants, clearly seen as the aircraft circled low. The injured man had been taken to hospital and was soon able to take up his duties on the rock again.

When the excitement had died down and Earraid resumed its seclusion, I began to think about going back to Glasgow. As I still felt out of sorts my mother sent for the local doctor. She was worried and I was secretly pleased when he shook his head. There was nothing he could put a finger on, but I was certainly not fit to go back to school. He prescribed iron pills and suggested I should stay at home for a while yet.

January passed and with it my twelfth birthday. I felt an odd mixture of pleasure at having my stay at home extended, and misery at feeling so unwell. In February I suffered bouts of sickness and at the same time a "running" ear. My mother nursed me patiently and three times a day poured the prescribed peroxide into my ear, which did absolutely nothing to cure the condition.

After three weeks, I woke up to find the room swimming round, whirling in a frightening way as though I was on some mad roundabout. I screamed in terror and when my mother came I could only hold on to her tightly until the vertigo subsided.. My ear had stopped "running", but it felt as heavy as lead. The doctor, who had been hurriedly summoned, took my mother aside. I tried to listen to their murmurings catching words like "hospital" and "Glasgow" and, horror of horrors, "operation." I lay quaking until he left; then my mother said I could get up to see how I felt. Apart from my left ear feeling peculiarly heavy I came to the conclusion I had been imagining what I heard. If I was really ill, I wouldn't have been allowed to get up and dress. Later that day my mother started to pack a couple of cases, so my fears quickly returned. I knew before she told me, that I was going away to hospital. My father was ashore and was given permission to take me to Glasgow. I am sure he sacrificed his three weeks summer holiday, as we both remained there for that length of time.

It was still dark next morning as we set off. At the door my mother gave me a quick hug and a peck on the cheek, her parting words being, "Now mind and do what you are told!" her standard parting speech. I've no doubt she sat down and cried before we reached the end of the Street, but she'd have hated anybody to know. The Street was dark and silent as we wended our way to the pier by flashlight, accompanied by the other shore keeper, who was to ferry us across to the waiting car. I was unaware that my illness, a mastoid infection, was serious, resulting in at least some brain damage if not dealt with quickly. Nowadays, the same thing can be cured by antibiotics. The journey to Glasgow by car, boat and train would take almost the whole day. The only bit I recall was being transported out by motor boat from Craignure to meet the *Lochinvar*, which couldn't tie up at the pier, there being not enough depth of water. We clambered aboard the steamer with the help of crew members. Normally I'd have thought it great fun, but my head was sore and I felt rotten.

In spite of the supposed urgency of my case I wasn't admitted to hospital that night. We spent the night at Wee Granny's, taking the tram next day to the Ear, Nose and Throat Hospital, where I was suddenly abandoned by my father and left to the mercies of strangers. I objected to being given a bath because I'd had one at Wee Granny's the night before, and because the nurse insisted on washing me like a baby. I was then dressed in a white nightie and taken to the ward.

I had never seen the inside of a hospital so I was somewhat unnerved when I was led into a huge room in which were long rows of brilliant white empty beds. I was deposited firmly but kindly in the one nearest the door and left alone in the empty white silence. I began to feel afraid. Time passed. Nobody came near and I felt I was going to be forgotten, to die eventually of loneliness and starvation. I fell asleep from sheer boredom and tiredness, and woke to find that the ward was no longer empty. I learned later that the ward had been closed for fumigation, and I happened to be the first admission. I was also the only child in a ward full of women.

Later that day another indignity was heaped on me. Half of my beautiful hair, the only feature of which I was proud, was shaved off. I cried. No explanation or apology was given. I was examined, poked and prodded at intervals all day. I was glad when the lights were lowered and I was left in peace, though I felt so homesick and ill that I cried myself to sleep. Next morning everyone was given breakfast except me. I was told to get up and taken along a maze of corridors before being ushered into a darkened room. In the middle a pool of bright light was centred over a high table round which stood several people in strange clothes and masks. Somebody said, in a voice muffled by his mask, "Come on, lassie, climb up here and lie down." Remembering my mother's parting advice, I reluctantly but obediently did so, whereupon something like a sieve was put over my nose and mouth and I was told, "Keep your eyes closed and breathe in!" Needless to say, when I smelt the suffocating chloroform, I instinctively opened my eyes. The last thing I was aware of was my eyes stinging before oblivion took the pain away. I have had operations in more recent times, preparatory to which I have thanked God that methods have changed since those days. I was still only twelve.

I came to in my bed. I felt sick from the chloroform and it was some time before I was able to sit up and take a little nourishment. Then came the next unpleasantness. I was handed a glass containing a castor oil sandwich, a layer of that most revolting laxative floating between two layers of orange juice. I said simply but firmly, "I can't drink that! I'll be sick!" "Nonsense," said the nurse briskly. "Drink it up!" I argued that I'd never been able to keep the horrible stuff down, but I had no option but to obey. "Now lie flat and you'll be all right," said the nurse. I lay flat and ten minutes later the nurse cleaned up both me and the bed. Not to be thwarted in her attempt to dose me, she brought a grey aluminium cup full of equally grey liquorice, which was another thing I disliked. I refused it doggedly. It was eventually left on my locker with sharp instructions to drink it. The other patients tried to coax me to drink the filthy stuff, but it was still on my locker next morning. The nurses gave up and took it away. I proved later in the day that I didn't need a laxative anyway.

For the next week my head was swathed in an enormous bandage like a turban. I felt much better and enjoyed my food, making a mental note to ask my mother why she had never given me steamed fish in white sauce mixed with mashed potatoes, which I thought tasted like nectar.

Came the day the bandages were taken off and the nurse told me she was going to "take out the packing." It was painless and fascinating. All I felt was an odd tickly sensation and heard inside my head a sort of swooshing sound. Curiosity overcame my fear and by swivelling my eyes to the left, I could just see what seemed to be a mile of orangey-yellow string slowly emerging from my head. I wondered how there had been room for it. The bandage replaced, I was once more escorted to the theatre to have stitches inserted under anaesthetic. Knowing what was coming I struggled, but was soon on my back with the mask on my face and whirling off into nothingness.

I was released from hospital a week later, when the stitches had been removed. It was 22nd March, Jean's eighth birthday. In spite of being a bit wobbly on my legs, I insisted on going to "Lewis's" to buy a present for her. My father was so relieved I was well that he agreed and I chose a canopied doll's cot which cost 5/11d (30p). Jean was delighted with her gift when we arrived home, and that cot remained in the family for years.

The doctor back home advised a long convalescence which resulted in my secondary schooling being abandoned for the rest of the school year.

Earraid

*A*fter the Easter holidays I joyfully rejoined the Earraid children at school. Some of them were strangers because they were periodically shifted about all over Scotland. Somehow this didn't seem to have an adverse effect on their education, as many lightkeeper's children became doctors, teachers, nurses and even authors. I spent my time revising the work I had done the previous year. By the summer I was fit and my cropped hair had grown in just as wavy and shiny as before. In my new-found state of good health, I joined more energetically than ever in the many diversions of the wee community, though I was aware that the pleasure was only temporary.

Relief day had its own ritual. Early in the day the *Hesperus* called to pick up the two keepers who were going on to the rocks. If we weren't at school, the entire juvenile population foregathered by the gate at the end of the Street, watching the brow of a hill. Suddenly two masts would glide along the top, whereupon we would give voice. "He-e-e-sprus, He-e-e-sprus," we chanted, until the womenfolk came out of the houses to go down to the pier with the two keepers, to greet the ship's launch and wave farewell to the two out-going men. Later in the day we went through the same performance with even more gusto, as two families were about to be reunited with their men for a couple of weeks.

We were, of course, greatly excited by the advent of visitors which were few in winter, but come summer a remarkable variety of people came to Earraid. Sometimes the "tinkies" came, selling clothes pegs and heather brooms, and

*The author with sister Jean
at Earraid.*

always asking for clothes "for the wee ones." My mother tried to find something they could use although we didn't have a vast wardrobe. My father's pay wasn't all that much, and Wee Granny lived on a widow's pension of 10/- a week (50p), so we had a sort of rota of everyday clothes. My summer dresses came from a friend in Glasgow whose daughter was a little older than me, then they went back to Glasgow for Mae, and finally to Jean, by which time they were the worse for wear. Once we found the things my mother had given the tinkers floating in the sea! We had a good laugh at my mother's discomfiture.

Whenever possible the local minister conducted a service in the school room. It was one of my father's regrets that he had so few opportunities to attend a church service throughout his service life. Once or twice at Earraid we had the pleasure of meeting a fine man, the Reverend George F. McLeod, later Lord McLeod of Fiunary, who was involved with the idea of restoring the crumbling and neglected Iona Abbey. Little did we know then how successful his project would be as the Abbey is now a thing of beauty and attracts thousands of visitors.

An annual visitor was the coal boat, *Alpha* and, unlike other vessels, she was able to sail right up to the pier. She came like a thief in the night, to be discovered in the morning, much to the delight of the children, but causing the adults to sigh, as it heralded several days of back-breaking work. We youngsters swarmed aboard and took up residence, having to be prised off to go to school or bed. We'd sit in the bows, watching the crane swinging down into the hold to emerge full of coal, then depositing its load in a welter of dust in the waiting cart. The cart, pulled by a big Clydesdale horse, had crossed the Full Vake at low tide from the farm. The men soon looked like pitmen, but most of the dust seemed to gravitate towards us. We had to wash and change every time we reluctantly went home for a meal. The mothers accepted this philosophically as they knew we had little enough excitement in our lives. Mr. McCorquodale and his crew were tolerant, joking with us and sharing their coal-dusty pieces with us while waiting for the empty cart to return.

The *Alpha* stayed at least three days as a great amount of coal was needed to last for a whole year. Each keeper had a generous allowance of about ten tons and the two principals a bit more, as their houses had an extra room. Then there was the teacher and Hughie the postman. One morning we'd wake up to find the puffer had slipped away, leaving nothing but coal dust sparkling on the pier and a few nuggets of coal that had fallen off the cart. We were at a loss for something to do for a wee while, but we were soon off on another ploy.

Every so often we were visited by some Very Important People. The flagship of the lighthouse fleet was the *Pharos*, based in Granton near Edinburgh. Each summer she'd set off on a cruise carrying the Commissioners. These were the Lord Advocate, Solicitor-general for Scotland, various Lord Provosts, sheriffs and magistrates. They cruised around the coast combining pleasure with business, calling at various lighthouse stations to inspect the premises. It was supposed to be a surprise visit but as the *Pharos* left one station, the keeper there would find some means of sending a message to the next port of call, saying, "The *Pharos* has just left heading your way." I'm sure the Commissioners knew that we knew, but they had little need to worry. The keepers took pride in their work and the womenfolk kept their houses like new pins.

We children loved the visit of the Commissioners, although at that time we had no idea who they were. It was cupboard love! Each of us was given a wee cardboard satchel full of the delectable, melt-in-the-mouth, pastel-coloured Edinburgh Rock, which was savoured down to the last crumb. While some of the V.I.P.s examined the premises, others walked about near the pier and made a fuss of us. The gentlemen looked out of place as, dressed in city suits or natty flannels, they sat on rocks or boxes, basking in the sun. I remember one who held us enthralled as we listened to the tune played by his pocket watch. We were sorry to see the *Pharos* steaming away, and as soon as possible, someone would send off the message, "They've just left heading your way!"

It was one of the Principal's tasks to submit a requisition for stores. Another highlight of our year was the day the *Hesperus* brought the stores from Oban. Earraid, housing more than the average number of personnel, needed a large amount of stores. It meant a great deal of hard work for the shore keepers as everything was piled into a store near the pier to be sorted out later for distribution. The horse and cart were not brought over but instead a big handcart was pulled by one man, while his opposite number and other helpers pushed from behind. It was another source of entertainment, with a gang of excited children anxious to help. We congregated round the door of the store, hopeful of being given something to deliver. Such a sense of importance I felt when the waiting housewife thanked me. The men were tolerant, only shouting at us if someone really got in among their feet. Perhaps we were useful as small beasts of burden.

My mother and the other ladies were supplied with a great variety of goods. When a man first joined the service he was issued with a plentiful supply of blankets, sheets and other bedding which were replaced as they wore thin. Most years everybody got at least one pair of blankets and several strong twill sheets. We loaded ourselves with dish towels, floor cloths, dish cloths, dusters and shammy leathers, Brasso for the lamps, black lead for the range, yellow soap and soft soap. The last-mentioned looked and felt like axle grease, but was marvellous for getting clothes clean and for shampooing. My mother never had to buy any basic household equipment, like pots and pans. All this largesse was given because it ensured that there was no excuse for having a scruffy station or a dirty house.

It was late summer when my mother started dropping hints that I'd have to think about going back to Glasgow to resume my education. I was in a better frame of mind because I felt better, but I wasn't keen on the idea.

This time I was going to stay with Wee Granny. The wee flat was only a "room and kitchen," with a box bed in each room so Aunt Jean and Granny would have to share the bed in the kitchen while Mae and I would sleep in the front room. We were cramped, but in all the years I lived there, never once was I made to feel a nuisance.

These good people came to Earraid that summer for a holiday, after which we travelled to Glasgow, except for my father, who had sacrificed his holiday when I was in hospital. Thus I embarked on yet another change in my life style. I was twelve and a half.

Back
to Glasgow

Since leaving the steel houses, Wee Granny had lived in the tenement at 1098 Shettleston Road. The local Methodist Church separated her home from the wee house where she had lived when we were at Inchkeith and directly across the street was the building she had come to as a bride. "Ten-nine-eight" as we called it, was an institution in our family. At various times and in various flats, the close housed my sister Jean with her husband Eric and daughter Christine, my mother and father in their retirement, and finally my cousin Peter and his wife.

Shettleston Road was long, winding its way from Beardmore's to the eastern outskirts of the city, en route for Coatbridge. The green tram (all Glasgow's trams were colour-coded), whined past Granny's window on its journey between Airdrie and Paisley Road Toll. The walls of the close were painted brownish-green (or was it greenish-brown?) but the stairwell was partially tiled to a height of about four feet, making it fairly desirable. The building was of red sandstone and three storeys, housing shops on the ground floor. In both directions, the same pattern was repeated, broken only by side streets at intervals. There must have been hundreds of little shops doing a roaring trade six days a week. Our building housed a barber, a greengrocer, a newsagent, a dairy, a draper, a grocer, and a "tally" chip shop. This was the environment in which I was to spend most of the next five years, and my heart sank as I climbed the stairs to the first landing. The shops still looked dingy, the street looked grey and the sky seemed very far away.

Wee Granny's house was typical of its era though the bathroom made it superior to some. The sink in the kitchen window gave Granny great pride, as it had two brass taps. It was quite a luxury to have hot and cold running water. Just inside the kitchen door was the coal bunker and once a week the coalman's call of "cooooe-ll" echoed up the close as he climbed the stairs with a hundredweight sack on his back. Granny removed anything which might get covered in coal dust, as the contents of the sack were dumped unceremoniously into the bunker, throwing up black clouds and leaving dirty streaks on the lobby wall.

Granny had a range for cooking and heating, and on its top was an ingenious gas appliance to augment the fire. It lifted vertically out of the way against the side of the range top, folding down only when needed. When I first stayed there I had difficulty in adjusting to the smallness of the rooms. As well as the bunker, the kitchen held two armchairs, a big square table with dining chairs, and a sideboard, after which there was no room to swing a kitten, far less a cat.

The front room was perpetually dark, the windows faced north and were covered by an assortment of draperies. Spotless white lace curtains hung on the lower half of the sections. Yellow linen blinds with fancy lace edges were pulled down to a carefully measured level, while framing the whole were dark green chenille floor-length curtains. As though to mask the light even more, the window ledge held several aspidistras. Every time I went "ben the room" I felt claustrophobic. The flat was on the first floor, just above a corporation tram stop and Granny couldn't abide the idea of passengers looking in her window.

This room was meant to be a parlour. It was dominated by a huge mahogany wardrobe and an equally cumbersome tallboy. The bed recess where Mae and I slept was hidden by more heavy curtains. The kitchen here was cheery with its sunny aspect overlooking some playing fields, just over the wall from the drying "green". We had a panoramic view over the rooftops to the Cathkin Braes, which on a sunny day looked attractive despite the soot-laden clouds which rose from the Clyde Ironworks.

I felt bereft when the others went back to Earraid, and I was back at Eastbank to repeat first year. Having gone through the ritual before, I was able to guide my new classmates through the intricacies and hazards of finding their way about in the first weeks. This time I made friends with a few of the girls.

I liked most of my subjects, barring history and games. In the coldest days I was expected to cavort about the exposed playing field, having divested myself of the layers of warm clothing which Granny deemed necessary. Apart from the usual vest and regulation black knickers, I wore a thick fleecy liberty bodice. It was a waistcoat equipped with numerous rubbery buttons and from four of these hung suspenders which held up my thick black stockings, though so loosely I felt they would fall round my ankles. I constantly hitched them up, usually by shrugging my shoulders. On top of all that I wore two woolly jerseys, an old one under my blouse and a decent one on top.

On the hockey field I shivered in a short-sleeved blouse, short cotton socks on my goose-pimply legs. To make matters worse, I knew nothing about the game. I was terrified of the heavy sticks and even more so of the hard ball. I avoided contact with these two objects, by loping up and down the side lines trying to look keen and unafraid and failing miserably. I just turned more and more blue with cold. The gym teacher soon gave up any attempt to rouse enthusiasm in me.

Gymnastics was another matter. I loved the gym hall with its dark varnished wall-bars and strong ropes hanging from the ceiling. Here I was in my element, having developed agility in the store at Earraid and on the rocks and hills. Once I forgot my shorts and was made to do the exercises wearing my black knickers as a substitute. I was mortified, having been brought up to believe it was rude to expose my nether garments to the public view. What bothered me most was the classes of boys who passed by sniggering on their way to an art lesson. Eastbank had no mixed classes until fourth and fifth year, so every opportunity was grasped to giggle or snigger when the sexes crossed paths.

We were segregated in the playground by a high railing. At playtime there was always a faction congregating along the railings chatting each other up or, more often, being rude to each other. A few of the older ones stood holding hands and whispering sweet nothings through the bars until the duty patrolling teacher broke it up. I had enough difficulty in forming friendships with girls so I just watched and wondered.

The girls were a bit contemptuous of me until the day I showed my true colours. One girl had a habit of tormenting the younger ones. I noticed her one day moving around the playground jabbing unsuspecting bystanders with the business end of a cheap brooch. She caught me unawares and stuck her pin painfully into my rump. My temper rose. I chased her round the playground several times before I got hold of her and walloped her unmercifully. Tearfully she threatened she would bring her mother to see the headmaster. I went home at dinnertime shaking in my shoes but I heard no more about it. From then she stopped bullying and I was treated with a little more respect and was no longer looked upon as a namby-pamby hick from the sticks.

There was nothing spectacular about my school work but I kept a little above the average. I became sophisticated enough to refer to the teachers by their nicknames. Miss Hogarth, the geography teacher, was Hoagy; Miss Nichol, who taught Maths, was Biddy and the headmaster was known as Gandhi for the simple reason that, given a dhoti, he would have been the spitting image of that revered gentleman. I never knew why the assistant head, Mr. McKenzie, was called Snudge.

In the thirties education at state schools was free, but all equipment had to be bought. This was not as costly as might be imagined. Down the street from the school was a shop specialising in school supplies. At the end of each session I sold my textbooks to the shop and bought the next year's prescribed books, which could be second, third, or even fourth hand. It worked well, the shop making a small profit with little or no outlay, and the parents content with the economy of the scheme. There was always a crowd of us in the shop, carefully choosing pencils and rulers.

Near the school was the inevitable tuck shop, where I could pick from a wide range of sweeties, buying four different kinds for one penny: maybe acid drops, dolly mixtures, conversation lozenges and cherry lips. The last-mentioned when rubbed on the lips gave an appearance of lipstick, which decadent make-up I and most others were forbidden to use. When the Shirley Temple films were all the rage, the tuck shop did a roaring trade in the first spherical lollipop, called "the Good Ship Lollipop", after the hit song of the same name.

It was difficult to adapt to the dirt and grime of the city. On the islands I only had to wash my face once a day, but in Glasgow I had to perform my ablutions several times a day, while my hands needed washing so often I was sure I'd wash them away. I hated the black rim of soot that collected around my nostrils. Granny's house, fronting the main road, was bombarded day and night by the noise of trams, buses, and lorries. It was some time before my brain adapted to the disturbance, but soon I slept like a log, and then found it hard to adjust to the silence at Earraid.

Mae initiated me into going to the pictures. Once, when I was very young, I had been taken to see Charlie Chaplin. During a scene in which he was supposed to be loading a block of ice into an ice-box, he mistakenly shoved it in the hot oven from which it naturally shot out again carrying him across the room with it. I thought he was going to be hurt and had hysterics. I had to be removed before I wrecked the pleasure of the more normal audience.

The first talkie I saw was *Roman Scandals*, a hilarious comedy, and I quickly became an addict. Shettleston rejoiced in three picture houses, the oldest one being the Premier, which was reputed to be a bug-house. We patronised the Palaceum, an old but clean establishment which showed the best films, and on rare occasions had stage shows starring such famous comedians as Tommy Lorne and Tommy Morgan. The Palaceum was popular in winter since they had an inside waiting room in which customers could queue in comfort. The Broadway was the height of comfort and luxury and was only a few hundred yards from Wee Granny's. There I first saw *Snow White and the Seven Dwarfs*, and was entranced by the colour, music and magic of the cartoonists.

I was taken there to the Saturday matinee on my first date with a boy. We were both fifteen; I was long and lanky, he was short, stocky and cross-eyed. We met outside the sweetie shop where I was given the choice of having a quarter of sweeties and sit in the cheap front stalls or go to the better seats and stay hungry. I opted for the better seats because in the front stalls the characters were distorted and the picture ruined. The experiment was not repeated. I was happier and more relaxed going with Mae, when I was able to munch sweeties as I drooled over Nelson Eddy and Jeanette MacDonald, or laughed at the Marx Brothers. Sometimes Granny or Aunt Jean took us to an evening showing, and afterwards for a special treat in winter to Demarco's for hot peas and vinegar. This simple dish was delectable. It was only a saucer of peas sprinkled with vinegar and pepper, sold by the "tallies" when ice cream wasn't in season. The memory makes my mouth water.

Mae and I had to help with the chores. On Saturdays we dusted the front room and washed and polished the aspidistras before going for the messages. At Templeton the grocer's, I watched as the assistant cut chunks out of a huge lump of butter, patting it into shape with a pair of wooden bats. Cheese, also in a huge chunk, was sliced with a bit of fine wire and was seldom more or less than the customer asked for. Sugar was weighed and poured into thick blue paper bags, the tops folded neatly in. All the youngsters got a sweetie from the shopkeeper. Next, I was usually sent downstairs to Greig's the greengrocer, where I'd ask for "threepence worth of vegetables for soup," and would be given carrots, turnip, leeks and parsley, none of which were weighed. A quarter of tatties, shovelled into scales resembling a coal scuttle, completed my purchases before I went to the butcher's. I usually tried to arrange that Mae would take it on as I was embarrassed by the things I had to ask for, like "Pope's Eye" and "a bit off the thick (or thin) of the runner." At the tobacconist-cum-paper shop I'd buy fire-lighters and pipe clay, the latter for the weekly stair-washing ritual. Granny, like all tenement dwellers, had to take her turn of the stairs. These housewives were proud of "their" stair, and as they scrubbed they decorated the sides of each step with intricate whorls and scallops of pipe clay. It was applied while the steps were wet, and woe betide any of us who went downstairs too close to the sides, disturbing the artistic handiwork.

On Saturday afternoon we were free, and as we grew we were allowed to take the tram into Argyle Street to Lewis's and Woolworth's. Here we decided what to spend our sixpence on. Once I acquired an "emerald and diamond" bracelet for sixpence, which glittered satisfyingly on my wrist. I wore it often, until the stones began to fall out.

Sundays were quiet; we had a long lie before going to church after the customary ham and egg breakfast. The Reverend Donald Johnston with his strong Highland accent made me feel homesick. Mae and I were often bored by the long sermons, and we found ourselves yawning in spite of Granny's supply of mint imperials. Mae devised a plan to combat this. On Friday nights we sneakily applied clear nail varnish, knowing that by Sunday it would be just right for peeling off. We sat in church, heads bowed, picking at the nails of one hand while Mr. Johnston discoursed on the topic of the week.

After dinner it was back to the church hall for Sunday School. After that, I had to pay my duty visit to my other grandparents. They had moved to a more convenient flat only one stair up and in the next close to Uncle Jack. Here I had tea with the family before going to the Methodist Church, which my father's family attended. I liked the cheerful hymns and the lively sermons. Later I walked home alone to Shettleston, the streets usually being thronged with families out for a Sunday walk if the weather was fine.

I went home to Earraid every school holiday. I'd sometimes sigh and say to Granny, "Oh! I wish it was Christmas," or Easter or whatever. Always her answer was the same. "You're wishing your life away, lassie." When the longed-for time came round, Mae and I eagerly helped pack our cases. We were still a bit young to travel on our own with so many changes of transport, so Granny usually accompanied us.

On the day, Granny was up before six, making the huge breakfast that she declared we needed. Mae and I were dressed in our Sunday best amid dire warnings not to get our clothes dirty. The suitcases weighed a ton. We staggered down to the tram stop, where we worried that there would be a hold up in the flow of trams as one broken-down tram stopped all those following. Granny shepherded us and the cases on to the tram under the eyes of the early morning workers, who were unused to seeing people dressed up on a weekday morning. On arrival at Buchanan Street station, we dragged the cases to platform 12, the furthest one from the entrance. There we awaited the arrival of the train, wrapped in travelling rugs, partly for warmth, but mainly to keep us clean. After an hour's wait, we were so cold and stiff we could scarcely move. The train was cold, too, so although we had the pick of the seats, we were well on our way before we thawed out, even in summer.

In spite of that, I enjoyed the trip to Oban, soon heading for the greener countryside of rolling hills and small mining villages towards Larbert. After Stirling the scenery changed, the hills giving way to mountains and the land becoming more rugged. Above Lochearnhead, the train chugged round the side of a mountain. I had to strain my eyes to glimpse the top of it, but on the other side was one of the finest views in Scotland. Below in the valley, beyond a graceful viaduct, lay the village of Lochearnhead and the loch from which it takes its name. Alas, neither of these lines now exists.

Beyond Crianlarich, the land was wild and almost uninhabited until we reached the beautiful ribbon of water that is Loch Awe. We had been told that the Pass of Brander on Loch Awe side was dangerous, enormous boulders on the mountains being held up by chains to prevent them rolling down on to the railway line. Mae and I sighed with relief when the land became more open on the last lap to Oban, and Ben Cruachan was left far behind. We lowered the window by its leather strap and soon the familiar smell of salt water, fish, oil and tar filtered into the carriage, as pleasing to my nostrils as the scent of the most expensive perfume. We sniffed deeply as the train, brakes screeching, ran down the last incline into the station at Oban. Our holiday had now truly begun.

Travelling with Granny was always different and often an entertainment. One summer she insisted on wearing a heavy musquash coat she had acquired as the result of a small legacy. The weather was scorching, but nothing would persuade her to leave it at home, in case it was stolen. When Granny ducked to emerge from the taxi at the station she couldn't see her feet for her furry apparel, tripped over the step and plunged headlong towards the pavement. I had got out first and made a quick grab to save her. Unfortunately it was her face my hand made contact with, a sound like a mighty slap. I broke her fall, but nearly broke her neck as well. We all burst out laughing, unable to hurry for the train. Next time we travelled she left the fur coat in the care of a trusted neighbour!

The journey back to Glasgow wasn't so enjoyable. As we approached the city we could see the pall of smoke, and I knew I would be fighting the grime again. After one such trip we were met by Aunt Jean, who said she had a nice surprise waiting at Ten-nine-eight. I rushed in eagerly, only to find that electricity had been installed. I couldn't have cared less and to everybody's surprise I burst into tears and was inconsolable for ages.

Once a week I diligently wrote home. My mother and father must have suffered, knowing how much I disliked the city as it must surely have come over in my letters. My mother missed out on a lot of pleasure which a mother should be able to experience. She never saw any of my school reports. She wasn't around when I collected my first pay packet, nor did she see me in uniform when I was first called up during the war. She didn't even meet my husband-to-be until four days before the wedding.

Letters from home said most of the time that life was going on smoothly enough with only the occasional interruption. One such was when Jean developed jaundice, turning a peculiar shade of yellow. It was attributed to her having "taken a scunner" at eggs. There was no particular treatment, Jean was kept warm and given bland food until she recovered.

During Jean's illness someone brought her a beautiful blue half-Persian kitten from Iona to cheer her up. It helped her recovery, giving her an interest for the first time in weeks. The kitten was christened "Puss", but Jean kept adding bits to the name until it must have had one of the longest cat names ever – Pussabossomstissergochie. However, she was still called Puss for short and lived to be twenty-two. There were never any suitors available at the islands, so she had no kittens to take her place.

Earraid had its share of tragedy, too. The shore keeper had crossed the ferry for the daily supply of milk, taking with him his two wee boys. The boys were left playing on the safe side of the stile that we used to climb over the three-wire fence. The seven-year-old had strict instructions not to go near the sea. He promised, but soon succumbed to the temptation to throw stones in the water. Knowing his wee brother couldn't climb the stile, he assumed he'd be safe. He didn't realise that the wee lad could easily crawl under the fence. Wee John did just that and toddled after his big brother.

From the other side of the ferry, the mother looked across to see if there was any sign of her husband returning. Horrified, she saw her littlest one fall in the water, to float away unnoticed by the older lad. The poor woman, powerless to do anything to save him, screamed, and soon all the women rushed down to the pier in a panic. The father, could be seen wending his way back from the farm, taking his time to avoid spilling the milk, unaware of the shock that awaited him. It was his dreadful task to fish the body of his son from the tangle of seaweed that had kept him from floating too far away. The couple were broken-hearted and the whole community was shocked. As soon as possible the family was moved to another station.

My father, too, had a serious accident. He was breaking up large lumps of coal when a tiny splinter flew into his eye, causing him a great deal of pain. My mother had to send for the doctor, who agreed he had to go to the Eye Infirmary in Glasgow. By the time he reached hospital his eye was badly inflamed, watering so badly he could scarcely see where he was going, and his head fit to burst. A small operation removed the offending object and he returned home a few days later. He confessed later he had been convinced that, like his father, he would end up with a glass eye. Even worse, he would have to leave his beloved lighthouse service.

Back in Glasgow, life went on in a monotonous round of school, housework, picture shows and church-going. I had no idea that history was in the making; that events were taking place that were to change forever our peaceful existence. I knew vaguely that a man called Adolf Hitler was making a name for himself in Germany, and that our own King George V, was growing old. Happy in my ignorance I still lived only for the holidays. Granny was so busy trying to make ends meet that she had little time to concern herself with world affairs. I was thirteen when the country celebrated the Silver Jubilee of our King and Queen. Glasgow Corporation treated the schools to a day trip "doon the watter" to commemorate the event. I was excited as it meant that for a few extra hours I could escape the city streets. I didn't realize how lucky I really was. Many of my classmates hadn't been outside Glasgow in their lives.

A day or two before the trip I began to feel out of sorts. Nothing specific; I just felt odd, with a dull ache in the pit of my stomach. I told no one, in case I missed the trip. When Granny asked me why I was going about like a half-shut knife, I straightened up and denied I was in pain. On the morning of the trip I set off to join the milling throng of excited school mates, feeling absolutely miserable. Granny and Aunt Jean maybe knew the cause but I was in complete ignorance.

The pupils in the playground were marshalled into order, and shepherded into the line of waiting trams that were to take us to one of the Clyde steamers. At the docks we streamed out like ticker tape and swarmed up the gangways. We had been warned not to lean over the ship's rail or to open portholes, so the teachers gave up hope of firm control and walked round the deck, keeping a wary eye open.

It was a glorious day, with a cloudless sky, and not a breath of wind. What a pity I couldn't appreciate it. I sought out a secluded corner on the promenade deck where I sat nursing my sore stomach. The few friends who tried to persuade me to come with them, were greeted with a sullen refusal. I saw none of the scenery as we sailed to Lochgoilhead. Once there, I had to rouse myself and walk with the others to a field which seemed miles from the pier. There we were issued with paper bags of food and our school milk. Afterwards there were games and races, a display of Highland dancing and such like, before we were allowed some free time. I wandered off to find a secluded spot where I sat thinking miserable thoughts of home. What a shame! It really was a super day well worth happy memories.

On the return journey I re-ensconced myself in my hideaway seat. A lot of subdued screaming was going on somewhere. I was roused from my misery by curiosity as girls appeared from the lower regions of the steamer looking flushed and slightly dishevelled. One of my classmates stopped to sit beside me to put me in the picture. Below decks some of the more adventurous boys had blacked out the portholes by leaning against them, while others captured any unsuspecting girls, and attempted to pull their knickers down. As word got around, more and more girls "happened" to pass that way and a good time was had by all. That, as far as I know, was the full extent of the caper. It was a daring thing to do in those days. The teachers were unable to catch anybody because when warning was given of the approach of a teacher, the "blackouts" merely stepped away from the portholes and stood about looking the picture of innocence.

The next morning I discovered the reason for my aches. I had "grown up" and was now a young woman. How thankful I was when everything was made clear to me by Aunt Jean. I made up my mind that if ever I had a daughter, she would be told in advance the necessary facts of life!

The next year, 1936, was marked by two major family events, which took place at the same time. Early in March, something happened which nearly wrecked Wee Granny's life. When her own three children were growing up, she had adopted an unwanted baby boy. David became her youngest and most dearly loved child. He grew up handsome and intelligent, and on coming of age decided to seek his fortune in America. He had been gone ten years, had worked his way through university to obtain a degree in engineering, and was about to embark on a prosperous career, when he took ill and died of peritonitis on his thirty-fourth birthday.

On that Saturday morning, I heard Granny rise from her bed and open the outer double doors that were always locked and bolted at night. Then she closed the door and all was quiet. I put on the bed light and sleepily noticed it was only six o'clock. On Saturdays Granny had a "long lie" until eight, so I wondered why she was up so early. I asked at breakfast what had roused her so early. "I thought there was somebody at the door," she said, "but I must have been dreaming." None of us gave it another thought. At eleven o'clock a cable arrived stating baldly that David had died and the sender needed instructions for the funeral. Granny sat down in her favourite chair, threw her apron up over her face and for the rest of the day rocked back and forth crooning over and over again, "Davie's deid!" It was only some days later, when she got a detailed letter, that we realised her beloved Davie had died at the time she had risen to open the door. She swore from that day that she had been letting in his spirit.

My mother had been told the sad news but she couldn't come to comfort Granny, as she was in the throes of packing. That was the second major event. My parents had opened the official letter hopefully. They prayed for a station on the mainland, as Jean was approaching secondary school age. The shift was to the Rhinns of Islay, another outlandish place, my father to take up his duties on 10th March. The flitting stopped my mother from thinking too much of the loss of her brother, but it was with a greater sense of sadness than ever that the family said goodbye to their neighbours. I was at school and wouldn't get home to say goodbye. I was sad at the thought, but I was growing away from the pleasures of childhood now that I was fourteen, and was surprised to find myself looking forward to the Easter holidays when I could go home to a new island waiting to be explored and new people to be met.

The Rhinns of Islay

The lighthouse known as the Rhinns of Islay is on the highest point of the small island of Orsay off the southwest tip of Islay, one of the biggest and the most southerly of the Inner Hebrides. On a clear day looking south you could see the houses on Rathlin Island and the coast of Ireland. The stretch of water in between was one of the busiest sea routes to America, hence the need for a lighthouse.

My mother saw how small and bare Orsay was, and realised she was still not going to have an easy time shopping or going on holiday. My father, on the other hand, could put all these problems aside in his pleasure at returning to an old familiar spot. When his father was keeper at the same station, my father had attended the local primary school. He could hardly wait to find out if any of his old classmates were still around.

It was a few weeks after the shift before Mae and I made the acquaintance of the new home. Granny, Mae and I set off on a new but equally long road to the isles; one with which we were to become very familiar, as my father stayed there longer than at any previous station. The train from Glasgow Central took us to Gourock, that popular holiday resort of Glaswegians. There we boarded the MacBrayne's steamer *Columba,* for a voyage through one of the finest waterways in Britain, crossing to Dunoon, on to Innellan, Rothesay and Tigh-nabruich, before passing through the Kyles of Bute towards our next change of transport at Tarbert Loch Fyne. I had no time to admire the picturesque town, as waiting for us was the bus to take us across the isthmus to West Loch Tarbert

The Rhinns of Islay lighthouse.

and our next steamer. There was a rush for the gangplank with Granny being afraid we wouldn't get on the bus. Mae and I were herded ahead of her with cries of "Hurry up and get in front of that big woman," and similar embarrassing instructions. Breathless, we threw ourselves into the nearest seats, and were soon on our way. Scarcely had we got our breath back than the bus screeched to a halt. To my astonishment we were at the next pier. It was then I learned exactly what the word isthmus means. The neck of land between the two piers was only about two miles wide, making Kintyre almost an island.

Waiting at the pier was the *Pioneer*, an ancient paddle steamer which looked too old to make any kind of voyage, far less one of four hours duration. We were to learn in the next few years that she was capable of crossing in any weather barring a hurricane.

For the first hour we steamed down a fiord-like loch with hills and mountains close on either side, until the loch opened out into the Sound of Jura. Ahead was the green isle of Islay, to the right the unmistakable and aptly named twin mountains, the Paps of Jura, were silhouetted against the clear blue sky. The *Pioneer* stopped near the wee island of Gigha, where a small boat came out to pick up sundry passengers and bundles, some of which wriggled. Farmers found the most convenient way to transport calves was to tie them loosely into sacks, leaving their heads free. This mode of travel didn't seem to worry the wee beasts as they lay on deck contentedly chewing the cud and gazing placidly at the passers-by.

On we went towards Islay. The steamer service alternated between Port Askaig in the north, and the much larger town of Port Ellen in the south. This was one of the Port Ellen days. We were intrigued by several factory-like buildings which seemed out of place in such a beautiful setting. They were distilleries and formed the most important industry of Islay. One of them had a huge white horse painted on the roof.

I was surprised at the size of Port Ellen, with its many hotels and shops. At the pier we were met by the car my father had sent, and soon we were on the second-last leg of our journey. A few miles out of town the road stretched ahead in a seemingly endless straight line. It was straight for seven miles and was known locally as the "Seven Miles Straight." Halfway along this phenomenon was an airport. On the landing strip stood a little plane. It was the first time I'd seen one close to and on the ground. What excitement! I found out later that many of the local people who were used to seeing planes had never seen a train.

We drove through Bowmore, with its round church, before skirting Lochindaal and heading south at last. While Mull is dominated by rugged mountains, Islay is softer, with rounded hills and lots of grass. It was a pleasant prospect all the way, but we were all getting tired, hungry and impatient by the time we turned a corner and suddenly saw before us the white tower that was to become so familiar.

When we drove through Port Wemyss, the road disintegrated into a narrow earthen path which fell haphazardly down a steep slope to the slipway. It was necessary to descend the slope like crabs to where the rowing boat waited to take us across. It wasn't easy for Granny, but with much grunting and help from the boatman, she was eventually seated in the boat. We waved like mad at the entire population of the Rhinns standing on the little pier on the other side of the narrow sound that gave us the most hair-raising five minutes of the day.

The sound was only a few hundred yards wide, but through it ran a powerful current, making it difficult for the experienced to negotiate and downright dangerous for anybody else. The current varied depending on the state of the tides. At that particular time it was at its height. The boatman had to row strongly, parallel to the shore against the current, until he reached a choppy bit of water which swung the wee boat sickeningly round to be swept rapidly back the way we had just come, the boatman rowing as strongly as he could at right angles to the current. In this way he reached the other pier safely. I was relieved when we landed all in one piece, but my father soon mastered the art and later even Jean and I were able to take an oar in the wee boat we kept on the island for fishing. We still had an uphill walk ahead of us before we could regather our strength with one of my mother's famous meals. Although the Rhinns was only a holiday home for me, it was where my mother and father lived, and so it soon became very dear to me. Earraid was already as though remembered in a dream.

On Islay with the author (second from left) are cousin Jean, and author's sister Jean (fourth and fifth left).

The Easter holidays passed happily and quickly in exploring the new island. Compared to Earraid it was tiny: a low, green place, treeless and apparently devoid of interesting features. It boasted three little sandy beaches, all of which we came to regard as our own, feeling somewhat resentful when we found visitors from the city disporting themselves on "our" sand.

Some way up from the pier was the usual "park" which contained the main garden and the henrun. Another behind it contained a small ruined chapel, in front of which stood a handsome Celtic cross. According to the local populace St. Columba was supposed to have landed on Orsay when he sailed from Ireland, and built the wee chapel intending to use it as his base, until one clear day he saw his homeland in the distance, felt homesick, and moved further north, finally settling on Iona.

Near the park was a deep gully known as the Geohore. (Unfortunately I have no idea of the correct spelling or pronunciation). In stormy weather with the wind in the right direction, it filled to a depth of maybe twenty feet with yellowy sea foam. Jean and I stood as near the edge as we dared, looking down and wondering what it would be like to fall in. Fortunately we never found out.

The Rhinns suffered from a great deal of thick, impenetrable fog, so the station had three keepers. In foggy weather, one man was on duty in the lightroom, one was asleep and the third was in the engine room looking after the fog horn. With only three hours off duty out of nine, they dreaded the foggy season. I found the engine room fascinating in spite of the noise. Three huge gleaming engines took up most of the floor space. I was wary of the great fly wheels, each of which weighed upwards of two tons, pounding round, pulsing rhythmically while the engine produced compressed air for the foghorn perched high up on the rocks facing the Irish Channel. Every three minutes the huge replica of the trade mark of "His Master's Voice" emitted three successive moaning blasts, muffled by the fog. We heard it loudly enough in the house, but we soon became unaware of the noise. Somebody would say after a while, "Listen! Is that foghorn still on?" Everyone would stop and be quiet and a minute later the loud moan would be heard.

The other two lightkeepers and their families proved to be every bit as friendly as previous neighbours. As with any group of people forced into close proximity, there was the odd incident that sparked off a temporary disagreement, but it soon passed and harmony was restored. I'm sure that the men were chosen as much for their ability to live in harmony as for any technical knowledge.

When the weather allowed, the ladies made frequent excursions across the ferry to the twin villages of Port Wemyss and Portnahaven, which were separated by a few hundred yards of rough road. The houses of Portnahaven lay in two tiers round a harbour which at one time had boasted a fair number of boats, but at the time I speak of, was occupied only by a few small rowing boats and the occasional skiff. There was one hotel, a Post Office-cum-general store and two other quaint shops which sold everything from a needle to an anchor. Port Wemyss had no harbour, only two shops and there was no Post Office. The two villages shared a hall, a school, and two churches. The first two and one of the churches were sited together at the apex of a triangle formed by two roads leading from the villages to the rest of Islay.

Going shopping at Islay.

The local people were very friendly towards the lightkeepers, taking each new family to their hearts. I seldom heard the native Gaelic spoken because if a non-Gaelic speaker happened along, the villagers immediately switched to English out of courtesy. I was envious of the bilingual prowess of even the smallest child, who, if spoken to in Gaelic answered in Gaelic, but equally fluently answered in English if one of us spoke to them. I only ever learned a few phrases in Gaelic, mostly everyday greetings and commands for sheepdogs, like "Come here, boy!" and "Stay!" gleaned from a local farmer.

Our official boatman lived in Port Wemyss. He was a tall rangy man of indeterminate age, who had been a sea captain. We knew him only as Captain John. He was an excellent seaman who could be trusted to ferry us safely "ofer across" as he called it, in his wee rowing boat, the *Staghound*, named after his last ship. If Captain John said we couldn't go, we couldn't go. Nobody argued with his judgement.

Once we knew him better he used to tease us unmercifully. He'd row the *Staghound* into the tide race, then ship his oars, announcing, "Chust wait until I light my pipe." He'd take what seemed an interminable time to strike a match and suck on his pipe, before leisurely putting out the oars at exactly the right moment to head for the pier. Sometimes in calm weather he'd let the boat drift past the pier as though heading for the open sea, whereupon he'd leer at us and say, "Now I haf you in my power!" When we dutifully looked worried, he'd laugh and turn the boat for home. He wouldn't have harmed us for the world.

Jean, now ten, had to attend the local primary, a sturdy one-roomed school like the one in Orkney and there she soon acquired a lovely Highland lilt. Dialects are so easily picked up that Jean and I finished up with an almost unrecognisable accent: a composite of Manx, Orcadian, Highland and Glaswegian, with a touch of East coast Scots thrown in for good measure.

My mother and father had problems getting Jean to and from school. It was easy enough in calm weather apart from the ever present tide race. Captain John rowed her across. She was often absent in really fierce weather, but the touch and go days were the worst. My father escorted her down to the pier to help her aboard the boat, which often heaved up and down as it waited, and rocked from side to side into the bargain. Captain John stood holding it as steady as he could, while Jean waited for the order, "Run!" whereupon, though hampered by oilskins and wellingtons, she sprinted across the pier to take a flying leap into the *Staghound*. Captain John could be trusted implicitly to time his shout so that Jean never missed landing safely in the wee boat.

Although I still disliked Glasgow, I was thankful that my daily journey to school wasn't fraught with such obstacles. Back in Glasgow for the autumn term of 1936, the country was stunned by the death of King George V. The Prince of Wales became Edward VIII but the country had scarcely started to think of his coronation when things began to go wrong. I picked up the rumour that the new king might have to abdicate and shortly before Christmas, I found myself listening to the speech in which the King said he was giving up the throne for the woman he loved, but who could never be queen. I failed to understand, but knew it was important as everyone looked so solemn, Wee Granny shaking her head and tut-tutting. Now I had to get used to yet another king, this time the younger brother of Edward, who was to be known as King George VI. I was even more confused because until then he had been Albert, Duke of York.

May 12th, 1937, was set for the Coronation of the new king and queen. Glasgow broke out in a rash of red, white and blue, months ahead of the date and new streamlined trams appeared on the streets in honour of the occasion. Mae and I were more interested in these than in the Coronation itself. Until the novelty wore off we'd let the old trams go by in order to ride on these yellow and green liveried beauties while the older folk preferred the more easily recognised colour-coded old faithfuls. I remember being given an emblazoned Coronation mug, which has long since vanished.

The summer holiday after the Coronation was a happy time. One thing spoiled it for me. I suddenly noticed that my mother looked older. Her hair had turned grey and her face had become lined. Maybe I was just growing up and starting to pay more attention to other people, but my father remained unchanged apart

One of our summer amusements – the Bandy Pool.

The family at Islay – around 1938 or 39.

from being a bit fatter. I worried silently about my mother, feeling sure I was going to lose her altogether, and as always she said nothing about herself.

In spite of that we enjoyed the peace and quiet of the island. Several times a week we'd go "over across," making the most of the balmy days, and it was on one of these jaunts that we acquired our second pet. We were in Georgina's wee shop in Port Wemyss, which was really only a room in her house, when I noticed a miserable tiny kitten, no more than six weeks old, slumped inside a fireguard. Georgina had put it there after she caught her toddler using the poor wee beast as a ball, bouncing it off the wall. I pleaded to be allowed to take it home. My mother, not an animal lover, though she always said she "wouldn't be ill to one," said, "Well! Please yourself, but your father'll probably throw it out and you with it!" I knew my father would do no such thing, so the wee kitten was tucked inside my cardigan where it cowered, shivering, all the way home.

As I predicted, my father was no problem but Jean's cat was! Having never seen another cat, it took a few days before she stopped hissing and spitting, and accepted the wee one by licking it all over. The newcomer was named Stripey. She recovered from her bad start in life, becoming sleek and healthy, but never grew to full size.

Apart from the cats, the island supported the usual hens and for the first time in our experience, ducks. My father found a nearby pond which looked ideal, so he bought several duck eggs and set them under a "clocker," resulting in a near nervous breakdown for the hen when her brood suddenly took to the water.

There was also a small herd of goats, six or seven nannies, and one ferocious and evil-smelling billy. The goat's milk was handy and we all became accustomed to its strong flavour. The nannies duly gave birth every year, keeping the milk supply flowing, but sadly only one or two of the kids could be kept. Excess nannies and any unfortunate enough to be males, were put down. My father said that was the most difficult and unhappy job he ever had to do. Unwanted kittens were disposed of in the same way; otherwise the villages would have been overrun by cats.

We kept one kid, a beautiful pure white nanny. She was perfect except that her horns turned inwards. She was taken from her mother, otherwise she would have taken all the milk that was needed by us. I was home at the time so I was given the job of feeding her. We had no teats for a bottle so my father taught me how to manage without. I inserted my middle finger into Whitey's mouth, in as near as possible to the natural position from which she would have suckled her mother. After a few abortive sucks my finger would suddenly feel as though glued to the roof of her mouth. Once firmly in position, I lowered my hand into a pot of warm milk, which disappeared as it was sucked up via my finger. I ended up with callouses on my knuckles caused by Whitey's sharp little teeth.

She became so tame she came into the house every time she found the door open and settled down on the settee to chew the cud, until my mother chased her out. Whitey was so used to sitting on my lap to be fed that she still tried to do so when she was almost full grown. Whitey lived to a ripe old age, until she eventually took to the wild at my father's last station. My father used to see her and two other goats high up on the hill. She never forgot her surrogate mother! After several years absence I only needed to call her name. She'd lift her old head, and come down the hill to greet me, nuzzling me, asking me to scratch between her horns as I used to do. She came down for no one else.

Each station seemed to provide us with a new delicacy for the table, entirely free. The Rhinns lay in the migratory lanes of many species of birds. When this was in season, dozens, and sometimes hundreds of birds committed hara-kiri. Attracted to the light, they literally hurled themselves at the windows, breaking their necks or stunning themselves so that they fell to the ground and were killed. There was no point in wasting this manna from heaven, said my mother, so we dined off roasted golden plover feeling like the aristocracy. They were delicious.

Fishing was good at the Rhinns. In all but the worst of weather my father was able to catch lythe and podleys and when he couldn't take the boat out he fished with a rod from a promontory near the pier. This became so habitual that the spot became known in the village as Petrie's Point. I sometimes joined him and learned to cast a reasonable line. More often, though, Jean and I preferred to accompany him in the boat, the best time being at dusk. My father rowing, Jean and I trailed lines over the stern, drawing them back and forth in a steady rhythm, making the rubber eel spin invitingly in the water. There's an odd sensation of elation when, after trailing a line for some time, you feel the little jerks as the fish takes the bait. Sometimes the jerks were anything but little, a lythe weighing up to fourteen pounds. When a big one took the bait a tug of war took place to bring it close to the side of the boat, far less lift it bodily into the boat. The lythe is a beautiful fish, the skin and scales a lovely reddish gold with fine markings. In the right season we could run into a shoal of suicidal mackerel. They launched themselves in dozens on to the waiting lines and we could have filled the boat, but only took as many as we could eat in one go, practically having to fend off the silly things.

At the end of the evening we rowed home. As we neared the pier we could see the two cats outlined against the darkening sky, tails erect and pacing regally to meet us. They knew where we had been. My father always gutted the fish in the sea by the pier, the cats purring round his legs asking for a bite to eat. Then we'd walk home a bit stiff and cold to where my mother would be waiting with a big pot of boiling water ready for the podleys. We ate them with our fingers. The bigger fish were kept for the next day, but nothing tasted quite like those podleys fresh from the sea at midnight.

I learned another exciting form of fishing at the Rhinns, that of flounder fishing. These wily flat fish are experts at camouflage. When they sense danger, they wriggle just under the sand and lie still, so that it takes a practised eye to spot one. My father made a glass-bottomed box which he held in the water over the stern of the boat to let him see the seabed clearly. In his right hand he held a line to which was attached a weighted three-pronged spear. This was allowed to drift above the sand while he watched for the tell-tale puffs of sand that gave away the flounder's position. The most difficult and frustrating part was giving instructions to the unfortunate person rowing. My father, who seldom swore in front of us young folk, usually did at this time. If I was at the oars he'd call out, "Back! Back a wee bit! Not so far! No! Left a bit! Forward slowly! Damn it, not so far!" Eventually, the spear landed on its prey and another tasty tea was brought to the surface It was all good exercise with the added advantage of healthy eating at the next meal.

Even the winter holidays held their own simple pleasures. In frosty weather the duck pond froze over. Mae, Jean and I skated there, but wearing wellingtons instead of skates. One day, my father devised a new game for the ice. He carried a big tea chest and a length of rope to the pond. Tying the rope round the box, he stood at one side of the pond holding one end of the rope while one of us did the same at the opposite side. A third person climbed into the box and was whizzed back and forth across the ice. Mae was a bit on the plump side so when her turn came the ice gave way when she was halfway across, catapulting Mae into the cold muddy water. The pond wasn't more than a foot deep so she was in no danger, but she couldn't get to her feet for giggling, and by the time she reached dry land, helped by us, we were all muddied and wet, and roaring with laughter.

The laughter ended abruptly when we arrived home trailing the smelly and bedraggled Mae, with mud oozing out of the top of her wellingtons. My father got the sharp edge of my mother's tongue, while she was cleaning her up. She gave us all hot soup to revive us but that was the end of our skating careers.

We had a lot of stormy weather in winter. Jean and I loved to lie, dressed in oilskins and souwesters, on a particular rock which sloped away from the sea. Behind it we were safe from the huge breakers, only our heads showing above the top. The noise was so deafening we had to shout to each other as we counted the number of waves between each big one. We went home from these expeditions rosy-cheeked and hungry.

After such enjoyable holidays Glasgow was tame but one new interest took my attention. My cousins Alec and Agnes, both that wee bit older than me, had left school. They were both musical, and together with friends formed a mandolin band similar to and copied from the famous band of that era, Troise and his Mandoliers. Alec's band was really good. They wore uniforms of brightly-coloured Russian type blouses and baggy trousers, and were in great demand at local functions. I used to be allowed to attend rehearsals, enjoying the music and desperately wishing I could join in.

A week or two before the end of each term I perked up. I didn't realise how lucky I was compared to those poor souls who never had a holiday and especially those who never lived long enough to grow up. One school friend developed the ever-present scourge of that time, tuberculosis. I watched her fade away until at the age of fifteen she was no more.

I at least had the pleasure of going home three or four times a year. By the middle of the thirties Mae and I were seasoned travellers, trusted to travel to Islay unaccompanied. We liked the freedom of being able to go where we liked on the steamers, unhindered by injunctions from Wee Granny, and throwing our crusts to the screaming sea gulls which kept pace with the ship all the way. We had the most fun on the old *Pioneer*, where we made friends with the crew, sharing cups of stewed tea while carrying on what we thought was clever repartee with the burly engineers, in parts of the ship where other passengers were barred.

We grew to know every sound the engines made. On one occasion, we were puzzled to hear a change in the normal rhythmic thud, thud, thud, made by the paddles as they turned. They were now going thud, thud, clonk. We followed the sound and discovered a seaman standing near one of the paddles wielding a huge mallet. At the end of every revolution of the paddles he thumped one of the blades with his hammer. We watched for some time before asking the reason. Between thumps the man told us that one of the rivets was loose and as the ship couldn't be stopped to fix it, the only alternative was to beat the rivet back into place each time it appeared above the surface. The performance went on until we reached Port Ellen. Not long after that we heard that the *Pioneer* was being retired and a bigger and newer steamer was to be put on the Islay run. We felt as though we had lost an old friend, but were left with many happy memories of the old lady.

My horizons widened as I grew older. The first signs of interest in the opposite sex appeared, albeit hesitant and suppressed. The local young Islay men mainly followed two widely different paths as they grew up. Either they joined the merchant service and went to sail the seas or they went to university, becoming doctors, teachers or ministers. During the summer, a number of them came home to the villages, as there were numerous concerts and dances. Mae and I were allowed to attend these functions, sometimes accompanied by my mother and father, sometimes on our own. They were great fun, and followed the traditional routine of that time. The men sat on one side of the hall, with the ladies ranging themselves gracefully along the opposite side. Each lot looked disinterested in the other, the girls chattering like starlings in a tree, the boys smoking and trying to look man-of-the-world. When the official M.C. announced the next dance, the men rose as one, stubbed out their cigarettes, and moved in a body towards the waiting girls. No girl would refuse to dance with one lad and then get up with another. If she didn't fancy the first one, she sat the dance out. I was still rather gawky and shy, so I wasn't the most sought after girl in the hall although a number of friendly, polite lads always asked me up for a duty dance.

When the dance ended in the wee small hours, the contingent from the island was always sure of being safely escorted home. Mae and I, along with Annie the principal keeper's daughter, would walk to the slip at Port Wemyss accompanied by a number of young seamen and students, all singing and disturbing whatever lieges were abed. All but the very old had probably been at the dance so nobody was upset. The local young men were well acquainted with the currents and therefore could be trusted to row us across. Sometimes the boat was perilously low in the water, being full to overflowing with passengers, but we all knew not to caper in such circumstances. The rower took it steady and no harm was done, though I felt uneasy at times, sighing with relief when we reached the other side. Everyone disembarked, giggling and laughing as we walked up to the station where we knew my mother would be waiting with scones and cups of tea. Sometimes if the moon was up we'd make a detour into the chapel park which looked ghostly in the silvery light. The lads would regale us with ghost stories, including the tale of one MacKay, whose grave was supposedly marked by the mysterious Celtic cross near the chapel. On one occasion they frightened the wits out of us, when a divinity student stood near the cross, raised his hands heavenwards and cried out in a deep sepulchral voice, "MacKay! Come forth!" I was convinced his spirit would materialise, and we all took to our heels and ran the rest of the way home followed by roars of laughter from the lads.

The highlight of each summer was the distillery dance in Port Charlotte, some seven miles away. We were allowed to go under the chaperonage of Duggie, the local postman. He was a bit older and a steady sort of man, liked and trusted by my parents. A crowd of us drove to the hall in two cars. The event was held in the loft of the distillery, a vast, low-ceilinged place. Across the roof space stretched at intervals huge beams which made for many a bump on the heads of those above average height. It was an entertainment in itself to watch the ducking and swerving which took place during the energetic Eightsome reels or Strip the Willow.

The hall was so long that when the music stopped the dancers had only traversed one length of the floor. When I think of it now, the loft must have been a fire hazard, there was so much wood in its construction and as far as I could make out, only one exit via a wooden staircase.

Any expeditions further afield than Portnahaven involved the use of a hired car and driver. Donald McAllister of the post office ran such a service, so he was usually booked when, on rare occasions, my father had a whole day off. We'd set off for a picnic to one of the most magnificent beaches in the country. Kilchoman Bay, on the west coast of Islay, could only be reached by a narrow twisty road. At the road end lay a wide sweep of golden sand open to the Atlantic and completely deserted. When the tide was out the water seemed miles away and we contented ourselves with lying on the sand, listening to the silence, broken only by the wheep of sandpipers and the occasional cry of a gull. Springtime visits to Kilchoman were breathtaking, the dunes bordering the sand were covered by a pale yellow carpet of primroses growing in such profusion it was impossible to walk without crushing hundreds of them into the ground. They had bigger blooms and longer stems than any primrose I've ever seen.

We picked bunches of these gorgeous flowers and carried them to a walled area nearby. On our first visit to the spot we found to our surprise that inside the wall was a neatly kept war cemetery. Rows of white gravestones mark the last resting place of the crew and passengers of an American troop ship which was sunk nearby during the first world war. All who were found were buried there facing their homeland, there being no other land between Islay and America. We put our bunches of primroses on the graves in memory of them.

Not all our excursions were for pleasure. There was the inevitable difficulty in visiting the doctor's surgery at Bowmore, some fifteen miles away. There was no dentist on Islay at that time so emergency dental treatment had to be dealt with by the doctor.

I had one memorable trip to the doctor. I wasn't a patient but went along for the ride. My father had developed, of all things, housemaid's knee, which didn't respond to rest and heat, hence the hire of Donald's Wolseley 14 to take him to Bowmore. It so happened that Duggie the postman had been suffering bad toothache, as had Jean, so all the appointments were organised to coincide. I waited in the car with Donald while the three hapless ones went into the waiting room. Time passed. My father emerged first, limping and looking decidedly green about the gills. He weaved his way unsteadily down the path and more or less fell into the car. When he recovered he told us the doctor had carefully inserted a long needle into the offending knee to draw off the fluid that was causing the swelling and pain. Unfortunately, my father had moved, and the needle struck the bone, causing him even more pain and making him feel sick. He sat in the front seat clutching his throbbing knee while we waited for the next patient. Jean, a bit of a stoic, had coped well with having her tooth out. Duggie, on the other hand, possessed extremely strong teeth of the type described by my mother as "paling stabs." The doctor had practically to kneel on the poor man's chest to gain enough purchase to extract the reluctant tooth.

We set off on the return journey like a mini-ambulance. The homeward journey was interrupted by muffled requests to, "Stop a minute! I need to spit!" from Duggie and Jean, and, "I'll need to get out! I feel sick!" from my father. These requests were seldom in unison and Donald needed all his patience for his patients. Luckily the trio made a quick recovery but all, including Donald, agreed later they hoped never to have to repeat the performance.

It was during one of those summer holidays that I had what I think was the most frightening experience of my life. Wee Granny, Aunt Jean and Mae were with us so the house was a bit crowded. Someone had to sleep on the settee in the parlour and I gladly gave up my usual place beside Jean as I liked sleeping alone. One glorious morning I woke suddenly at six o'clock. I had no idea what had disturbed me but I knew something wasn't right. I had a strong feeling that I was alone in the house. Everything was so still, there wasn't even a bird singing, though the sun was well up and the air warm. I rose and crept quietly through to the kitchen, where my mother and father slept in the recess bed. I felt a bit of an idiot but I just wanted reassurance that they were there. The bed was empty. I ran through to the other two bedrooms to find to my growing horror that those beds were empty, too. I was indeed alone in the house.

The tale of the mysterious disappearance of the three keepers on the Flannan Rock sprang to mind. In a panic I rushed across the courtyard to the other assistant keeper's house and banged frantically on the door. That house was empty, too. My legs had turned to jelly by the time I reached the principal's door and it, too, was deserted. There was a 'phone in that house but by that time I was a gibbering idiot so I didn't think of trying to 'phone the village for help. My old fear of being alone took over, made worse by the knowledge that though at all times one keeper must stay at the station, all were absent.

I headed for the pier, my legs trembling so I could scarcely put one foot in front of the other. On rounding the last corner, I saw to my relief the entire population congregated on the pier and staring silently across the water. I almost fainted with relief, as my mother, hearing my sobs, turned in time to catch me as I fell into her arms, my face as white as a sheet. I was taken home, given two aspirins, the household cure-all, and put to bed with promises that I wouldn't be left alone.

When I recovered, I heard the whole story. The keeper on duty in the tower had heard a terrible scream and, realising something was wrong in the village, he quickly came down from the tower. It was broad daylight so the light wasn't lit and he was at liberty to do so. He roused the others to investigate. I was left undisturbed as I was nervous and might be upset if something dramatic was taking place. Little did they know that I was to be far more upset as a result of their concern.

On reaching the pier they witnessed the end of a tragedy. A local woman, wrongly thinking she had an incurable disease, had decided to end it all. She rose early, dressed herself, walked to the point and simply jumped into the water. It so happened that someone else had risen early and saw her jump, but being at the opposite side of the bay, was unable to help. She it was who had screamed. The village rapidly came alive, but too late to save the unhappy woman.

The local men who had the task of recovering the body, said later it was a gruesome job. The tide race eddied at the point, with the result that the woman was found held bolt upright almost exactly where she had jumped in. They could see her standing looking as though she was going shopping, her hair and clothes swirling about her as if in a stiff breeze.

Glasgow Again

I seemed to live in two different worlds. Back in Glasgow after the summer holidays I no longer felt completely miserable. I was learning to make the best of what couldn't be changed. Mae and I had only been familiar with the places between Shettleston and Argyle Street, but in the late thirties we began to explore hitherto unknown parts of the city. Our favourite Sunday adventure, only allowed when there was no Bible class – we had graduated to that from Sunday School – was to take a tram ride to Elderslie Mills, Paisley, or to Knightswood. On Sunday the trams weren't busy so we could usually choose our seat, the favourite being on the top deck in the small secluded section above the driver. It was separate from the main compartment and from that vantage point we had a good all round view of the streets ahead.

On a sunny day it was a pleasant ride. The streets in the city centre were almost completely devoid of people and traffic. How different Glasgow looked when we had time to see it undistracted by the normal noise and hurrying crowds. I realised that Glasgow wasn't composed only of tall buildings. There were trees and bridges and, surprisingly, a multitude of birds.

Sometimes we were the only passengers, and carried on a shouted conversation with the invisible driver who, bored by the solitude of his platform, was glad of the diversion, while the tram ground and clanked its way over the Jamaica Bridge and on to less familiar places. At the terminus we were supposed to get off and wait while the tram was "turned round," but sometimes the conductor let us stay on to help him in this, to us, interesting job. The seat backs were on a swivel. We walked along the passageways pushing them noisily and enthusiastically into the opposite position, while outside, the driver, using a long pole, unhooked the rod connecting the tram to the overhead electric wires, and swung it round to work in reverse. Then he headed for the opposite end of the vehicle where another set of controls awaited him. He clocked in his time on the terminus clock, and with a clang of the bell worked by stamping his foot on a metal plate, we were off. The conductor then solemnly collected our return fares. The whole trip of about two hours cost us each 5d.

In spring and summer when the days were long, the young folk congregated on the main streets on Sunday evenings for the Sunday Parade. Everyone, dressed in their Sunday-go-to-meeting clothes, walked in small groups, girls and boys separately, each group pretending to have not the slightest interest in the others, but eyeing the opposite sex furtively. After several laps of the course, the more adventurous and bold mingled and continued the parade in mixed groups. I was far too shy to mingle.

I remember one Sunday outfit at that time was a long light grey coat with wide revers, a red halo hat and a red and white spotted scarf tied in a pussy bow, the whole ensemble completed by a pair of matching red gauntlet gloves. One odd fashion point was the habit of wearing the coat unbuttoned.

I was never allowed to choose my own clothes, being told that when I was paying for them I could choose for myself, but not before. I never thought of rebelling. In spring my mother sent money to buy a new "best" outfit; last year's was relegated to Saturdays and the one before that to weekday trips to the pictures or whatever. The same ritual was repeated in the autumn. I would never have dreamed of wearing my best things during the week.

At school I started preparations for my Highers. The final two years at Eastbank were devoted to studying seven subjects I had to pass in, so I had little time to spare for frivolities. I felt relaxed while studying, yet I've been told since that I was always nervous about exams. I don't remember feeling that way. I confess I worried about almost everything else in my life.

It was about that time that I learned the real reason for my mother's ageing appearance that had worried me for so long. It seemed that for some time my mother had been suffering terrible bouts of severe pain which was diagnosed as gallstones, making an operation essential. The N.L.B. took good care of their employees, paying all medical and surgical fees not only for the men but their wives and children up to school leaving age. The only stipulation was that patients who needed an operation had, whenever possible, to travel to Edinburgh where the N.L.B. had endowed a bed in Chalmer's Hospital. So it was arranged that my father would take his holidays to accompany my mother there. Once my mother was deposited in Chalmer's Hospital my father came to stay in Glasgow, commuting on visiting days.

The operation went off smoothly enough. My mother was strong and otherwise healthy. She was making a good recovery when I created an incident which could have caused a relapse. My father took me, along with a lady friend of my mother's, to visit her. The memory of my own not very happy time in hospital was still vivid so I wasn't too keen to go, but I didn't want to let my mother down and I did want to see for myself that she was all right.

That morning I had no appetite for Granny's "traveller's" breakfast, and I only ate a bit of toast. We arrived in Edinburgh in the forenoon, hours before visiting times, as my father wanted to show my mother's friend, Agnes, a few of the sights. We walked to the Castle, explored it and the Shrine, then on to Holyrood. It was all very interesting, no doubt, but suddenly my father realised we had to get moving as it was near time to see my mother. We walked to the hospital, by which time I was trailing my feet and felt dog tired.

Visiting was from two until four. The time seemed endless. About three o'clock I became aware that all was not well with me. The idea of hospital was bad enough and the disinfectant smells coupled with the faint aroma of chloroform that hung in the air upset me, but I didn't expect to find the world suddenly growing dark. Having never fainted in my life, I failed to recognise the symptoms. Agnes took me outside for fresh air when I turned pale and began to wilt. I leaned against a wall but the world stayed dark like a badly tuned television picture with the brightness turned down. A passing nurse took me to see one of the doctors, who asked what seemed like dozens of irrelevant questions. "Have you ever had scarlet fever, diphtheria, rheumatic fever, etc., etc.?" I could truthfully say no to all of these. He sat silent for a moment, obviously puzzled, before asking me, "When did you eat last?" When I told him I'd had nothing since my mini-breakfast, he sighed, and said, "You're hungry, my lass. Go and get something to eat!" My father was told off for not having taken us for a meal. A nurse gave me a cup of tea and some thin bread and butter which I ate ravenously. Afterwards my father took us for a fish supper and I was cured.

Unfortunately there must have been a hiccup in communications as my poor worried mother wasn't told the outcome of my fainting for an hour or two, during which time she almost worried herself into a relapse. She was able to rise above it, only mentally raging at my father for being so daft. It was a sheepish man who crept into the ward next visiting day, but at least he had the sense to take a present to soothe my mother into forgiving him. Soon the patient was back in Glasgow for a rest before tackling the long journey home. I was pleased at the unexpected bonus of having my mother nearby for a week or two.

Back on the island, the doctor gave her strict instructions not to lift anything heavy for at least six months. This was difficult as most of her chores involved lifting drinking-water buckets, coal buckets and all the other buckets. My father had his work cut out to prevent her from disobeying orders, sometimes catching her in the act of taking out the slop bucket.

The biggest problem was washing day. Washing was still done in big wooden tubs which sat on trestles. These had to be filled by the inevitable bucket. So did the boiler. The whites were boiled first, then had to be transferred by means of a long stick to one of the tubs. In turn they were scrubbed on a washing board, then passed through the Acme wringer into yet another tub to be rinsed, back through the wringer, and folded ready for hanging out on the green. All in all washing day was a day of hard work and strenuous lifting. The boiler then had to be emptied, the fire cleaned out and the place left ready for the next person to go through the routine.

My mother against her will hired a woman from the village to do the washing, although she used to say, "I wouldn't see anybody in my road." On the first day she supervised the job to show the woman the ropes. The following week she stayed out of the wash house as long as she could, but eventually popped in to see how it was going. She discovered that the whole washing had been done in one tub of water which by then was the colour of strong tea. She watched in silence as her "helper" proceeded to rinse the whole lot in another single tub of water. My mother was unused to dealing with an employee and was too polite to say anything, so she paid her, thanked her and sent her home, before rolling up her sleeves and doing the entire job again. My father was furious and they had a row, but my mother was adamant that she wouldn't let anyone from outside do her washing again. Her only concession was to let my father do the heaviest lifting and the turning of the wringer handle. He was very patient, as was the principal keeper, who gave him time off from his forenoon duties to do this.

The year 1938 brought a new excitement to life in Glasgow. That was the year of the Empire Exhibition. For months, preparations went ahead in Bellahouston Park. It was a resounding success, attracting countless numbers of visitors from all corners of the world, and bringing trade to Britain. Not that I was at all interested in the economics of the project. As far as I was concerned it was an exciting place to visit. As often as we could afford either the time or the money, Mae and I took the tram to Bellahouston and wandered through the pavilions for hours, seldom seeing anything twice. We didn't have much money but most of the exhibits were free. We had fun at the fairground just watching the laughing sailor poised over the gate. The automaton was so realistic and his laugh so infectious there was always a crowd standing around laughing.

My favourite exhibit was the Clachan, a stylised mock-up of a highland village with low thatched cottages, heather and the unforgettable fragrance of burning peat. I'd stand with my eyes closed, sniffing deeply, my spirit transported to the islands. I suspect I wasn't the only visitor to act like that. Glasgow was full of exiled highlanders who had been forced to leave their homes to find work.

*My father and mother at the
Empire Exhibition during
1938 in Bellahouston Park.*

The Clachan boasted a Post Office where visitors could buy and send postcards, each with the official Clachan postmark and a sticker affixed to it as a souvenir, one of which has remarkably survived to be one of my small prized possessions.

Scattered throughout the park were small pavilions tucked away behind the more imposing ones. We loved the milk and bakery pavilions especially as they gave away samples of delicacies like cheese, biscuits and wee rolls. We watched fascinated as loaves of bread were sliced and wrapped mechanically, and elsewhere we watched goggle-eyed at seeing cigarettes marching along a production line to be packaged.

I had one great pride in the Exhibition. I had two exhibits displayed in the Scottish pavilion. The schools had picked out the best efforts in the needlework and arts and crafts departments. My contributions were a nightdress I had designed and sewn and a flannel matinee coat. I'd wander about nearby hoping I'd hear somebody admire my work. Nobody ever did, at least not in my hearing. I hovered full of homesickness over another display in the same pavilion, a relief map of Scotland laid out on the floor surrounded by an unnaturally bright blue sea. At the spot where each lighthouse is situated stood a tiny model tower. I hung over the low wall that protected the display for ages until Mae, impatient with my moods, hauled me away to see something more interesting.

It was a sad day when the Exhibition closed. It had given many thousands of people a great deal of pleasure during a worrying time politically, with the threat of war hanging over the whole world. I remember seeing on the cinema newsreels, Mr. Chamberlain waving his little bit of paper, promising "peace in our time," but the significance of it went right over my head.

In the summer of that year, Aunt Jean was married. She had been widowed for almost sixteen years when she met a widower with four grown up children. They hit it off at a wedding and soon set the date for their own. This meant one important change for the rest of us. Granny would be left with more room in her wee flat that she'd had since I came to stay. Mae moved away to live with her mother and new step-father in Carntyne, only about ten minutes walk from Granny's. Granny's breathing space was to be short-lived. Jean was ready to start secondary school and what more natural than that she would join Granny and me at Ten-nine-eight. I was delighted to have my wee sister for company as we had always got on well.

I don't think Jean was any more enamoured of living permanently in the city than I was but she was a different character altogether, more philosophical, less nervous and much more stoical. She soon settled in and adapted to the new routine quickly. Or so it appeared, until one day a first year girl ran up to me in the playground with a worried expression on her face. "Come quick," she gasped. "Your wee sister's round at the front and won't tell us how!" I translated that statement into "Jean is standing in the forbidden area at the front of the school and won't tell anybody why she is doing so." Dashing round the corner I found Jean, facing the school wall, head down, fending off a crowd of concerned classmates. The more they badgered her with questions, the more angry she became. I sent them all away and waited until Jean gave up acting like the proverbial ostrich and informed me that she had toothache. That was her way, preferring to suffer in silence rather than admit to pain.

Winter passed uneventfully and spring came bringing with it not only warmer weather and longer evenings, but the first chill hint of what might lie ahead. In Europe, Hitler was making demands for more and more territory. I still didn't appreciate what it could mean to me personally. We only knew that we had to go to a school in Parkhead to be fitted with gas masks. It was a fine spring evening when we queued up outside the school, wondering what a gas mask was like and if we would ever have to use it. Inside the school, I watched those in front of me having weird close-fitting rubber things pushed on to their heads. They had a snout-like face piece which contained a chemical which supposedly filtered out deadly gas, leaving enough air for the wearer to breathe. The thing was held tightly in place by rubber straps. The more I watched and thought about it the more claustrophobic I became and as I heard the person in front being told how to care for hers, I realised that I didn't care for mine one little bit! When the Civil Defence worker had managed to put mine half over my head I felt suffocated and tore it off. He didn't argue. He simply pushed it into my unwilling hands and said, "Next." I carried it home in its wee cardboard box, shoved it into the far recesses of a cupboard and forgot all about it.

That spring my mind was more taken up with exams which would decide my future. I had ambitions to go to the "Dough School," as we called the Domestic Science College, to study needlework with a view to teaching it at the end of the three year course. I was the only candidate from Eastbank that year for that particular subject, so my teacher, Miss Duthie, was able to give me individual tuition. I had always been a wee bit afraid of her, until one day I earned a sharp telling-off for spilling a whole box of tiny pins on the rough wooden floor. I wasted most of the precious period picking every one of them out of the crevices between the floor boards, Miss Duthie looking daggers at me. Shortly after I had resumed my interrupted sewing, Miss Duthie managed to spill her box of pins. We both silently got down on our hands and knees to retrieve them, looked at each other and both burst out laughing. From then on we were firm friends and remained so until she died a few years ago.

The exams over, everybody relaxed during the long wait for the results. As usualI began to count the days until the holidays. Eventually Jean and I set off for Islay. Mae wasn't with us because she had left school and started work. It seemed strange without her. I felt a bit odd, too. In all probability a phase of my life was over. I was seventeen and if I passed the exams I would no longer be a schoolgirl. I wasn't at all sure that I was ready to face the adult world. That could wait, though. As soon as we reached home all I could think of was the

The family at the Rhinns, about 1939.

warm pleasure of being with my mother and father again for nearly ten weeks. The fresh air and freedom relaxed me. Time enough to think of the future when the exam results arrived at the end of the summer.

The holiday was spent going to the local dances, fishing, picnicking, and our newest form of entertainment, playing tennis. My father had been an ardent tennis fan, but had been unable to keep it up in the service. One day he was idly leaning on the balcony rail outside the lightroom after polishing the brasses. His mind was drifting as he looked at the island scenery when the thought entered his head that a piece of unused ground in the corner of one of the parks looked like a tennis court. It was flat and just the right size. That afternoon he examined the spot more closely, then went home and informed my mother he was going to make a tennis court. For weeks he laboured shaving off bumps in the grass and using the turves thus obtained to fill in the hollows. Next he mowed and rolled the site regularly until it was reasonably smooth so that by the time we came on holiday we were the proud owners of a tennis court. He measured it out and marked it with lime wash of which there was always a generous supply for whitening the tower every year. My mother and others who had scoffed at the idea began to realise he had made a good job of it.

For two summers our homemade court gave us endless pleasure. The local people came over to play and visitors being shown over the tower commented on it with the result that many of them came back for a game. Tournaments were organised. We had some hilarious games with unexpected results because, owing to the unevenness of the ground, the ball was inclined to shoot off at surprising angles catching the receiver unawares. My mother did most of the work which my father's grand tournaments involved. On blazing hot summer days she'd spend a whole forenoon baking scones, cakes and mounds of pancakes.

Tennis at the Rhinns.

She even made enormous clootie dumplings, sweating uncomplainingly over her self-imposed task. We carried all this largesse to the tennis court, where my mother, ensconced in the famous Tent, distributed the food among the hungry enthusiasts. The results of her hard work vanished like snow in the desert. Those who came over from the village didn't accept this selfishly. They brought large quantities of biscuits and chocolates, and large bottles of lemonade to wash it all down with.

That summer of 1939 I was in my usual euphoria and the tennis tournaments were still going with a swing when the fun stopped abruptly at the height of the season. The holiday makers packed their bags and vanished overnight, the local young men rushed off back to their ships and the place became as quiet as though it was winter. My father and the other two keepers started measuring out strips of wood and mysterious lengths of black cloth out of which they made shutters to fit every window. The atmosphere was strangely subdued, yet there was a feeling of excitement and tension in the air. There was a crisis. War, mobilisation and bombing were the main topics of conversation throughout the rest of August. I experienced a feeling of unreality. This kind of thing only happened in films. It would all fizzle out and we'd be able to laugh at it.

The only reality about that time was that the results of the Highers had come through and I had failed. In those days you had to pass every exam in the group. Fail one and you lost the lot. I had failed history by one miserable mark. I'd have to go back to Eastbank to try again. Jean and I were due back in Glasgow on 2nd September ready to start school on the 5th. The crisis changed our plans, my father wisely deciding we should wait and see what happened. This suited me fine as it meant I'd have at least a few more days at home.

On Sunday, 3rd September, the atmosphere was electric as we waited by the wireless, watching the hands of the clock moving round slowly towards eleven o'clock, at which time the Prime Minister was to speak to the nation. It sounded ominous. I stood with my elbows on the kitchen window ledge watching the cats bursting bubbles in a puddle in the courtyard, while the solemn voice of Mr. Chamberlain told us that Britain was now at war with Germany. I don't remember much more about that day except that my mother, practical as ever, went on cooking the dinner. The wireless went haywire. Normal programmes were cancelled and replaced by records and still more records interspersed at frequent intervals by news bulletins until it became monotonous.

War

For several nights now our windows had been covered by the blackout screens made by the men, a ludicrous precaution as the powerful beams still flashed out brightly every five seconds. Looking across to the villages we missed the twinkling lights. We had come to the end of an era and the future was uncertain. My father had decided that neither Jean nor I would go back to Glasgow to resume our schooling. As far as I was concerned my school days were legally over now that I was seventeen, but Jean would be obliged to attend school for another year or two.

Meantime we were too taken up with wondering when and where hostilities would start. We weren't left long in doubt as to who would strike the first blow. Within twenty-four hours came the shocking news that the liner *Athenia*, carrying evacuees to America, had been sunk by a German submarine. We mentally prepared to do battle. Germany was now truly our enemy.

It took a few days for the wireless to become more organised. The spaces between the interminable news bulletins were filled heroically by Billy Cotton and his Band, keeping up a steady stream of cheerful music and comic patter, which helped more than anything else to raise our morale. Soon Billy Cotton was relieved of some of the pressure by another great laughter maker, Tommy Handley, whose programme gave us our first real catch phrases, like "Can I do you now, sir?" and "This is Funf speaking," taking the mickey out of the Germans. We all sang the propaganda songs, "Run, rabbit, run" and "We're going to hang out the washing on the Siegfried Line." Unfortunately the enemy overrode the small countries around its borders and that was the end of that bit of propaganda.

As far as we on the island were concerned, we knew little difference to begin with. The keepers were allocated one additional duty. A copy of "Jane's Book of Ships" arrived, with instructions that all personnel were to learn how to recognise the outlines of our ships which had started to pass in convoy along the northern coast of Ireland. The man on duty was to take note of all ships and a report had to be sent regularly. The whole family became hooked on the study of ships, searching the North Channel for convoys and peering at them through the telescope, comparing the silhouettes with those in the book and arguing over who had got the ships' names right.

German radio began to broadcast "news" bulletins in English, purporting to tell us the truth about how the war was going. The news reader, known to us only as Lord Haw-Haw, possessed a soft persuasive voice which gave us an additional source of amusement. We at the Rhinns knew he wasn't telling the truth when he'd report such items as the sinking of the *Ark Royal*, when the next day we'd see the aforesaid aircraft carrier steaming past unscathed. I think that particular ship was "sunk" three times before it was finally torpedoed.

My mother's most immediate problem was getting Jean to school. The nearest secondary school was at Bowmore, sixteen miles away. Catching the local school bus would be practically impossible in winter. Instead, Jean settled happily into lodgings in Port Wemysss, coming home only at weekends. She had a cosy room with a deep soft feather mattress, a luxury compared to our horsehair mattresses at home.

Important happenings remain vague. I can't remember in which order events took place. I know we had a visit early on from the Man from the Ministry, who issued us all with pale blue identity cards, bearing name, address and identity number. Rumours of rationing arose, rumours which caused my mother sleepless nights as she wondered how she would manage. Self-sufficient though we were in many ways, she had always relied on keeping a substantial stock of items like flour, sugar, tea, lentils and so on. Tinned meat and milk were essentials when stormy weather prevented her from getting over to the villages.

I selfishly felt that the war had at least done one good thing; I didn't have to go back to the city. I was content to stay at home and keep my mother company. I had no fear of boredom. I wasn't aware that at seventeen I was probably missing out on the best years of my life. There was certainly plenty of knitting and sewing to be done, although the colours were not those I'd have chosen. I was restricted to three colours, khaki, air force blue and navy. We did our bit for the war effort, by joining the W.V.S. and Red Cross, who provided the wool to knit "comforts" for our forces. That winter my mother, Jean and I knitted dozens of balaclava helmets, mittens, scarves, socks, seaboot stockings and bedsocks. The latter were for hospital use along with shapeless white gowns we sewed for the wounded. As we sat by the roaring fire, well away from the field of war, we couldn't help but think of the soldiers, sailors and airmen who would eventually wear our contributions.

One of the instructions that came quickly from the office was that no more visitors were to be shown up the tower for reasons of security, not surprising in view of the convoys. The keepers resigned themselves to a fairly substantial drop in income from tips, as well as missing the many pleasant interludes chatting to the visitors.

Not long after that edict, we were astonished to see walking up from the pier, a well-dressed couple who had the look of what we called "county" about them. Dressed in tweeds and brogues, and carrying parcels, they headed towards the lighthouse. My father assumed them to be friends of the principal keeper so he just carried on with his chores. In a few minutes he saw the couple being ushered in the tower door. About half an hour later they reappeared, thanked the keeper profusely and left. Later, my mother was handed a pheasant and a lovely pot plant with the message that the visitors had brought presents for everyone. My mother accepted them gracefully. She wasn't one for turning down a good dinner. Neither she nor my father were happy about it, but decided the incident was best forgotten.

A week or two later, the same couple reappeared bearing more gifts. They had enjoyed the previous visit so much, they said, in beautiful English with a trace of foreign accent, that they had come back. My father was highly suspicious of their motives, especially as he had checked the names in the visitors book and found them to be German sounding. He would never have allowed them in, but he wasn't in charge and thought it best to keep his own counsel. Much to my father's relief they never reappeared after the second visit, and shortly afterwards we heard on the local grapevine that they were indeed aliens and had been interned in the Isle of Man. Local rumour had it that they were well-to-do Germans, connected to one of the big banks, who had for several years rented a big estate on Islay. My father remained convinced they were spying on the convoys.

We had a good Christmas that year. Before the war my father had set a hen on several turkey eggs and had managed to rear three birds, two hen birds and a bubbly jock. Turkeys are notoriously difficult to rear, especially during the first six weeks when they often fall prey to chest complaints. Once past that age they were healthy enough to dislike roosting indoors. They took to roosting in all weathers on some rocks near the henhouse, where they obstinately remained even in the winter. When the time came to kill the birds for the table, my father had to creep down at dead of night with a torch, grab one of the unsuspecting hen birds and perform the dirty deed. The process was repeated a few nights later with the other hen, both of which were sold to someone in the village.

On impulse my mother decided we'd hold a party for some of our friends in the village along with the rest of the station complement as the remaining bird looked far too big for one small family. When the time came to do his stuff, my father set off yet again at dead of night. The bird must have realised in his dim brain that every time the light of the torch appeared one of his mates went missing. Try as he might, my father was unable to capture the huge bird that night or the next. He'd have to lure it in the daytime. With Jean and me as beaters he set off, and herded the bubbly jock into one of the parks. For over an hour that bird defied our efforts to corner him, utterly exhausting hunters and hunted. Finally captured, he put up a good fight. By that time my father was swearing as well as sweating, and vowing never to rear turkeys again.

The bird weighed twenty-two pounds and it was all my mother could do to fit it in her roomy oven. On the big night my mother greeted the guests at the door. As each one appeared out of the darkness of the blackout, he or she pressed into my mother's hands a box of chocolates, until her arms were piled high with sweets. They had got together and raided the local shops, buying up all the fancy boxes left over by the sudden evacuation of all the summer visitors. It was a final gesture before austerity set in. My mother was overcome and for once I saw tears glistening in her eyes. We had a wonderful party and there was enough turkey left over to feed us for several more days.

It was as well we enjoyed that festive season as it wasn't long before we had to tighten our belts and submit to strict rationing. The first foods to be rationed were as my mother had feared; sugar, fats, tea, cheese, bacon and meat. We, like most people, got into the habit of leaving the books with the shop-keeper. I was horrified when my mother told me I'd have to spread margarine on my bread. Margarine was only for baking! I was sure I couldn't eat it, but when our first ration of butter turned out to be rancid and full of green bits I was glad to use the dreaded margarine. How naive I was. There was a lot worse to come. Not as far as I was concerned, as it turned out, but the next five years was to bring a lot of heartache and hardship to millions. I was to be one of the lucky ones.

My mother had to cope with the shortages as best she could. Trying to make a few ounces of bacon go a long way wasn't easy, and she missed the sugar and fats that she relied on so much for baking, but she was luckier than most. Lightkeepers were classed as seamen and therefore were allocated a bigger ration of items like tinned milk and meat. At a time when eggs were rationed to one per week, we still had our own supply of that versatile food, limited only by the availability of hen food. It was difficult to get the normal mixture of grain for them, which had contained Indian maize as well as oats.

Winter passed uneventfully and the following spring we added another voluntary task to our war effort, gathering vast quantities of the sphagnum moss which abounded on our island. We spread it out in the sun, turning it like hay every few hours until it was thoroughly sun-dried. If a rain cloud appeared we rushed out and raked it into a mound which we covered by a tarpaulin until the shower had passed. Once dry, it was packed in big sacks and delivered to the W.V.S. to be sent away. We were told it was made into mattresses for field hospitals as it wasn't only soft but very absorbent.

What came to be known as the Phoney War continued for some time. We began to experience a sort of anticlimax as no real fighting was taking place except at sea. Then everything erupted, and before we knew it our troops in Europe were being pushed back and cornered on the beach at Dunkirk. We were aware it was a turning point which would probably decide the final outcome of the war. We could only listen to what were now called communiques on the wireless, and wait while our troops remained trapped, literally between the devil and the deep blue sea. We heard how every ship and small boat available had set off like an armada to rescue as many as they could. Pleasure boats, yachts, and anything that could float rallied round. I little knew that the man who was to become very dear to me a few years later was on one of these ships, the minesweeper *H.M.S. Hebe*, picking up as many soldiers as the ship could carry.

The full realisation of the hardships suffered there was only brought home to us when the local men involved began to drift home on sick leave bringing

Robby, aged 24, on board the minesweeper H.M.S.Hebe *in Malta (during the siege).*

with them the sordid details. We heard of one Islayman who had for so long been unable to take his boots off that when finally he found time to do so, his socks had fused to his feet, needing hours of soaking before they could be peeled off.

The Dunkirk evacuation took place in June, and we had just settled down after the excitement had faded, when something more personal took up our attention. My father got a shift. Once more he opened the letter in anticipation of being sent to a mainland station. Once more he was disappointed. He was going to Lismore. The small consolation was that it meant promotion to Principal Keeper, which meant more money and more responsibility. One thing especially bothered my mother. There would be no handy school for Jean. At least not one she could go to on a daily basis.

The move was to take place in July during the school holidays. We packed our belongings, which through the years had grown to a substantial amount. At Earraid we had acquired a three-piece suite, my mother's pride and joy. She had sent to Oxendale's mail-order firm for it at great expense. It cost eight guineas (£8.40), which included delivery all the way from Manchester. I was entrusted with the job of sewing the precious suite securely up in sacking, using rough string and a long curved needle. I can still recall the smell of the jute and the numerous hacks the rough material left on my hands. It was far removed from my usual fine embroidery.

Gradually, during the next three weeks, the house became more and more uncomfortable, until we were down to the bare essentials. We looked forward to the move with mixed feelings, the excitement of change tempered with the sadness of again leaving many good friends. The *Hesperus* arrived to pick us up and there was no time for regrets. All our energies were directed towards making sure we left nothing behind except the standard lighthouse equipment.

We embarked with a wee menagerie, taking with us not only the two cats, but three nanny goats: Whitey, now full grown; her sister Pansy, so called because of her facial resemblance to the flower; and Pansy's daughter, Patchy. On board ship the bewildered goats were tethered on deck where they stood looking miserable. These three certainly were subject to seasickness. Shortly after we set sail the poor beasts began to look even more dejected despite the sea being almost like a millpond. They stood there, heads lowered, ears drooping, with saliva trickling slowly and steadily, unheeded onto the deck.

In normal circumstances we would have steamed in open sea up the west coast of Islay towards our destination, a wee island near Oban, but due to the remote risk of meeting a U-boat, the Captain took the scenic, though longer route between the island and the mainland. The scenery was beautiful, the weather likewise. That evening we dropped anchor in a small secluded bay in Jura, hidden from possible danger. I was none too happy about any sea trip in wartime, but it was proving uneventful. That night we all stood leaning on the deck-rail, breathing in the soft balmy air and watching the sun go down in a blaze of glory. My father remarked, "You'd never know there was a war on." For a wee while at least we felt at peace.

Early next morning we steamed north again towards Lismore. We had seen it often enough in the past as it was on the route taken by the *Lochinvar* out of Oban towards Mull, so we knew it to be a tiny lonely place. We were shown over the ship and introduced to some new technology. We stood amazed, watching the latest equipment searching the seabed for obstacles. On a graph we saw outlines of what looked like hills and valleys, also large dotted areas which we were told were shoals of fish. I was relieved to see nothing resembling the outline of a submarine. My father was interested in all new gadgets and wanted to know all about the intricacies of the device. Even more so he wanted to find out about the very latest safety measures against submarines. This was apparently something called degaussing, meaning the ship was ringed by an antimagnetic cable which could repel any magnetic mines which had been scattered about our waters by the enemy.

Soon we passed the tip of Jura where someone pointed out Corrievreckan, one of the most dreaded currents in Britain, culminating in a whirlpool. Ships gave it a wide berth. It made the fierce currents at the Rhinns look like a mere ripple.

It wasn't long before we steamed up the Sound of Kerrera. Oban suddenly appeared on our right and my mother began to wish we were headed there. She'd have given almost anything to live in a town again, especially one as pleasant as Oban. Instead the *Hesperus* turned its stern on civilisation and shortly afterwards dropped anchor beside the tiniest island we had so far encountered, Eilean Musdile.

Lismore

The island of Lismore lies between the mainland of Argyll and the area called Morvern, at the south end of Loch Linnhe. It is shaped like a badly made cigar, and the wee bit that looks as though it had been broken off the southern tip was where my father was to take up his first more responsible duties as Principal Keeper. The little strip of land seemed to rise no more than a few feet out of the sea, the tower at the southernmost end looking like a timid giant standing with his feet not quite in the water.

We landed at the slipway on the east landing. When we walked up the slip there was a narrow strip of grass from which the other slipway led down to the sea again. It was possible to throw a stone from one side of the island at that point to land in the water at the opposite side. My father commented he had seen rock stations built on bigger islands. We were greeted by the keeper who was being replaced, and the other keeper, a single man who had his mother as housekeeper. The ship's launch started its usual shuttle service, bringing ashore one load of our belongings and returning to the ship with a load of the other man's stuff. We meantime were enjoying a meal and getting to know the other inhabitants, before the *Hesperus* steamed away with the usual farewell blast on her foghorn.

The new house was almost identical to the one at the Rhinns. The cats and goats were turned loose to carry out their exploration. The goats made a remarkably swift recovery from their seasickness, bounding off to eat some of the lush grass that covered most of the island, the first food they had eaten for

Lismore.

two days, having refused all offers of hay and oats en voyage. Meantime the two men barrowed our furniture up to the house hampered by the ubiquitous assortment of hens and cockerels which clucked and scuttered among their feet.

After tea that evening we all went for a walk. The island widened out beyond the slipways. Nearby stood the hen houses and a store and beyond a big walled park which appears to be a statutory adjunct to all stations, in this instance left to lie fallow and neglected with nothing to be seen but wild grass about two feet tall. We walked round the west side of it on a narrow path which only allowed single-file progress, the sea being a few feet away. Once past the park we came on a puzzling feature of the island. A fine stone bridge similar to the old Wade bridges joined our island to an even smaller one, devoid of any amenity other than grass and rocks. It was ridiculous that where this useless appendage ended there was a narrow stretch of water which frustratingly separated us from the big island of Lismore, but there was no bridge spanning it.

My mother's furniture being landed at Lismore, 1940.

The opposite shore looked bare and uninviting. Only a rough road winding round a hill showed signs of the presence of other human beings. Our neighbour had told us it led to the nearest habitation half a mile away where two young shepherds lived. Just above the stony beach across the water stood a big square box set on a pole. This was our mailbox. An unseen postman put the mail in it and he raised a white painted flap on the box. The keepers, on seeing the signal, took it in turns to row across and pick up the letters, at the same time depositing the next lot of out-going mail. If, the white flash showed at an unscheduled time, it usually meant a telegram, though in some cases it turned out to be a present of a brace of rabbits from Baldie and Duggie, the young shepherds.

The first time my father went to collect the mail we all went. We walked as far as the farm and introduced ourselves to the lads, who became good friends and neighbours. Back on the island we took stock of how we were to get enough exercise and avoid boredom in such confined quarters. Although the station was a two-man one, not having a foghorn, there was always plenty of maintenance work to keep the men busy and the usual lack of labour-saving equipment gave the women plenty of housework. Stretching our legs was the problem. It was decided that except in the worst weather we'd walk the full length of the island every day. It was a boring kind of exercise following the narrow path all the time with no access to the miles and miles of glorious scenery that surrounded us. What we would have given to tramp over the Morvern hills away over to the left! Even more frustrating was that Oban was a mere six miles away. We could see the traffic on the streets, and the puffs of steam that indicated the arrival of trains.

On one of our restricted walks we found we had company. The path was so narrow we had to go in single file, my father leading the way followed by my mother, then me with Jean bringing up the rear. Jean started to giggle. She had glanced behind to find tucked on the end of the line, the three goats, followed by two cats, with behind them, a cluster of hens. An onlooker could have been forgiven for thinking he had come across a latter-day Noah leading the animals into the Ark. We wondered why we had been honoured by the presence of the beasts until my father suggested maybe they were hopeful that we'd lead them back to the familiar and relatively wide open spaces of the Rhinns. Whatever the truth, the performance was often repeated.

My mother wasn't entirely deprived of shopping in Oban, but she had to be content with a weekly trip by motor boat, weather permitting. Her first trip was to register with a grocer and butcher for our rations. Jean and I went, too, to make the most of the opportunity to browse round some real shops. The snag was the limitation forced on us by wartime shortages. My first priority was for wool and embroidery threads, so far unrationed. With a good supply of these I could sit out the winter.

Jean didn't go back to school. She was fourteen and entitled to leave if she wanted to. She could have gone to Oban High School, but we were still unsure of how the war would go. The Phoney War was still in operation. The bombing of cities that we had feared had not materialised, nor had our country been invaded. Jean and I were therefore quite content to stay on the island and keep my mother company.

Although we were isolated, there was always plenty of passing traffic. Every time the *Lochinvar* passed on its way to or from Mull, we'd go out and wave to the passengers just for the sake of making a small contact with other people. Numerous ships congregated in Loch Lhinne near Oban from time to time, ready to move off in convoy to America. Apparently it was an ideal spot for the purpose, surrounded as it was by high mountains which made things difficult for enemy planes to spot the ships.

Oban was the shore station for Hyskier, one of the lonely west coast rock stations. The houses, similar to those in Port St. Mary, were situated half way up a steep road leading to Pulpit Hill, a local beauty spot. Occasionally, if the opportunity arose, my mother stayed overnight there especially if the weather changed for the worse while she was on one of her shopping trips. Towards the end of that summer, my mother and father were invited to a wedding in Glasgow. Deciding to make a proper holiday of it, my father took a week of his annual leave. They left Jean and me at the lighthouse buildings in the care of one of the wives who had previously been a neighbour at the Rhinns. Money changed hands for our board and lodgings and, after the usual injunction to us to behave and do as we were told, the two set off with an easy mind. Jean and I were delighted and settled in with high hopes of having an enjoyable spell in a safe and civilised seaside resort.

At our first meal we were served with reconstituted dried fish. The men at the rocks often spent their time fishing, and dried and salted those they couldn't eat immediately, to take home to supplement the rations. Jean and I found the meal unpalatable and very salty. However, we had been taught not to be fussy about our food and never to complain when eating out, so we washed the fish down with tea, helped with the dishwashing and went off to explore what to us was an unfamiliar town apart from the pier area which we had grown used to when we lived at Earraid. Back hungry for our next meal, we were presented with more dried fish. To our great disgust, we had the same uninteresting food for most meals all that week, varied only by what accompanied the fish. Toast at breakfast, potatoes at dinner-time and bread and butter for tea.

Not daring to complain, we escaped as often as we could to visit places like McCaig's Folly, the huge amphitheatre-like structure that dominates the town. We wandered round the shops, but couldn't buy anything. Our pocket money only allowed us a couple of visits to the pictures. It was there we saw "The

Wizard of Oz," which had just been released, and which helped us for an hour or two to forget about the horrors of war and dried fish.

On the day our folks were due back, we were treated to a lovely breakfast of porridge, boiled eggs and toast. When we had been reunited with the holiday-makers we enjoyed an equally pleasant lunch, after which we set off for home amid grateful thanks on the part of my mother and father to the lady for having looked after us so well. Jean and I waited until we were safely back on the island before spilling out our tale of woe. At first disbelieving, and then angry, my father sat down and wrote a letter to our hostess, asking what she meant by such treatment. Back came an even more incensed reply casting up such things as "after all I have done for you," and, "looking after them out of the goodness of my heart." As a parting shot she enclosed a kirby-grip which one of us had left, as she wanted nothing to remind her of us. It was fortunate that the two families never had to be neighbours again, and it was to be many years before the quarrel faded. To this day I detest dried fish.

All seemed to be well in Glasgow and apart from the nationwide difficulty in making a little food go a long way, the war appeared to be having little or no effect on everyday living. The biggest nuisance was the blackout. City dwellers were not so accustomed as us country folk to going about bearing a torch after dark and many suffered a black eye or worse from colliding with a disused lamp post or unlit bus stop. To make matters more difficult, the torches had to be covered over except for a little strip of light in the middle and had to be held pointing downwards at all times. My father said we'd be surprised at some of the changes. At the front and back of every close stood a brick baffle wall, to limit bomb blast and flying shrapnel if the need arose. These were the only protection the tenement dweller had in the event of an air raid.

It was decided I'd risk going back to Glasgow, mainly because I was a financial burden on the family. I would soon be nineteen and had until then contributed not a penny towards the household budget. Granny was on her own, too, and I'd be company for her. As for the war, it was almost nonexistent and therefore not worth worrying about. Jean, not yet fifteen, would stay at home and keep my mother company. So it was arranged. Before winter set in properly, I packed my bags and set off to face wartime Glasgow. I was sad and not a little apprehensive in spite of reassurances that nothing terrible was happening in the city.

Glasgow
at War

*I*t was with mixed feelings that I boarded the train at Oban. I soon realised things were going to be different. The light fittings in the carriage were shaded and the compartment had an air of neglect. It was dark when I reached Buchanan Street Station, the last part of the journey having been travelled blind. I had only known what station we were at by the shouts of the porters announcing stridently, "Stirling," then "Larbert," and so to Glasgow.

I was thankful to be met by Aunt Jean as I was confused by the blacked-out streets and tramcars. The whole city was apparently dead. The tram we took to Shettleston was even more dimly lit than the train and it was difficult to know where to get off. The conductress – nearly all the conductors had gone to war – called out the stops. I thought I'd never get used to this and wished I'd stayed at Lismore. I had to be guided round the baffle wall to find that the stair was also shadowy, making the walls look even grimier than before. My depression deepened. Inside the house, however, the kitchen was bright and the welcome warm, and I was ashamed of my miserable thoughts. After all, Granny, now getting old, had put up with it all since the war began, so who was I to feel resentful and unhappy?

In daylight there seemed to be less to like than before. The row of ugly baffle walls stretched in both directions. The familiar shops looked half empty. More and more items had disappeared from the shelves as the months progressed. Onions were nonexistent unless you grew them yourself. People had become used to eating their meagre ration of meat without the mouth-watering flavour of that humble vegetable and I appreciated how lucky we were at the lighthouse to be able to grow our own.

I spent the first few days finding out about these minor irritations before having to decide how to earn my keep. I had given up the idea of going to college. I was too old to go back to school, and further education was unheard of without Highers. Thinking it over, I realised I only had one asset, the ability to knit and sew. Before the war I had often bought wool and embroidery threads from Smith's, the wool shop in Sauchiehall Street. I walked into that shop, looking, I hoped, more confident than I felt, and asked to see the manager. To my surprise, word came back that he would see me. He was an aloof, disinterested man, the kind who says "Yes?" without looking up from his papers. Quaking, I announced that I would like a job either in the wool or needlework departments of his shop. Maybe he was impressed by my initiative. Maybe he was in need of a member of staff, but he didn't turn me down. Saying he had no vacancies in these departments, he offered me the job of lift attendant, with the promise that the next departmental job would be mine. I grabbed the chance. The pay was £1 a week, and I'd be supplied with a uniform. I was desperate to rush home to tell Granny the great news. I started work the following Monday in a green uniform that fitted only where it touched.

I had given scant regard to the fact that I was terrified of lifts. I had always felt claustrophobic, expecting the things to break down between floors with me trapped inside. It was only after I had been shown how to work the thing and left to myself that the full implication of what I was doing hit me. I was tempted to run off and forget the job, but the idea of being seen running along Sauchiehall Street in a blind panic and an ill-fitting green uniform stopped me from making a complete fool of myself. I stuck to my post and once the customers began to ply me with questions, I started to enjoy the sensation of importance.

It was six months before a vacancy arose in the needlework department and I was able to do work more to my liking. It meant a rise of 10/- a week. I gave Granny half of my wages and the rest was mine to spend or save. Some of this vast wealth went on tram fares, the rest on clothes and trips to the pictures. At last I was independent. Unfortunately, my mother wasn't going to benefit, but at least she wasn't having to feed me. The amount doesn't sound much, but it went a long way. A good pair of shoes cost about 12/6 (62½p) and stockings could be bought for little more than the equivalent of 5p.

I grew used to travelling in the blackout. My brain developed its own system for knowing where we were. I came to know the sound of every twist and turn of the route home from work, so that when I heard a particular screech of the wheels I came out of the semi-comatose state brought on by the dimness of the lights, in time to leave the tram at the Chester Street stop. Home was just across the road.

It wasn't long before Jean decided to follow me to Glasgow to try and make a useful contribution to the world. She found a job in a shoe warehouse, not really to her liking, but at least she was earning. Some time later a vacancy arose in the wool department of Smith's which she successfully applied for, joining me on my daily journeys. As we had always been friends as well as sisters, we arranged to share lunchtimes and tea breaks.

Granny passed the evenings going to whist-drives, which were as popular then as bingo is today. Sometimes as a change from the pictures, I went with her. Sometimes she went with us to the pictures, a fine way of escaping the war. How we envied the characters in American films who seemed to have unlimited access to the sort of food we hadn't tasted for ages. I remember one night on the way home from the pictures, Granny saying wistfully, "My! But I'd love one of those juicy apples they were eating tonight. My mouth watered every time that girl bit into hers." We hadn't seen a Macintosh Red since the war began.

I had resumed my visits to my other grandparents in Wellshot Road. Granny Petrie was beginning to look frail, although her bulk hadn't decreased. More and more she sat by the fire letting Aunt Meg and Aunt Jean look after the house. Grandad was still as alert as ever and ready for an argument, his solitary eye gleaming with delight when I took the opposite view in a debate.

Aunt Jean Petrie decided it was time she got a job. Until then she had merely kept house to the old people. Wee Granny heard of an elderly lady who was looking for a housekeeper-companion on a daily basis, so one dark night I found myself guiding Aunt Jean to the big house in Mount Vernon for an interview. I think we were both in need of a guide, as we stumbled along the long, pitch-dark, unmade-up road aided only by the slit of light from the regulation torch. The house was at the far end of the deserted road. We felt our way up the drive to the villa and rang the bell. The lady was so tall and stately I felt I ought to bow to her. I was quite disappointed when she introduced herself, not as a duchess, but simply Miss Robertson. Aunt Jean got the job there and then, and we went home elated.

Life went on with little variation. We listened to every news bulletin on the wireless, sitting impatiently through the playing of every national anthem of the Allies, which preceded every news broadcast. The war was in earnest now and we'd hear, "A raid was carried out on — last night." "Ten of our aircraft are missing," or "Nine ships were lost when one of our convoys was attacked by U-boats," were common items in the broadcasts. We in Glasgow had suffered only sporadic air raids, nothing compared to cities like Coventry and London. We lived as normally as possible, only wondering when it was going to be our turn. Each night without attack was a bonus, especially as we were surrounded by munitions factories and other manufacturing places. The luck was not to last.

Granny, Jean and I came home from a whist-drive one night in March, 1941, in time to switch on the wireless for the nine o'clock news. As Big Ben struck the hour, we heard in the background the wailing of the sirens announcing another raid on the capital. Sympathetically, we said, "That's London getting it again." The words were scarcely out when the sound of Big Ben was blotted out by the rising wail of our local siren on the roof of the nearby Police Station. We just stared at each other in disbelief before taking action. Would this be just another of the minor raids we had become used to? We couldn't take a chance on it, so we headed for the close, someone carrying a chair and a travelling rug for Granny. The stair echoed with the clatter of feet as the other five families joined us. We disposed ourselves as best we could in the close, the wind whistling through the tunnel-like passage which was open at both ends except for the baffle walls. Some of us sat on the bottom stairs, causing Granny to become agitated. She was afraid the landing window would be blown out sending shards of glass flying into those in the direct line of fire. It didn't seem to bother her that if the four-storey building received a direct hit we would all be buried by hundreds of tons of solid stone blocks. The close was neither the safest nor most comfortable place to be, but it was all we had.

Granny sat ensconced, wrapped in her fur coat, not so much for warmth as for fear she'd lose it. In her hand she clutched an ancient tapestry bag containing all her insurance papers. The rest of us sat or wandered up and down in our cold prison, listening to the easily recognised irregular beat of the enemy aircraft. Somebody wondered why Germany, with its great reputation for engineering skills, couldn't make aeroplane engines with a steady rhythm like ours. Listening to the ominous whine and crump of bombs, I remembered being told that if you didn't hear the approach whine you were sure to be killed by a direct hit, and I wondered how anybody knew that.

It was obvious that this was no short term raid. It was equally obvious that Shettleston and its environs were not the main target, as most of the planes passed well into the distance before unloading their deadly cargo. Far to the west we could hear the sounds of a concentrated attack and we prayed for the poor souls who were catching the full brunt of it. Extra loud bangs signified the dropping of a landmine All I knew at the time was that after one such noise I became aware of some unseen force making me sway back on my heels in company with others who were near me. It was a weird sensation caused by blast. The landmine had landed several miles away. It must have been very powerful.

It was almost dawn before the noise subsided and the siren sounded the all clear. We all tottered back to our homes. Not to go to bed, though. There was just time to have some breakfast before setting off to work. Strangely, nobody thought of staying at home to make up for lost sleep. We had no idea what we would find in the city centre, but the trams were running as usual, so I reckoned it hadn't been too bad in spite of the racket during the night. That day I remained in a zombie-like state as I supplied the customers with embroidery threads. How strange that people should still be concerned with such peaceable pursuits as sewing, after a night of fear. I began to wonder how the Londoners, who had been suffering terrible nightly raids managed to keep going.

As soon as she could that morning, Aunt Jean came to see how Granny had fared in the night. Nothing amiss had taken place in her household either. The family had spent the night in the Anderson shelter buried in their back garden. Aunt Jean had apparently kept the rest of the family from being too frightened by unwittingly making herself the butt of a great deal of hilarity. Some months before, we had discussed what we would do in the event of a big raid. Aunt Jean said she would try to keep calm, and had already laid plans for such an eventuality. She made sure all her prize possessions were in an easily accessible cupboard near the door, ready to be lifted as soon as the siren sounded. The raid duly started and everyone repaired swiftly to the shelter where it was discovered to everyone's glee, that Aunt Jean was clutching only one item, her spare corsets. She never lived it down.

A few days later, when I visited the grandparents in Wellshot Road, I recounted the tale of the corsets. My other Aunt Jean laughed and then told her story. She had also laid plans. Granny Petrie, by now slow and infirm, needed help with dressing. She spent most of her time in bed. If Aunt Jean was in bed when the sirens went, she would throw her own clothes on quickly over her nightdress, thus giving her a minute or two more to help Granny. That first night of the big raids there was no problem, as it started before bed time, but the next night they had all gone to bed early to make up the sleep lost the previous night. When the siren went, Aunt Jean leapt out of bed, wrapped her corsets round her, then pulled on her stockings to find to her horror that she couldn't fasten the suspenders because of the bulky nightie. She had to start all over again with the result that the raid was well under way by the time she got Granny dressed and down to the close.

After that first big raid, word filtered through that Clydebank had been the main target, with terrible loss of life and property. Very few buildings were left standing and no family was left unscathed. That evening Granny, undeterred, went to her usual whist drive, arriving home full of excitement. She had been talking to an air-raid warden. He was sure there would be another similar raid that night, but reckoned the sirens wouldn't sound until about midnight when the moon rose. We asked sarcastically if he was in touch with the Luftwaffe, which remark went straight over Granny's head. She was too busy with her own strategy. Jean and I were ordered to bed immediately, still in our day clothes to save having to dress at midnight. We were to try to get some sleep. Granny would stay awake to stand guard. Sure enough, we slept soundly until she shook us at midnight. We leapt out of bed and dived towards the door, only to be stopped by Granny. "No!" she said, "the siren hasn't gone yet. I've just wakened you to get ready." Reluctant and shivering, we repaired to the close which Granny had meantime in some way furnished with several rugs and chairs, together with a flask of tea and sandwiches. We were to be more comfortable this time than last night.

The rest of the city was still wrapped in slumber as we sat in silence waiting for the alert to sound. At long last Granny came to the conclusion her informant must have made a mistake; so we carried all the gear upstairs very quietly so as not to disturb the neighbours, and went to bed, this time in our pyjamas. We had just lain down when the siren went. At that moment I could cheerfully have strangled Granny and her unknown air-raid warden. We spent the rest of that night and the next two in the close – waiting and wondering if it was to be our turn next. Thankfully we were to be let off lightly.

After that, raids were few and far between, and of short duration. Perhaps the enemy had decided it was too far to fly to Glasgow. We became a bit blasé, not bothering to go down to the close any more. When we heard the siren we congregated in the windowless lobby, sharing it with the family in the house above, whose baby slept blissfully through it all in the safety of Granny's coal bunker. A cushion covered in an old pillowslip was placed inside it as a comfortable mattress for the little one. Granny, who hated wasting time, would boil the next day's soup or make a dumpling since she was awake anyway, never thinking that if a bomb landed nearby she would be covered by scalding vegetables or sticky hot fruit as well as being blown to bits.

At work we were given an additional duty, fire-watching. One night in ten I had to stay in town. Bunks furnished with freezing air mattresses were roughly knocked up in a cold, depressing stockroom on the top floor of the shop. It seemed a bit daft to sleep just under the rafters, which would be the first place a bomb would hit, but we were in more danger from rats. We were there to deal with incendiary bombs. Everybody was trained in the use of the ubiquitous stirrup pump with which we were supposed to quench the fire bombs. The business end of the pump was stuck in a bucket of water. You stood on the footplate and pumped furiously on something that closely resembled the handle of a garden spade, while someone else directed the jet of water thus obtained at the flames. I felt it would be much more effective just to heave the water straight out of the bucket as I watched the pathetic wee trickle, which was all my puny strength could muster, issuing from the nozzle of my stirrup pump. Fortunately, I never had to put it to the real test.

After some time our sleeping quarters were transferred to a safer and more comfortable venue. A door in the basement which I had never noticed before, led to a vast concrete vault. No ordinary bomb could have penetrated there. When I got around to asking why it existed, I learned it belonged to the bank next door, only they didn't appear to have any use for it. The vault proved to be a much more comfortable bedroom than the attic floor, and had the advantage of being rat free. It had one big disadvantage, though. It was so solid we wouldn't hear the sirens at all. So much for efficient fire-watching.

Until bedtime we on duty sat round a cosy coal fire in the second floor tearoom frequented in the daytime by genteel townspeople seeking refreshment before embarking on a round of the shops in search of goods. It was a luxurious olde worlde room, with ornate lighting and hung with heavy velvet curtains. As I sat sewing or knitting I imagined myself to be a great lady in her mansion. The dream was spoiled a bit by having to don a steel helmet and do rounds to check that all was well. During a raid, we had to be on the top floor in readiness. I enjoyed my firewatching nights, even though we were not paid extra. The only perk we had was a meal in the evening and breakfast next morning before work.

I didn't feel resentful about having to spend my teenage years in this way. If there had been no war, my late teens would have been a dead bore. I was too shy to break out of the routine I was used to even if I had gone to college. When restrictions were lifted, years after the war ended, I began to realise how much I had missed out on in the way of freedom and how many small luxuries I had been deprived of by rationing. The war to me was a kind of exciting adventure, sometimes worrying, sometimes full of small pleasures, like finding in an out-of-the-way shop a lovely wee silvery powder compact from prewar stock. It was like finding treasure, as the normal way of buying face powder was in a plain cardboard box, providing you could find it at all.

Stockings were hard to come by. We evolved all kinds of deceptions to make bare legs look as though covered in silk. Chemists sold bottles of "liquid stockings," similar to tanning lotion, which was applied with a wad of cotton wool. There was a knack in doing it so that the liquid went on smoothly without leaving telltale smudges of uneven colour. When it was dry, it was handy to have a chum at hand with an eyebrow pencil, to draw a straight line down the back of the legs to look like a seam.

One Saturday morning in June I was dressing for work when an announce-ment was made on the wireless that as from midnight that night all clothing would be rationed. It was hardly surprising that the shops were mobbed that day. Anybody who had money to spare was out to buy up all they could afford before the deadline. Having to work until the shop shut at one, I was on heckle-pins all morning in case there was nothing left by the time I was free. I headed straight for Lewis's where I elbowed my way through the milling throng to emerge triumphant with a clerical grey suit.

From then on things became more difficult. Even knitting wool was on the coupons. I ripped down jumpers I had grown tired of, wound the wool into hanks and washed it to take out as many wrinkles as possible, and re-knitted it in a different design. We became ingenious and inventive over the next few years. Dresses for special occasions could be made from spare curtains, and coats from dyed blankets. We were only allowed twenty-four coupons every six months. A dress cost eleven of these, so it was obvious we were going to have to look after our clothes carefully.

I queued one day in Daley's, the smart department store next to Smith's. Word had reached us via the grapevine that a consignment of real silk stockings had been delivered to that shop. The entire staff of Smith's took it in turn to nip next door to spend some of our precious store of coupons on that most coveted commodity. The queue was long and I was tired by the time I reached the head of it, but both Jean and I went home that night jubilantly waving two pairs of black silk stockings each.

Now that Jean and I were working we found it more difficult to visit Lismore, having only two weeks holiday and a day or two off at Christmas and New Year. As a result, I didn't get to know the people of Lismore apart from the two boys at the farm. This didn't bother me. Maybe I was growing up and away from country life at last. I still missed my mother and father and the passing years seemed etched more strongly on my mother's face when I saw her, which was mostly when she and my father came to Glasgow for a break. I think she had given up hope of ever being shifted to a mainland station. My father never looked any different, apart from having broadened out as he grew older. He loved his work and was content to be a lightkeeper. He found plenty to interest him: fishing and gardening and inventing gadgets. He invented a wool-winder simply because it saved my mother having to wait until he could hold the hanks of wool for her.

The summer after the Clydebank air raids Jean and I went home for a break. We cheated our employer for the first and only time. We were supposed to work on Saturday forenoon, but that meant not being able to travel until the Monday, thus losing two precious days of our holiday. We took a chance on travelling on the Saturday, leaving Granny to make up some excuse for our absence. We were still feeling guilty as we took our seats on the train. To our horror, a few minutes later we saw passing our carriage window, the Boss, followed by a company of scouts, off for a day's outing. By sheer coincidence they were travelling on our train. Jean and I shrank down in our seats, sighing with relief when the train started with no further sign of Mr. Allen. At Stirling one of the frequent changes in the timetable occurred. "All change," called the guard. We had to pile out and get into another train as our engine had developed a fault. I was sure we'd bump into Mr. Allen, so I rushed as quickly as possible to the nearest carriage on the other train, hoping to disappear from sight before my boss could catch a glimpse of me. Unfortunately, besides my usual luggage I was hampered by a fishing rod that some idiot was sending to my father. It wedged itself across the carriage door and refused to budge. I had to be rescued by a porter who bundled me unceremoniously into the train under the amused eyes of other passengers. Thank goodness Mr. Allen wasn't among them. At least I presume he wasn't, as nothing was ever said when we came back to work. He must have got off the train at Larbert as he certainly wasn't aboard when we reached Oban. I came to the conclusion I wasn't good at deception and that it was best to remain honest.

That holiday was nearly the last Jean and I were ever to set out on. We took the opportunity of accompanying my mother's neighbour one day to Oban for a few hours, while my mother caught up with the extra washing. The day promised to be fair, but as time passed the wind rose and by the time of the return trip, the weather had definitely worsened. In Oban Bay it wasn't too bad, but once out of the shelter of Kerrera Island, the full force of the wind hit us and we were in for a rough crossing. The waves were topped by ferocious white horses. I wasn't at all happy, but we had to put our trust in the boatman and providence. Jean and I held firmly on to our seats to avoid being thrown about as the small craft dived into the oncoming waves, throwing great sheets of spray up on both sides. That six miles was the longest I've ever known, so it was with no small sense of relief that I saw through the spray the figures of my father and mother standing on the slip waiting for us. As we neared the pier, my father waved as though signalling. Mr. Cowan knew what he meant. We were not going to be able to land.

Turning back meant turning broadside on to the waves for a time, a dangerous manoeuvre. The sea looked more menacing than ever from our low level just above the water and for a few fraught minutes we all but capsized. Thanks to the boatman's skill we made it without sinking, and soon we were heading back the way we had come, the waves now pushing us at a spanking pace towards Oban and safety. We spent the night at the Hyskier shore station, and the next day dawning clear and bright we made for home. When we eventually reached the island, we were greeted by my mother, for once with tears in her eyes. Visibility had been so bad the previous day that when we turned back the boat had been swiftly swallowed up by the haze, leaving my mother and father not knowing if we had made it safely to port, and with no means of finding out until the weather improved. They had spent an anxious night.

The rest of the holiday was peaceful, the weather kind, apart from one morning when we woke to find the sun blotted out and the world shrouded in dense fog. That being the routine day for going across to collect the mail, my father swithered about the wisdom of getting the boat out. He was well aware of the danger of fog. After a while he decided there was enough visibility if he kept close to the shore. I went with him as an extra pair of eyes. On the way back I had my first practical lesson in how deceptive fog can be. Several barrage balloons were always anchored in the sky above Oban as they were over most cities and towns. "Look!" I said to my father. "The fog must be lifting. There's one of the barrage balloons." As I pointed toward the silvery-grey roundish object it made a movement. What I was seeing was the head of a grey seal swimming silently only a few yards from our boat. I had been deceived over both height and distance, since when I have been extremely respectful towards fog.

The fortnight soon passed and it was time to say goodbye again. I was used to farewells, having been saying them at regular intervals since I was seven. I'd give my mother a peck on the cheek and say, "Cheerio, then," and that was that. Jean hated saying goodbye. We went back somewhat reluctantly to Glasgow and the prospect of more air raids, while my mother and father settled down to what showed signs of being a long boring winter. It turned out to be not quite that.

One day in early winter a mysterious parcel arrived at Ten-nine-eight, the enclosed note merely saying, "Here's a wee present for you all. I'll explain when I see you." Not like my voluble father, I thought. It was some months before we saw anyone from home, so we remained puzzled as to how we came to acquire a number of beautiful luxury manicure sets, the like of which had not been in the shops since the war began. Covered in expensive-looking blue or black leathercloth and fitted with zip-fasteners, each contained a selection of nail varnish, polish remover, and all the other appurtenances of nail care, and all with the famous Cutex label.

Only when my mother and father came for their next holiday did we hear the story behind this largesse. One night a fairly large convoy waiting in the Firth of Lorne was attacked by enemy planes, which swooped unexpectedly over the mountains. One ship, at least, was sunk and many badly damaged. A bomb had dropped unerringly down the funnel of one ship, blowing it and its crew to kingdom come. The helpless quartet at the lighthouse had a grandstand view of the mayhem. My mother said it was like a horrible fireworks display. My father had to decide whether or not to extinguish the light, which was still shining from the tower. He dowsed the light and hoped he had done the right thing. Next day a message came telling him not to light it again, and the tower remained in darkness until the war ended.

It was a day or two before the flotsam of the raid began to drift ashore, among which was the box that turned out to contain the manicure sets. My mother thought it a pity it hadn't contained food. Her mind was always set on filling her larder. My father suddenly realised he could expect a visit from the customs officers any day. Also washed up on the island were hundreds of pit props which when salvaged were piled up against a wall outside the station. Sure enough, the sound of a motor boat made itself heard at a time when the normal supply boat wasn't expected. It was the custom boat. The officer simply asked where the pit props had come from and when told, said, "It would cost us more to take them away than to get some more to replace them, so just make use of them yourselves." Whereupon he departed. My father, still wary, kept the box of Cutex intact for a while before distributing the booty among the family.

A much more valuable cargo was washed ashore in other areas nearby. Race horses reputed to belong to the Aga Khan had been on board one of the ill-fated ships, en route to America like the human evacuees earlier in the war. Those horses which survived the attack, swam safely ashore; and some were still in their wooden horse boxes. None of them appeared on our wee island. My father wouldn't have had a clue how to handle them. Goats were his limit.

They had one other adventure which was recounted on that same holiday. One dark foggy night, not long after the light had been permanently extinguished, my father went to shut the hens in for the night, finding his way by the light of a dim little torch. Backing out of the henhouse he became aware of the sound of an engine close at hand and coming nearer. Peering through the murk he could see nothing for a few minutes, then suddenly a huge shape loomed high above him. It was the bows of a ship heading straight for the island and disaster. Frantically my father waved his torch and shouted at the top of his voice, aware that his puny effort was unlikely to be noticed. Maybe someone did see or hear his warning. At any rate the sound of the engines changed and he could hear the water churning as the ship went into reverse, coming to a halt just a few feet from the rocks near the slipway. There it stayed, thankfully undamaged, until the tide rose and it slipped away.

One of the advantages of living in the city was that the weather had little or no effect on day-to-day living, unlike on the islands where everything revolved round the weather forecast, but there was one day during which the weather played an unusual trick on us. I woke to find the noisy city had become deathly silent. No bus or tram drew up outside our window and there was no sound of footsteps echoing on the pavement. I wondered if I had gone stone deaf overnight. When I rose to look out of the window, the street and the dingy tenements had been transformed into a scene of glittering white. The snow looked to be several inches deep. I had to get to work, a twenty-minute tram ride away, and there was no sign of a vehicle of any kind. Instead, the middle of the street was filled with trudging workers, their footsteps muffled by the carpet of snow. It was like a scene from one of Lowry's paintings. After breakfast I joined them, hundreds of us walking along the tramlines into town. People who would have sat in silence in the draughty trams, blethered to each other as they walked; grumbling, no doubt, but no-one having dreamed of staying at home. It was about half past nine when I eventually reached the shop, my cheeks rosy and feeling as warm as pie, only to be told the shop was going to close at midday because of the weather.

The needlework department had one customer that morning, an elderly befurred lady who had walked quite some way to make her purchase. Her urgent requirement was one small embroidery transfer of a monogram to decorate a handkerchief. They cost 1d each. We stocked three types and she spent a happy half-hour swithering over which one she preferred. By lunchtime we were all bored stiff and glad to be free even if it did mean a long walk home. I set off but had not gone far when Sir Galahad, in the guise of a bus driver, drew alongside on his way to Shettleston, his steed the first double-decker bus to have got on the road again.

The only other incident that relieved the monotony of a wartime winter was not so pleasant. A foreign seaman had brought the dreaded smallpox to Glasgow. Immediate arrangements were made to have all citizens vaccinated, a daunting task for the medical services. We queued at the local surgery. I had been vaccinated three times as a baby, but in my mother's words "it had never taken." Granny gave the doctor this bit of information and I passed out into oblivion vaguely aware of the doctor saying, "Give her an extra strong dose." I wasn't the only person who fainted in that queue. I soon came round, but a few days later I became ill with what was diagnosed as vaccine fever. I babbled for a number of days, during which I remember I thought I was sleeping on a makeshift bed, made from two small uncomfortable chairs, a physical impossibility, as I realised when I regained my senses.

I celebrated my twentieth birthday in January, 1942. There was no party and few presents. Nobody could spare coupons to buy sweets or clothes of any kind. It was then I realised that soon my life would once more be unavoidably changed. I'd be eligible for call-up to the forces. I tried to put it to the back of my mind, but found the thought intruding every time I wanted to plan ahead. One Sunday in spring I paid a visit to one of my mother's friends. On this occasion I had an ulterior motive. Isa's husband worked in the Labour Exchange and I wanted to pick his brains. I asked him how and when I was likely to be sent for and where I was most likely to be directed. He was very helpful. If I waited until I was called up, I'd have a choice only between nursing and the A.T.S. I knew I'd make a rotten nurse and I didn't fancy the Women's Army Corps. He told me that if I volunteered for one of the other services in advance of call-up, I'd be accepted. I went home armed with an application form to volunteer for the W.R.N.S. He also advised me that if I put a 'phone number – anybody's would do – on my application, it would make all the difference. I had never spoken on the 'phone, far less owned one, but I asked permission of one of the few people I knew who had possessed that status symbol, if I could use her number. My application was posted off and I sat back to await an answer. I had a long wait.

Meantime a letter came from home at Easter telling us that my father was being shifted from Lismore. It came as a bit of a surprise as he had only been there two years, about half the average spell of duty. The letter from the office invariably began with the words, "We are pleased to inform you that you have been transferred to ..." The office may have been pleased and the man my father was replacing may have been pleased, but my mother and father certainly were not. They were leaving the claustrophobic wee island for a bigger, but even more isolated one in the Outer Hebrides. I looked up Barrahead on the map and found it to be a tiny smudge at the most southerly tip of those islands on the far side of the Minch.

Jean and I were never back at Lismore. The next letter we got said simply that they had arrived safely at the new station and were both well. It was only as I read the rest of the short letter that I realised just what was in store for my mother. We would only get a letter once a fortnight in future, as the supply boat only called at Barrahead every fourteen days with fresh meat, bread and groceries as well as the mail. There was of course no fridge, so once the fresh meat and bread was finished my mother would have to resort to tinned meat and bake her own bread or scones. Coping with rationing would be even more difficult than before.

It was May when the letter with O.H.M.S. on the front came, informing me I was due to start war service. I answered right away saying I had volunteered for the W.R.N.S., after which I heard nothing for a month. Another letter came saying I had been accepted and asking me to present myself at a building near Glasgow Green a few days later for a medical. I was delighted. I had chosen the Wrens because I felt I was bound to be stationed somewhere near my beloved sea.

Barrahead

I had been well-trained by Granny and circumstances to be early for appointments, so on the day of the medical I arrived at the imposing old red building long before anyone else. I was directed into a big room furnished mainly with a huge desk behind which sat a fierce-looking woman in a white coat. Apart from the desk there was only a couple of filing cabinets and a door in one corner clearly labelled "Staff Only". As I sat on the end of a row of old chairs, a number of other candidates joined me.

It was then I wished I was not first in line. A white-coated attendant handed me a chamberpot and said baldly and loudly, "Give me a sample," and left me holding the embarrassing receptacle, watched by a sea of expectant faces. I looked wildly around and said, "What? Here?" "Of course not," said the disgusted nurse. "In there," pointing to the door marked Staff Only. Followed by titters and muffled snorts from the other victims, I obeyed, feeling a right fool and vowing never ever to be first again.

That over, the rest was easy. I was in good health. I was told to go home and await further instructions. I carried on working in Smith's, but had to inform my boss that I would be vacating my job in the near future. I was a little piqued by the cool reception given to the news. It was nothing personal, of course. A fair proportion of the staff had vanished in the same way from time to time, so it was now all in a day's work to lose yet another to the forces.

The W.R.N.S.

One sunny morning in August brought the letter with O.H.M.S. on the top. I was to report on 14th September for two weeks initial training at the Wrens depot in Mill Hill, London. The only time I had previously been outside Scotland, apart from when we lived in the Isle of Man, was when I went with a bus trip to Blackpool one prewar September holiday weekend. When I read the letter properly, I was glad to see that besides a travel warrant, it contained full instructions on how to reach the depot. There was also a list of things to bring with me, and more importantly, a list of things not to bring. I was glad of the latter, as Granny would have sent me off loaded with such necessary items as a hot-water bottle and a travelling rug.

I handed in my notice at the shop, and spent the rest of the waiting time feeling important and scared. My mother and father must have felt even worse. Their unworldly protected daughter was being sent out alone against the multifarious types of situations she would be meeting. My father gave me what advice he could when replying to my letter breaking the news to them. The gist of it was, "Watch how you go when in the company of men," and "Stay honest and as good as you have always been." I'm afraid my parents were unable to say anything that "wasn't quite nice."

I wasn't the only one in the family to be called up. My cousin Alec was already in the R.A.F. and his sister Agnes, a year or two older than I, was in the A.T.S. When I went to visit all the Petrie relatives I was told that the girl who lived next door to Uncle Jack was joining the Wrens the same day as I was. I didn't know her very well, but we arranged to travel down together. We were to meet on the platform at Glasgow Central Station to catch the overnight train to London.

I was escorted to the station by friends and relations, all giving me conflicting and unknowledgeable advice on how to find my way to the depot. The train was busy. Hundreds of people, mostly in uniform, milled about in the semi-darkness of the station, looking for seats. Train services were few and far between. I pushed and elbowed my way with the rest and found two seats. There was no sign of my supposed companion as departure time approached. I grew more and more agitated as numerous travellers tried to take the spare seat. I had to give it up eventually to a young airman, and I waved goodbye to my friends feeling more angry than anything else. Just as well, otherwise I might have made a fool of myself by crying all over Aunt Jean.

As the train rattled along through the dark, its passengers crammed like herring in the corridors as well as in the carriages, I started to worry again. How would I find my way unaided through the vastness of London? I was painfully shy, finding it difficult to talk to strangers, of which my compartment was full. Eventually I fell asleep, lulled by the train sounds and the poor lighting. I woke to find I had been using the unknown airman's shoulder for a pillow. He, gallant soul, had cramp from trying not to move in case he disturbed my slumbers. Although I blushed with embarrassment, the ice was broken and we talked quietly the rest of the way. I told him it was my first venture "abroad" and how bothered I was about finding my way to Mill Hill. When we arrived at Euston in the early morning, he carried my case and escorted me to the tube, where he explained how to read the route maps on the underground trains. I was to get off at the stop after Golders Green. I thanked him and he went out of my life.

I had always avoided the underground train system in Glasgow because I hated the closed-in feeling, so I sat suffering from the beginnings of panic as the tube train thundered through the tunnels. Suddenly to my astonishment and subsequent relief, we swooshed into bright sunlight. I didn't know it was only underground in the city, emerging to become an ordinary train in the suburbs. I enjoyed the rest of the trip, successfully boosting my morale by descending at the right station.

The morning was clear and fresh and smelled of moist leaves. I handed my ticket to a surprised ticket collector and asked the way to the depot. He cheerily said, "You're early." I might have known. I was first in the queue again! He added, "Most of the girls don't get here until the afternoon. They have a day's sightseeing in London at the expense of the government first." I hadn't even thought of that. Now I had to find my own way to my destination instead of following some better-informed person. I walked up a real English country lane set in real English countryside, another surprise as to all intents and purposes

I was still in London, which I had hitherto thought of as consisting of tall buildings and busy streets.

At the top of the lane I saw the building I was looking for. An enormous futuristic structure with "arms" jutting out in all directions. I'd never seen anything like it. It seemed unfinished. Work had started before the war to erect the imposing building to house the National Institute for Medical Research, but the programme had been abandoned when war began. The half-finished construction was now in the process of completion to house about nine hundred trainee Wrens, and I was about to join the throng, a small cog in a very big wheel.

Tentatively I pushed open the big door and I asked where I should report. Like an echo of the ticket collector, the Wren said "You're early" as if I didn't know! I was put through a long and involved routine of filling in forms and answering questions, and then directed to the "mess" for breakfast. Then I was collected and taken to the clothing store, or "slops" to be issued with a temporary uniform, a sort of overall dress, in navy blue, before being shown to my sleeping quarters. Each corridor looked exactly like the last and I wondered if I'd ever find my way out of the maze. The "cabin" was bare with raw plaster walls, but I had the choice of a dozen beds; sorry, bunks.

Free for the rest of the forenoon, I hunted for the recreation room and settled down in an armchair to make up for the lost sleep of the previous night. It wasn't until well after lunch that the main bulk of recruits poured in. Then I was glad I had arrived early as I watched them queuing to register. One of the last to arrive was my erstwhile travelling companion who had missed the train.

That night as I lay unable to sleep because of the strangeness of my surroundings, and the sound of muffled sobs from homesick souls, including the supposedly cool young lady from Tollcross, oddly, I didn't feel homesick. Maybe I was too used to being separated from my loved ones. In the morning, I awoke to the sound of a cement mixer loudly at work beneath the window. It was then, when I heard the workmen calling to each other, that I began to realise I was far from home. They were speaking in to my ears, beautiful cultured English, an alien tongue to one who had been used to hearing only broad Glaswegian from the lips of labourers. English was in my experience only for posh people in films or on the wireless.

The first week was one of constant, though varied, hard work. At six in the morning, dressed in shorts and blouse, we ran to a nearby field where we practised the rudiments of organised physical jerks. "Arms stretch, knees bend." I hadn't enjoyed it at school, but this was different. The morning air was soft and sweet-scented, and we ran back with hearty appetites for a good breakfast. Half of us were set to work on menial jobs. I had to scrub corridors, using a bucket of water and a scrubbing brush. It was a lot different from scrubbing Granny's wee kitchen floor. Each corridor seemed endless, and when you came to a corner, there was another one of equally daunting dimensions. By dinnertime my back was fit to break and my soft hands were red raw. Afternoons were allocated to lectures. Rules and regulations, all of which started either with "you must" or "you must not," were most important. Then came Morse code, flag signalling, naval history, first aid, air-raid drill and such necessary items as recognition of the various ranks in the R.N.

There was a medical that week too. I made sure I wasn't first in line on that occasion, but I was still to be embarrassed. We had to strip to the waist, a dozen or so of us at a time, waiting our turn sitting on a row of chairs facing a huge window which was being vigorously cleaned by a man in overalls. He was apparently immune to the exposure of a variety of female charms on such a grand and free scale, but I'd have done anything to be able to hide. All I could do was fold my arms and blush. The doctor was a man, but he was no gentleman. He had a glint in his eye that shouldn't, in my opinion, have been there when he was simply doing his job! Thankfully, each of us was only kept a few minutes and all of us passed.

Evenings were free. I walked in the country lanes enjoying the peace and quiet and marvelling at how lovely England was. I was too shy to mix with the local soldiery, who seemed to materialise out of nowhere to the delight of most of the girls. Down one of the leafy lanes I found a Toc-H club in what had been an elegant house. I ventured in, hopeful of a cup of tea. I found it was a quiet haven frequented by the older and more sober-sided members of the forces. There I spent my evenings just sitting listening to the wireless and dreaming of home.

The second week was easier. It was time to swap over with the other half of the group. I was now to learn how to cope with officers. We were to act as "bat-women", each allocated a Wren officer to work for. Mine was a very pleasant lady who didn't overwork me. I woke her with a cup of tea, ran her bath, and laid out her uniform, brushed and sponged when necessary. I had to polish her shoes, make the bed and tidy up the cabin, and generally act as a lady's maid. Finally I had to wait at table in the officer's mess. This had one enjoyable perk. We were allowed to eat any extra food. I sampled some luscious puddings and cream cakes, the like of which I hadn't eaten for ages because of rationing, not to mention lashings of roast beef and Yorkshire pudding.

As I performed these tasks I wondered why everyone had to go through the same routine, especially as none of us knew yet what we would be directed to at the end of the fortnight. At one of the last lectures we were informed that if any of us became officers or held important posts we would be better able to understand what those under our command had to do day in and day out. It was also designed to bring us all down to the same level so that no one would think herself better than her fellows. It ensured, too, that the wren who washed the dishes knew she was playing as important a part in winning the war as the one who was sending urgent messages to a ship or driving the Admiral's car.

The first Sunday I spent there was not easy. Most of the girls were English and within reasonable travelling distance of home, so they had gone off for the weekend, and the depot was almost empty. After the church service, I hung about longing for the wee room and kitchen in Shettleston which after many years of dislike had suddenly become very dear to me. Scruffy, noisy Shettleston Road took on an aura of near beauty; trams, dingy tenements and all.

After a cold lunch I could stand it no longer. I had to do something to occupy the rest of the day. I still suffered my old fear of being alone but, determined to take the plunge, I set off by bus to the nearest town. Again I marvelled at the beautiful clear accent of the conductress, who spoke as though she had been to Oxford. It was so different from the "Come oan, get aff" tones of her Glasgow counterpart. Alighting at Mill Hill Broadway, I found myself near a cinema, which was open and showing "Beyond the Blue Horizon." I had never seen a cinema open on the Sabbath and I was faced with a dilemma. Here was a way I could spend a pleasant hour or two on a lonely afternoon, yet it went against the grain to do anything so frivolous on a Sunday. My lesser self won. I mounted the steps, looking furtively to left and right to see if anyone was watching, and feeling terribly guilty. Once seated in the dark auditorium I felt a bit better, but I can't say I enjoyed the show.

By the following weekend, I had made friends with a girl whose parents lived in a nearby town, and who invited me to spend the day there. The journey involved no less than four changes of bus. This seemed odd to me as I was used to the Glasgow transport system on which you could travel for well over an hour without a change. It was the most luxurious house I'd ever been in. It was actually a semi-detached house of modest proportions by today's standards, but it was a palace compared to Granny's room and kitchen. We ate in a dining room, and what a meal: roast beef and Yorkshire pudding, followed by something I'd never heard of, blackberry pie, which turned out to be made from what we called brambles. It was only later that I realised the lady of the house must have sacrificed her entire week's rations for the occasion. After dinner I was shown over the garden which included something else I'd only read about, an orchard. I never saw or heard from Betty when we all went our separate ways, but I have often thought about the kindness her parents showed to a passing stranger.

At the end of the fortnight we were asked if we still wanted to join the Wrens. If anyone backed out they could go home, but were still liable for call-up to serve in some other way. A few opted out and those who remained were called to a special meeting after we had signed on. This was the moment we'd been waiting for, when we would find out where we were to be stationed, and what kind of job we'd be doing.

Before I left Glasgow I had paid a visit to my old needlework teacher, Miss Duthie. When I told her I was joining the Wrens, she said, "Oh! Wouldn't it be lovely if you were sent to Inverary. There are lots of Wrens there." She had often raved about the beauty and peace of the area. Knowing I had little choice in the matter, I had put the conversation out of my mind. I only knew I'd like to go back to Scotland if it was possible.

At the meeting I discovered there was a degree of choice after all. The officer in charge would announce, "Six drivers are needed for.... Who would like the job?" When the requisite number had volunteered, they were asked questions on their suitability for the job. I sat until I heard her say, "We need three sail-makers for Scot...." My hand shot up almost of its own volition before she had completed the word. I was asked what qualifications I had as a sail-maker, answering that I was good at sewing and used to handling sacking at the lighthouse. I was accepted. In no time I found myself queuing to be issued with my uniform, marvelling at the amount of clothing and wondering how I was going to carry it all. It was a strange proud moment when I saw myself in the smart outfit and realised it suited me well. I had a problem with the tie, but we helped each other.

The office issued me with a pay-book with instructions not to lose it, on pain of dire retribution. I had parted with my familiar identity card and ration book reluctantly, feeling I was no longer the same person who had left Glasgow such a short time ago. When I was handed a travel warrant I stared at it in disbelief. Of all places, I was indeed going to Inverary, the Argyll village so enthusiastically praised by Miss Duthie.

In the train bearing three of us north I couldn't have cared less how dim the lighting was. We spent the night blethering and singing and wondering how we'd get on at Inverary. I knew when we crossed the border, although it was still dark. I know every time I travel even yet, that I have come home. Perhaps there's a change in the air or the scent of the countryside is different. I don't know. I'm simply aware of the fact.

In Glasgow we were taken to Queen Street Station from where we proceeded up the West Highland line. The scenery grew more and more beautiful as we left the banks of the Clyde and headed north towards Arrochar, a bonny wee village set among mountains at the head of Loch Long. The English girls were as awestruck by Argyllshire as I had been by London. The last part of the journey was by canvas-covered truck over the Rest and Be Thankful, one of Scotland's most spectacular passes. At that time a narrow road twisted and turned up a very steep gradient, culminating at the top in the worst bend in any road I had known. Fortunately, we in the back of the truck were blinkered by the canvas covering and didn't realise until it was over that the wheels came within a foot of a sheer drop as the driver changed gears for the final hairpin bend.

Down the other side of the pass we swept more easily through countryside apparently devoid of any habitation for miles. About an hour later we turned into the gate of what was to be my home for the next three years, *H.M.S. Quebec.* It was merely a collection of huts of all shapes and sizes clustered along the edge of Loch Fyne and surrounded by a barbed wire fence. I had no idea at the time just how important it was to be to the winning of the war.

We reported to the regulating office to sign in and go through the routine for newcomers. I had already come to the conclusion that from the time I signed on at Mill Hill I simply had to obey orders, keep to the rules, and everything else would be taken care of. I would have no worries about rations or clothing coupons, and my physical, mental and spiritual welfare would be taken care of. Travelling expenses would be arranged and met by His Majesty's government. I was content. I was to live in a lovely spot, only sixty miles from Glasgow and, best of all, the camp was on the shores of a beautiful sea loch.

At the regulating office we were asked why we had been sent there. When the three of us chorused, "To be sail-makers," the officer nearly choked. "I didn't know we needed sail-makers!" he laughed. "There are no sails on any of the boats we use and we're not likely ever to need any." He gave the matter some thought before going off, still chortling, to consult with some unseen person. By the time he came back he had managed to straighten his face into an expression more befitting an officer of the Royal Navy, and told us we were going to be stokers. This seemed to me even more ludicrous than sail-making and we went off to sort out our sleeping quarters wondering what on earth our duties would be.

The Wrens' quarters were a scattered assortment of huts, some of wood resembling outsize garden sheds, some of the tunnel-like variety known as Nissen huts and made from corrugated iron. Ours was a wooden one where I found myself in possession of a top bunk, and half of a small chest of drawers shared with the girl in the bottom bunk. The hut housed twelve girls. In the middle was a small circular stove, the only source of heating, but which proved adequate even in the worst of the winter weather.

The following morning I was initiated into the mysteries of being a stoker. We were shown to the generating station, a square utilitarian building of dirty grey brick, nestling beneath the brow of a little hill near the shore. From the open door issued a familiar sound. I was transported back in time to the Rhinns of Islay for a moment. Sure enough, inside I was confronted by two huge engines like those that worked the old foghorn. One was in action, its flywheel pounding round, the noise so loud we had to shout to be heard. The only difference was the smell. These engines were run on diesel, instead of paraffin.

So started another radical change in my life style. On duty I wore dungarees on top of bell-bottomed trousers while on my head I had to wear an unbecoming blue skip cap with a snood attached as a precaution against catching my hair in the machinery. The duties were not hard to learn, simply oiling specified working parts of the engine regularly and checking the dials on a console, stopping and starting an engine as required. To make things easier there would always be a real stoker on watch with two girls. He must have been disgusted to find himself encumbered with two females whose knowledge of mechanics wouldn't have covered a bus ticket, but he was stuck with us.

H.M.S. Quebec had been established as far back as 1940 as the naval wing of a new force to be known as Combined Operations composed of groups from all three services training together for raids on and the subsequent invasion of enemy occupied territory, from the sea. The army had to be taught sea warfare and who better to do so than the Royal Navy. The new style troops had been named Commandos. Loch Fyne, well off the beaten track, was the ideal place for such training along with several other sites on the west coast of Scotland. I was there some time before I learned something about it, and even then only as much as I needed to know, for the sake of security.

The morning after I arrived I was wakened in the traditional way by a lone bugler playing the appropriate call. I soon adapted to the habit of referring to everyday objects by the right naval term. I lived in a cabin, slept in a bunk, ate in the mess, and washed in the ablutions. In the afternoons, if not on duty, I was free to go ashore; in other words I could go out of the camp. On that first venture ashore several of us caught the "shuttle," a canvas-covered truck that plied back and forth regularly between the camp and Inveraray, a distance of about three miles. As we explored Inveraray, admiring its olde worlde white-washed tenements, we came across a hall bearing the legend "W.V.S. Canteen". We ventured in and found ourselves in a smallish dingy room bursting at the seams with khaki and green-clad men quaffing steaming cups of tea and eating sticky buns. The noise of their chatter stopped abruptly when they became aware of females in their midst. In no time we were surrounded by young men with alien accents, all clamouring for a date. I was in the midst of a division of the American army troops undergoing the Commando training. Lots of our own British troops were around too, but we girls couldn't stop our hearts beating a bit faster. Here was something new and extremely exciting. I was flattered, as I had never before found men attracted to me. I soon discovered it was simply a matter of supply and demand. The female population of Inveraray was vastly outnumbered by these troops, so if I'd been bandy-legged and possessing only one eye, I'd still have found somebody willing to make a date.

I found myself that afternoon going for a walk through the village with a gangling spotty youth who rejoiced in the name of Virgil Doe. We were both ill at ease, but when the time came to part company I realised he was going to kiss me goodbye. I had previously only been kissed perfunctorily by relatives so I waited in vain for bells to ring and stars to appear as his lips met mine. The only thought that went through my mind was, "Is that it, then?" I was not impressed. In fact I was downright disappointed. Poor Virgil! I'm sure he felt the same. I never saw him again.

That evening on the way back to camp in the shuttle with my new found Wren friends, we were treated to some caustic remarks from the sailors sharing the shuttle. They were piqued at having to compete for our attention with the glamorous Americans. One of these lads said to no one in particular, "You want to watch it! These Yanks are full of V.D." In my innocence I asked the inevitable question, "What's V.D.?" Gwen, nearest to me, gave me an almighty nudge and whispered, "Shut up!" In an uncomfortable silence I obeyed, returning to camp squirming with embarrassment without knowing what I had said wrong. That night while on duty, Gwen completed my education. She had attended an enlightened school in England which had taught its pupils the facts of life. I was given a crash course in the most mundane matter of fact way, for which I was forever grateful.

After that first abortive introduction to the world of dating we were inundated with requests from numerous American soldiers who wanted to take us to the pictures or partner us at dances. Watch-keeping allowed us a fair amount of free time, so sometimes we kept a date with two different soldiers in one day, afternoon and evening. We took to jotting the dates down in a wee notebook so as not to get muddled. In fact, I found the G.I.s I went out with were all extremely courteous, calling me "Ma'am" and only wanting to talk about their loved ones back in the States. We liked them, too, because they had access to luxuries hitherto only dreamed of, like wrapped chocolate bars. Ours, when you got it, was unwrapped. I was given a couple of cakes of Lux toilet soap encased in not one but two layers of silky paper. Our soap came stark naked. What a pleasure it was to unwrap each one slowly. I was introduced to the delights of the long sticks of Juicy Fruit chewing gum, which tasted different from our chewing gum, and the final joy was to ride in a real Jeep.

I learned to dance American style to the music of a band composed of ex-members of such famous bands as Tommy Dorsey, Glenn Miller and Harry James. It was a great band and a pleasure to dance to even though it was only in a big hut and everyone was in uniform. It was at one of these dances I met George, a sergeant in the U.S. Engineers. He was a quiet likeable man, a lot older than I was, and who was to be my constant companion for the rest of his time at Inveraray, a matter of two weeks. I think I was a bit in love with him. I cried myself to sleep the night we said goodbye, knowing that in all probability I'd never see him again. He had handed me a letter as we parted, with orders not to open it until he was gone. In it was a lot of good advice and three £1 notes, an advance Christmas present as he'd be far away when Christmas came.

I never heard from him again and never knew if he survived the war. About a year later I heard that when the 1st Division landed at Oran in North Africa, the Engineers were the first to go ashore, where they were wiped out almost to a man. I cried again at the thought of George perhaps lying somewhere in the desert.

Every two or three weeks there was an exodus of troops followed by an influx of new ones to go through the same rigorous training. The immediate environs of Inveraray were cluttered with camps, even in the grounds of Inveraray Castle. It was commonplace to meet tanks rumbling along the main road. They would suddenly turn off the road as if to drive straight into the loch. They were being driven on to the new landing craft whose bow doors opened to admit the tanks. Loch Fyne was dotted with these strange flat-bottomed boats of all sizes bearing letters and numbers like L.C.T. (Landing Craft Tank).

Overlooking the village was Dunniquaich, a high steep hill covered by trees and bushes, on the summit of which stood a stone tower, used in days long ago as a lookout post to warn the castle of imminent danger from enemies. The hill was put to use as a training ground for the infantry. Almost every day hundreds of men clambered up the steep slopes or hurtled downhill through the dense green cover carrying full kit. Although everyone was involved in these activities, few of us knew why it was being done. There were many wild guesses, but those at the top were tight-lipped. Even the postal addresses were anonymous. Mine was simply P.O. Box 2, Inveraray.

At *Quebec* I settled into a routine of watch-keeping. After an initial period of sticking strictly to the rules, I joined my fellow watch-keepers in what was not exactly the correct way of doing things at work. During the night watches, after the duty officer had done his rounds, we took it in turns to have a snooze in a cosy nest made from the heap of cotton waste in one corner, lulled to sleep by the rhythmic hum of the engines. I have been known to curl up on the wooden workbench, curled round to avoid the big vice in the middle, with my head on a folded coat for a pillow. I have always been able to sleep anywhere at any time since then.

We always brewed up on these long night watches. They were only four hours duration, but in the quiet when everyone else was asleep they seemed much longer. There was a particular knack in making tea in a tall enamel jug on a small electric ring. First the water was brought to the boil in the jug, then a handful of tea thrown in. After a minute or two the tea leaves which had been floating on top of the water, suddenly sank to the bottom. Sometimes we had a feast of fried egg with a tin of beans, made into sandwiches and washed down with tea. One day I took some left-over bread back to the cabin and toasted it later in the day. Yeough! It was uneatable, saturated with the diesel fumes from the "gen". We hadn't noticed it before, being a bit saturated ourselves. It's a miracle we didn't develop stomach ulcers or worse. We generator watchkeepers were apparently supposed to be issued with an extra pint of milk daily to counteract the effect of the fumes, but the milk never materialised in the three years I was there. None of us were any the worse for the deprivation.

I enjoyed being part of the services. Most of the people I worked with were congenial, but there was now and again some discord ... like the time when one girl who was less than fussy about her personal hygiene was reported to a higher authority by person or persons unknown, with the result that she was "sentenced" to report to the sick bay every day for a week to take a Dettol bath. It cured her and nothing more was said on the subject.

The one thing I disliked was squad drill. Not that it was difficult, merely marching and wheeling and practising all the well-known military exercises. What bothered me was the tormenting we were subjected to by any ratings who happened to see us performing. They did their best to distract our attention, all done behind the back of the Wren P.O. who was drilling us. It was extremely off-putting, especially as their mimicry of the P.O. nearly had us falling about in fits of the giggles at times.

Every second Thursday was payday. We stood to attention in alphabetical order, stepping forward in turn to salute and hold out an open pay-book, on which the paymaster placed, in my case anyway, the vast sum of 26/- (£1.30), my two weeks pay. At the same time we were issued with vouchers entitling us to buy duty-free cigarettes at the Naafi canteen. I didn't smoke, but most of my cabin mates did, so were delighted to make use of mine. Twenty Senior Service cost 1/6d (7½p).

My twenty-six shillings had to stretch a long way. Not only had I to buy odds and ends like shoe polish and toothpaste, but after the initial issue of uniform, I had to buy replacements at the Slops. The clothes were of very good quality, if unglamorous. Entertainment was also inexpensive. The Naafi in the village ran a cinema, which cost us only 3d a time, while a small cinema in camp was free. Both these places showed the latest films, but there was one snag. In the small hut in camp we only had a single projector so at the end of each reel there was a boring wait until the operator changed to the next reel. My money usually spun out to last the two weeks with even enough to allow me a cup of tea in the Temperance Hotel as a special treat. That wee hotel was extremely popular with the service men and women.

My first leave was at Christmas. I felt excited about that as my mother was coming through to Glasgow. Like the rest of the family she hadn't yet seen me in uniform. She had come off Barrahead with the fortnightly relief boat, leaving my father to his own resources. She was desperate to find out how her daughter was coping although when I arrived at Ten-nine-eight she, as usual, showed little of her feelings. I spent that leave visiting all the relations to show off my

In the Wrens, 1943

uniform, and going into town to have my photograph taken to preserve that uniform for posterity. The resulting photograph was somewhat marred by the fact that I wouldn't or couldn't smile properly, owing to the fact that one of my front teeth was missing. Not long afterwards the R.N. provided me with a neat wee dental plate which restored my nice smile. I was glad to be able to prove to my mother and Wee Granny that I was thriving in the Wrens and was, as my mother would have put it "behaving myself."

And so my leave whizzed by. Soon it was time to say goodbye yet again to my mother and go back to that strange mixture of a great social life and rigid discipline that was *H.M.S. Quebec.* Life was a mad whirl of dances, Ensa concerts and cinema shows. There was some kind of entertainment on every evening and I seldom went out twice with one man, owing to the constant turnover of troops. In spite of it all though, I still hankered after George.

The end of January brought a very important milestone in my life, my twenty-first birthday. Like most people I had often wondered what it would be like to get the key of the door. Never in my wildest imaginings would I have guessed the reality. The mail brought several cards and a Postal Order for 4/- from my grandfather, and presents from the family of someone called Harold. I've no memory of him. I celebrated my birthday by going to bed as soon as I came off duty, nursing an extremely painful and swollen left arm, the result of having been given an inoculation that morning against some obscure disease. There was no present from my own family. They had decided to club together to give me something I had always wanted, a Swan fountain pen. An order had been placed with a shop months before. Such were the vagaries of war it arrived eight months later.

In that first year at Inveraray, I met literally hundreds of ordinary young men who had been taken from their peaceful ordinary lives to serve their country. Inveraray rang to the accents not only of the Americans, but in their turn Canadians, Norwegians and numerous English, Irish, Welsh and Scottish regiments; not to mention, though in smaller numbers, Frenchmen and Poles. One evening at a dance I even encountered some husky Russian sailors whose ship was anchored temporarily in the loch. They caused a sensation when they appeared at the dance. I was with an English lad that night, who at the end of the dance escorted me back to the pier where the shuttle waited to transport us with other homeward bound dancers back to camp. As we sat waiting patiently for the driver, one of these Russians walking by shone a torch round the inside of the shuttle, making everyone blink in the bright light. It shone on me, wavered towards my escort, and then a deep foreign voice said simply, "Nice girl. You sleep?" Then there was the sound of several deep chortles and the torch and its owner were gone, leaving me mortally embarrassed and everyone else highly amused.

We found the Norwegians interesting not only because of their blond good looks, but because we could communicate quite well. There was a similarity in

My mother and Jean with the Wren, taken at Barrahead when I was on leave.

our languages. We learned quite a number of Norwegian words and taught them some English phrases. We kidded them on a bit, though, when they asked us to teach them a British song. One of my more exuberant friends decided we'd teach these unwitting souls one of the popular tunes of the time. It went thus: "Mairsy doats and dozy doats and little lamsitivy; a kiddlytivy, too, wouldn't you?" It gave us a lot of fun as these soldiers went off happily singing it at the top of their voices. Translated it goes, "Mares eat oats and does eat oats and little lambs eat ivy. A kid'll eat ivy, too, wouldn't you?"

The Canadians were my favourite people. I grew very fond of one of the handsome soldiers. He was tall, blond and had the deepest blue eyes. We went out together at every opportunity while we could and afterwards kept up a regular correspondence. I was never sure where his letters came from as they were postmarked only with a Field P.O. number, which could have been anywhere in the world. Time passed and no more letters came so I concluded that either he had grown tired of writing having found another girl or, horrible thought, he had been killed in action. Ages after I had given up all thoughts of hearing from him again, an air letter arrived in the familiar handwriting. It had been written from a field hospital somewhere in Italy. He had been badly wounded, he wrote, and was still having trouble with his left arm. He was being transferred back to England for operations and would write again as soon as he could. I was overjoyed and watched the mail every day, but it was several weeks before I got another letter, this time from a hospital in Colchester. He was doing well and waiting for a final operation, he said, and as soon as he was fit he was going to apply for leave and come posthaste to Inveraray. I never heard from him again. To this day I have no idea what went wrong.

I wasn't the only one to spend time yearning for a likeable young man who was never to be heard of again. Many must have wondered like me, perhaps for years, whether or not it was wise to get fond of someone whose future was so full of question marks. That was the way of wartime friendships and romances.

Barrahead

*I*t was summer 1943 before I was able to go home to Barrahead. I was keen to see it myself. A request for extra travelling time was submitted because the visit couldn't be undertaken in less than eighteen days, as the relief boat only went to the island once in fourteen days. My request granted, I set out, spending a night at Wee Granny's, before leaving with Jean on the old familiar route by train to Oban. The steamer for the Western Isles left from there, passing Lismore lighthouse on the way. Beyond Tobermory the scenery was unfamiliar. The steamer called at various small islands meeting small boats to exchange passengers, merchandise and wee animals tied up in sacks. In the islands time is unimportant. All told it was about ten hours before, having crossed the Minch, we swung round into Castlebay, passing Kisimul's Castle from which the busy "capital" of Barra takes its name. Two strangers, Mr. and Mrs. McNeil greeted us when we disembarked. Most of the inhabitants were called McNeil. We were given a meal and a bed for the night before setting out on the relief boat, a small fishing boat. We had fourteen miles to go, due south, passing Vatersay, the only other inhabited island south of Barra; then numerous large deserted islands, the final one being Mingulay, famed in song.

Beyond Mingulay was our destination, Berneray, which translated from the Norse means Bjorn's Isle. It was a monstrous lump, on top of which was perched the lighthouse station; the tower, from where we were approaching the pier, appeared like a tiny white pencil. As we came nearer, the island seemed to grow bigger and the tower smaller. I could see a narrow ribbon-like road threading

Barrahead lighthouse.

its way from the station down to the pier, at which waited the entire population: three keepers, their wives and surprisingly, two small children.

I knew then that Cape Wrath was not the last place on earth. Barrahead held that dubious honour. I have never seen such a desolate uninviting island as the one I landed on, that lovely calm summer day. We were greeted with more than the usual enthusiasm by my mother, and my father had tears in his eyes as he saw me for the first time in uniform. His wee girl had grown up. Introductions and greetings over, the men turned their attention to unloading the various boxes and packages and the mail bag, which bulged with a fortnight's accumulation of letters and parcels. Jean and I had time to look about. Close to the pier was the remains of a small hamlet which had been sensibly abandoned at the turn of the last century. The roofless houses were still standing but overgrown by grass. All but one were of the typical low style of the islands. The odd one which had retained its roof was a peculiar shape, the roof low at the front and higher towards the back. Later, when I asked about this phenomenon, my father told me it had been the home of a man of more than normal stature, the roof being adjusted to allow him at least part of the house in which he could stand upright, the remainder left the customary height for the rest of the family. It was now used as a store for equipment needed at the pier.

Waiting behind that house, I was pleased and relieved to see a lorry. The island seemed to tower thousands of feet above us. In fact it was only a matter of 650 feet. In distance we had to cover a mile and a quarter. The back of the lorry was fitted with bench seats. I sat petrified at an angle of nearly forty-five degrees, my heart in my mouth as I looked at the steep drop towards the sea. There was nothing to break the fall if the lorry went off the road. If we didn't break our necks, I thought, we would either be killed by the final drop into the sea or drowned. The higher we climbed, the engine protesting all the time, the more dangerous it appeared. After an eternity of anxiety, we reached level ground, to my great relief.

The house was identical to the others at previous stations and it was heart-warming to see all the old familiar furniture and ornaments, the brass tea caddy on the mantelpiece, cheek by jowl with the two brass shells my mother had made while on munitions during the Great War. The war seemed far away and I felt secure. My mother bustled about making one of her tasty meals, obviously delighted we were home. My father's tongue never halted as he plied us with questions and gave us all his news. I hadn't seen him for ages.

It was only after we had been there a few days that I realised what a hard life my mother was leading. She was secure from the rigours of war, but this was no place for a woman, far less one in her middle years. In one of her letters to me she had said, "This is a God-forsaken place. It's only fit for Hitler and Co." I now knew what she meant. The view from her windows might have been thought by some to be breathtaking. Far to the east on a good day could be seen the mountains of Skye. To the south and west there was nothing but the wide expanse of the Atlantic, while to the north was the straight row of uninhabited islands leading to Barra. It gave me an odd sense of unreality.

My mother's days were spent in cooking and cleaning. She knitted and sewed and baked and washed and ironed, day after day, the monotony only broken on "relief" days. She couldn't even forget her isolation by listening to the wireless. Barrahead was a fog station, not the traditional kind with the big moaning horn, but instead there was a radio signal in Morse code. It tapped out "--. --. ...." (D.D.H.). These dots and dashes came over loud and clear through every wireless programme, enough to drive you crazy.

In one of her more expansive moods my mother told us she sometimes changed the whole house around, making a bedroom into the parlour and vice versa, just to see something different. Never once did she think of complaining or giving up and going to the mainland. It was her job to stay and look after her husband through thick and thin. My father, knowing the strain she was under, made sure she left the island as often as possible, sending her to Glasgow for a spell and if that wasn't convenient she'd go to Castlebay if she could scrounge a lift from a passing fishing boat.

The island was magnificent. It was so exposed to the wild Atlantic weather it couldn't support trees, but it had a surprising variety of flowers and wildlife. Jean and I spent a lot of time sitting on the edge of the cliffs, which dropped almost sheer to the restless sea far below, and which was home to countless numbers of sea birds, mainly gulls, guillemots, razorbills and puffins. We loved the puffins. These sea parrots looked comical with their feathered morning suits and colourful parrot-like beaks. They were completely unafraid of us. While we sat on the grass at the top of the cliffs they wheeled about to within a couple of feet of us as if to satisfy their curiosity. I'd settle my eyes on one particular bird to follow its movements. It would wheel out to sea in a great circle, flying back to stare at me with its bright beady eyes, then repeat the whole performance time after time until it tired of the game.

When I worked in Smith's, the manageress of the shop had once, during fire-watching, spoken of the difficulty of keeping up a supply of home-made cakes for the tables because of a shortage of eggs. I mentioned this in a letter home, as a result of which my father supplied the shop with large numbers of wild birds' eggs as long as the nesting season lasted. The shop was delighted; none of the customers knew the difference and the keepers had a little extra in their pockets. I hadn't thought much about it at the time. It was only when I saw the cliffs the men had to climb down, protected only by a stout rope round the waist and held by the man at the top, that I realised just what a dangerous ploy it was. I shuddered at the thought. Fortunately no-one was hurt and the next year the shop didn't ask for any eggs.

Jean and I walked all over the island during the warm summer days, though there wasn't an awful lot to see except water. The vegetation was mainly coarse hardy grass, all that could withstand the onslaught of the Atlantic gales laden with salty spray. The cliff tops were covered with cushions of sea-pinks and clumps of sea campion, while the expanse of grass was dotted with splashes of colour from wild orchids, ragged robin and buttercups. It was hard to believe that in winter the full brunt of the wind hit the cliffs with such force that on occasion small, very dead fish had been found on the cliff top. They had been thrown up 600 feet.

During one of our walks in the deserted landscape, Jean and I stopped in our tracks when we heard a sound that raised the hair on the back of my neck. It was the cry of a baby. Knowing there was no such thing on the island we instinctively looked in the direction of the cry. It was a distinct ghostly sound made more so by the fact that nearby was a high circular wall surrounding a small graveyard in which were buried, among others, several small children who had died in years gone by of croup or other childhood illnesses, because there had been no medical help available. Jean and I were about to make a run for the safety of the lighthouse when, much to our relief, the mystery solved

A wider view of Barrahead lighthouse. If you look carefully you will see a man at the top of the radio mast!

itself. There on the rocks below we saw a movement. A number of seals were basking in the sun, their young crying out for food in much the same way as a human baby.

One small gate in the protective wall surrounding the station led to a spot on the cliff top where the rubbish was tipped into the sea. It was advisable not to rush headlong through that gate, the gate and the abyss being separated only by a few yards. There was, however, an intriguing old ruin out there which we cautiously investigated. We had no idea of its origin nor how it came to be built in such a precarious position. It was obviously very ancient. Only recently I read that when the Vikings were raiding and conquering the Western Isles, this could have been a lookout, perhaps housing a bonfire to be lit as a warning against the approaching long ships. On the other hand it could have been a beacon placed there by the Vikings to show the safe seaway for their own ships. At any rate it was a peculiarly fascinating structure, which we pondered during our visits home.

We made an expedition to another ancient and fascinating place on that holiday. The keepers had a small rowing boat. We did a bit of fishing to supplement the larder, but on a calm settled day we rowed over to the neighbouring island, Mingulay. My mother came, too, and brought one of her picnic feasts like the ones we used to have at Earraid. The sea was flat as a millpond as we rowed across the wide sound that separated the islands. There we landed, like castaways, on a deserted sandy beach in a sheltered bay, something which Barrahead couldn't boast of. Just beyond the beach lay the barely recognisable remains of the abandoned village that had once housed a thriving community. All that remained were the broken walls and scattered stones of a row of houses, almost buried under the encroaching sand and spiky grass. Only faint traces of a street were visible. We didn't linger too long. A fair distance up the hill stood the only substantial building on the island, a two storey house of much bigger proportions than the others. This had been the chapel and the priest's house. The door wasn't locked. What reason could there be for locking it? We went in to explore and found traces of recent habitation. It was apparently used as a bothy by visiting shepherds. We climbed the stairs to the upper floor. The doors were all of beautifully carved solid wood, the kind you would expect to find in some great house. My father said he'd heard they were originally ship's doors. They looked to me like the spoils of some old-time wreckers. The whole expanse of the upper floor was equally lovely. The floor of the single big room which had been the place of worship, was of parquet and in good condition. My own sacrilegious thought was that it would have made a perfect dance floor. The whole thing seemed out of place in such a setting, and we stayed to admire it for some time before reluctantly leaving it for the wild outdoors.

We didn't climb to the top of the island. When you live on the top of a mountain you have little desire to climb its neighbour just to see the same view of never-ending ocean. Instead, we had a long leisurely picnic on the beach and paddled awhile before rowing back home. It was a fine day out, the memory of which I recall every time I hear the "Mingulay Boat Song."

My leave over, I was reluctant to say good-bye to my parents. I felt bad about leaving my mother to resume her lonely existence, akin to imprisonment. The only company she had from one relief day to the next was the wives of the other two keepers. Both were friendly young women, each with one child under school age. The wee ones gave my mother great pleasure as she was like a granny to them, giving them sweeties when they came wandering into her house and telling them stories when they couldn't get out to play in bad weather. As I watched these two at play in the courtyard I was reminded of my own childhood days at Inchkeith. These two were lucky. They had each other for companionship. I felt it was a shame they should be isolated at the top of a potentially dangerous cliff, but soon they would leave to go to a school station in a more congenial spot. Meantime they were blissfully unaware, as I had been, that their life was anything out of the ordinary.

I spent only two more leaves at Barrahead, both in the summer when the weather was more likely to be calm. When Jean and I arrived the second year, my father was full of tales of events he hadn't wanted to write about. Even there they were conscious of the wartime cautionary slogan "Careless talk costs lives."

Life wasn't always dull it seemed. One happening was both sad and unpleasant. The two men who had gone down to the well by the pier for the day's supply of drinking water, had noticed two oddly-shaped objects undulating gently on the waves close to the pier. They launched the rowing boat and approached the objects with caution. It was unwise in wartime to go too close to anything floating in the sea in case it blew up. When they got to within a few yards they realised to their horror that the bundles were the bodies of two men. Carefully they lifted them on board and took them to the pier. The uniforms were those of our own air force. It looked as though they had bailed out, though with little chance of survival in the Atlantic.

The only way in which my father could report the grim find was to wait until the next appointed time for contact with Earraid by radio. Earraid then notified the proper authority on the mainland, who in turn arranged for a boat to be dispatched from Barra to pick up the remains. My father was relieved when it was all sorted out and the sense of responsibility was lifted, but it was a long time before the wee community could erase the sight of those pathetic bundles from their minds.

Not long afterwards the men again noticed several rigid box-like objects floating by. The sealed zinc containers about the size of a small chest, proved to be surprisingly light and easily lifted into the boat. The men returned triumphant with their spoils. My mother wanted to know what my father was so excited about as the boxes appeared to be empty, and in any case they were going to be difficult to open. No-one could figure out their original purpose, but my father reckoned they'd make good containers for hens' food or even blankets. How he opened them I don't know. It was a good job he tackled it outside in the courtyard at my mother's insistence, because as soon as the "lid" came off, out sprang an enormous amount of kapok, which expanded as it was released from confinement. What a job it was to get the volatile stuff under control in the windy courtyard. My mother raged about people interfering in things they knew nothing about and what were they going to do with it in the long run? Eventually it was gathered up and stuffed into sacks, appearing to take up about six times as much space as before. The birds had a field day collecting all the wee bits that still blew around the courtyard like snow. There must have been some very luxurious nests that year.

It was left to my mother and the other ladies to come up with a good use for the stuff. Jean and I found ourselves roped in. We were going to make soft comfy mattresses to put on top of the hard horsehair ones supplied by the N.L.B. Dressed in old clothes and with a silk scarf enveloping my head I joined the others, all looking like weird spacemen, in a shed where, with great difficulty, we filled two mattress covers with the wretched stuff. The kapok flew in wisps into every corner of that shed and stuck to our clothes, and we found it hard to breathe through the scarves. We also made pillows and cushions galore and still had some of the kapok left over. My father made wooden lids for the zinc boxes, which for the rest of his time in the service did duty as storage for the bran and corn given to the hens. I even had one years later for my children's toys. My father learned later the boxes were simply buoyancy floats for emergency rafts.

At the end of that leave Jean and I shared one of my mother's unusual modes of transport. A day or two before our holiday ended we were given the chance of a lift to Castlebay in a passing lobster boat. This would give my mother a couple of days in civilisation before coming back on the relief boat. During a seemingly endless trip we sat, our feet encased in Wellington boots, only inches from the snapping pincers of dozens of the blue crustaceans, all angry at being removed from their natural habitat. While we travelled, the fishermen waded casually among them tying their claws together, untill the clashing sound was reduced to a mere rustle.

My final visit to Barrahead passed uneventfully. There was only one tale for my father to tell that time. One day, one of the goats hadn't come home with the others at milking time. When he and my mother went in search of her, calling her name as they ranged along the top of the cliffs they heard a faint bleating. Peering over the edge they saw the animal, trapped on a narrow ledge. She was lying with one leg in an unnatural position, obviously broken, looking up at them and bleating pathetically. There was nothing they could do to rescue her without endangering their own lives. Only a goat could have got down there. Reluctantly they went home, my father wishing he had a gun so that he could put the poor beast out of its misery.

Every day my father went to look at her expecting to find her dead or the ledge empty. She was still alive for nearly a week, but one day the ledge was bare. A few days later, my father at milking time was met not by two, but three, goats. As though nothing was amiss, Patchy was blissfully and greedily eating grass as though trying to make up for lost time. She was minus one leg, but otherwise seemed fit. It proved that goats deserve their reputation for sure-footedness even on three legs. She lived a long and happy life after her narrow escape.

On the last day of that leave, as we set off down to the pier in the lorry, my father predicted a change in what had until then been glorious quiet weather. "The glass is falling," he said, shaking his head. "It's a good job you're getting away today." He was right. I wasn't long in Castlebay when the wind rose and rapidly developed into a full-scale gale. I began to feel apprehensive about crossing the Minch in such conditions. That strip of water between the Outer Isles and the mainland had a bad reputation.

The steamer normally called at Castlebay in the evening to deposit passengers, before going on north to her final port of call, Lochboisdale. Then it would return to Barra, picking up passengers there at one in the morning. On this occasion because of the deteriorating weather, I and the other luckless passengers for Oban got a sudden call to join the ship as soon as it reached Barra the first time, as it was going to cut the journey short by going straight from Lochboisdale to Oban.

Short was not the appropriate word. The whole trip which should have lasted less than ten hours, took more than eighteen. Going to Lochboisdale wasn't too bad as there was a following wind, though the ship rolled a lot in the heavy swell. Lochboisdale itself was calm, but once out of the shelter of the land the full force of the gale struck the ship broadside. It rolled and tossed, rising and falling sickeningly. In the saloon I was talking to some airmen who were going on leave from the local aerodrome. I didn't feel too good, a feeling that wasn't helped by the airmen teasing me, telling me I was going green around the gills and so on. However, one by one they paled and left, disappearing into the bowels of the ship. I began to long to lie down so I retired to the cabin I had booked, bumping off the walls of the passageway as I went. Thank goodness I had the two-berth cabin to myself. I climbed into the lower bunk still wearing most of my clothes. If I was going to be shipwrecked I wasn't going to be left shivering in a nightie. I swallowed two aspirins, my mother's cure-all, read *The People's Friend* from cover to cover, to the accompaniment of creaks, lurches and groans from the protesting ship, then fell asleep, having prayed I'd wake up still safely in my cosy bunk.

Around six next morning there was a tap on the cabin door. I called out, "Come in," noting at the same time the motion of the ship had steadied. The door opened, admitting the white face of a steward, who asked if I was all right. When I said I was fine and had slept well, his jaw fell. "Have you not been sick, then?" he enquired. When I said, "No", he told me I was the only one. Even some of the crew, the steward included, had succumbed. "You'll not be wanting any breakfast, though" he stated. "Well, no. But I could do with some tea and toast?" I answered to his astonishment. When I emerged on deck later, I found the sea had calmed down and we were steaming in the relative shelter of the Sound of Mull. All the same I wasn't sorry when the ship tied up at Oban and I could set foot on terra firma once more. As for my friends, the young airmen, they were still looking a bit sorry for themselves as they went down the gangway, while I at least still had some colour in my cheeks. I was glad I hadn't let the Royal Navy down by being seasick in front of a rival branch of the services.

Inveraray

At the end of that first leave at Barrahead I returned to Inveraray to resume my busy, full life in the bosom of the Royal Navy. Not long after that I and my oppos were moved en masse from the wooden hut to new quarters in one of the bigger Nissen huts. The cabin was much more roomy and airy, though the curve of the walls took a bit of getting used to, and presented difficulty in displaying the photographs of our families and boyfriends, which we liked to see on waking in the morning.

One advantage of the new hut was that we no longer had to go out in all weathers to reach the ablutions. A corridor led to the ablution area, a bare utilitarian place containing several toilets, a dozen or so washbasins and three bathrooms, shared by several other groups in other huts. One phenomenon I never fully understood was the mystery of the disappearing bath plugs. At first all the baths and washbasins had been fitted with plugs secured by the usual chains, but so many disappeared in a short space of time that those in charge gave up replacing them. The chains hung limp and useless, causing enormous frustration when someone wanted a bath in a hurry before a date. The local ironmonger, John Clerk, did a roaring trade as each Wren bought her own set of plugs. If someone was careless enough to leave one in the ablutions even for a minute or two, it vanished. I never found the solution to the mystery.

We were well fed and could supplement our diet for a few pence at the Naafi canteens, but we were always delighted when someone received a parcel of goodies from home. These were often sent at great sacrifice on the part of the

In the Wrens about 1944.
That's me on the left.

giver, who had to use up precious rations to bake a favourite cake. The spoils were always shared out among the cabin mates. I remember once eating a slice of cake which had a pleasant but unfamiliar flavour. We ate it like official tasters at a garden fete, with each bite we tried to guess the flavour. Someone eventually was inspired to say, "I know. It's banana." It was so long since any of us had tasted that common taken-for-granted fruit we had forgotten it. Although that cake had only been baked with banana essence, every morsel was savoured

There was no sign of a letup in the fighting. Troops came and went, giving us a lot of fun and teaching me a lot about life and people. Every minute was filled with either work, sleep or a variety of entertainment. Everybody had a goal to aim for, namely to get the war over and return to a peaceful existence.

I continued to make friends from all corners of the globe. Every time I said good-bye to anyone, promises were made to "keep in touch," very few of which were ever kept. Some of my Wren friends went off to pastures new, some got married and left the service to start a family. New ones arrived to replace them. There was a constant turnover. It wasn't easy for newlyweds to make a life together there. There was no such thing as married quarters and it wasn't easy to find accommodation outside the camp. Young couples were looked on with suspicion if they tried to find a room somewhere in the village. No-one would accept them unless they produced a marriage certificate. Those who married usually had to go back to their home town or stay separately in camp, as though still single.

I had no plans for marriage. I was content to stay where I was. I didn't have any ambition for promotion either. I simply carried on with my job as a stoker, or more properly speaking, a Generator Watchkeeper, trying to stick to the rules and keep out of trouble. Once I smuggled out a bag of sugar and some tea to give to Wee Granny to make life a bit easier for her. It wasn't a terrible crime, but how my conscience tormented me.

One commodity that was scarce was eggs. My father sent me regular supplies, a dozen eggs at a time, in specially made boxes. I had to return the empty boxes to be refilled. It was one of these that got me into trouble. *H.M.S. Quebec*, surrounded by barbed wire, was classed as a ship and as such had a form of customs to prevent contraband, like cigarettes and rum, being smuggled out. Every parcel that left the camp had to be taken first to the regulating office to have the contents examined before being wrapped up. Once passed and wrapped it was stamped with the official oval red imprint which carried the name of the ship and the date, without which nothing could get past the eagle eye of the duty officer at the gate.

One day as I was preparing to send back one of the empty egg boxes to Barrahead, I noticed that the wrapping paper, another scarce commodity, had been used several times, and therefore was emblazoned with the red oval stamp, albeit with an old date on it. I was in a hurry so I took a chance on not bothering to go to the regulating office. After all, it was just an empty box. I wrapped it carefully, making sure the red oval was prominently displayed. At the gate I flashed the parcel at the officer on duty and kept on walking. I had only taken a few steps when a voice commanded me to come back. "Let's see that again," he said in a voice that brooked no denial. My heart sank to my boots. "That stamp is six weeks out of date," he announced in front of an interested audience of people waiting for the shuttle. "What's the big idea?" I tried to explain, telling him I was posting an empty box. Needless to say, he looked at me askance. "Get that down to the regulating office," he ordered. I had perforce to trail back and open the parcel to prove to another sceptical officer that I was telling the truth. He also thought I was nuts. I missed the shuttle and just gave myself an awful lot of unnecessary bother. I never tried to avoid the dreaded stamp again. I was lucky not to be put on a charge and lose a day's pay.

Most of my leave was spent in Glasgow where some things had changed. Mae was married and the proud mother of a baby boy, and was expecting her second baby. She lived in a "room-and-kitchen" in Linthouse, not an ideal home, but she was lucky to have a home at all. Houses were scarce. There was little movement in rented houses during the war except in the case of those unfortunates who had been bombed out. Before the war there was a constant shifting and shuffling as the mood took people. It was never the same again.

Jean was old enough to be directed into war work. She was sent to a factory making small components of some sort. She never knew what she was helping to make. Jean didn't like the monotonous work, she missed the pleasant atmosphere of the shop. During the winter months she only saw daylight at the weekends and it began to affect her health though she was determined to stick it out. When I heard of Jean's problems I realised how lucky I was to be able to live and work in a healthy environment like Inveraray.

Wee Granny was always pleased to see me. She liked the extra company to break up the monotony of wartime Glasgow and she liked the extra food. I was allowed seaman's rations which was a lot more than the civilian population was allowed. I took with me an emergency ration card, issued to anyone when on holiday or at any other temporary address. My rations, if they didn't exactly fill Granny's cupboard, at least made it look not quite so bare.

Suddenly in the late spring of 1944 the atmosphere at Inveraray subtly changed. There was an air of tension. Equally suddenly the main body of troops vanished overnight and our hitherto large community shrank noticeably. The loch was no longer so busy with the now familiar flat-bottomed boats and the army camps took on a bleak deserted look. All leave was stopped. For several weeks we were not allowed to go beyond the village, and letters home were censored. All kinds of rumours flew about. It wasn't until June I learned the truth, when our forces invaded Europe on what was to become known as D-Day, June 6th. For some time everything hung in the balance as the Allied armies fought to get a firm hold on French soil and we all prayed or kept our fingers crossed according to individual beliefs. I wondered how many of the men I had met were involved in the landings which had cost so many lives.

At *Quebec* we were at last released from the stoppage of leave and began to get back to a more normal way of life. The atmosphere had changed permanently though. The army camps were no longer packed with troops. Training still went on, but not with the same intensity as before. There was more room at the camp cinema and shorter queues at the Naafi. My work at the "gen" was unchanged. Whereas before D-Day I had assumed that this was the normal way of life in future, I now began to hope the war would soon end.

On one leave in Glasgow I made the acquaintance of Bill Brown, an Ordinary Seaman in the R.N. He was a distant relation. I was flattered by the attention Bill paid me until the day I called at his house to find him so engrossed in the daily paper that he simply looked up, said "Hello" and carried on reading. His mother, annoyed, asked him if he was going to take me out or not. He sighed and did so, but from then I wasn't so enamoured of his company. We continued to write to each other. Maybe we were both doing it out of consideration for the two mothers.

In January 1945 I returned from leave during a blizzard, having just departed from Bill once more. At Arrochar I learned that our transport over the Rest and be Thankful had been prevented from crossing the high pass by the heavy snowfall. We paced up and down in the freezing waiting room until someone announced that we were to return to Glasgow until the next day. There were cheers all round. Ten minutes before the train was due, the now unwanted truck arrived and we had no option but to climb in and embark on what seemed to me a crazy attempt to cross the pass. We sat huddled together for warmth as the truck climbed up the mountainside. Apart from the cold and a few sickening skids we made it back to camp stiff but all in one piece.

That evening, Carol, one of my friends, suggested we go to a dance in the village Naafi to cheer ourselves up. She had recently married one of our Chief Petty Officers, but he was on duty and she needed company. We were standing on the fringe of the dance floor when a young C.P.O. asked Carol to dance. He still wore his hat, perched on the back of his head, round his neck was draped a blue and white spotted scarf which was definitely not uniform, and he looked tired and drawn. Carol refused his request as she was sure he was drunk, but nothing daunted he turned to me, bowed deeply and asked me to dance instead. I wasn't too pleased at being second choice, but my feet were tapping to the music so I agreed. With another gentlemanly bow he handed his hat and scarf to Carol to hold for him and we swept on to the floor.

For the rest of the evening we danced together as our steps seemed to fit well, and afterwards he escorted us to the shuttle. He told me that he had been at Quebec only a week, having been sent there to recuperate from a leg wound that had kept him in hospital for eighteen months. He danced so well I thought he was having me on. It was only as we walked to the pierhead that I realised he was limping a bit. Sorry for my scepticism I tried to make up for it by asking where he came from. "Arbroath," he said simply. I couldn't believe that either as his accent was very English. "My father was born in Arbroath," was all I could think of to say, and suddenly felt an affinity for this thin, slightly squiffy young man. He had been drinking a little, he informed me, to take his mind off the pain in his leg.

Before we parted he asked me out, but I refused as I had only left Bill that day and felt disloyal to him, although there was no definite "understanding" between us. One at a time was enough for me to cope with. Robby, as the thin young man told me he was called, had different ideas, though, from then on pestering me at every opportunity. It was easy for him to do so as he worked in the office in charge of the generating station. I was equally determined not to give in. Three weeks passed pleasantly in this way, while I enjoyed the feeling of being sought after. Then came the night of the St. Valentine's Dance. I went with a crowd of friends. At the door we were each given a pink cardboard heart with instructions printed on it, like "Juliet find Romeo." Of all people, I was Lady Macbeth, nothing as romantic as Juliet for me. The men had been issued with similar instructions on a blue heart. It was fun hunting for the right partner for the first dance. Suddenly I saw Robby advancing purposefully towards me. Sure enough, he was Macbeth.

We dutifully danced the first dance together, during which Robby, with his persuasive tongue, convinced me that fate had thrown us together in this way. I was romantic enough to believe him and eventually I agreed to go out with him. Years later, long after we were married, he confessed to having cheated. He had found out what name was on my card, then hunted for the real Macbeth, and persuaded him to swop cards. He was a very determined suitor.

From then on we went everywhere together. We were thrown together at work as in a way he was my boss. An engine room artificer, he was temporarily on light duties, doing office work while recovering from his injuries, received when his ship was blown up by a mine in the Mediterranean. Two-timer that I was, I still wrote to Bill and still saw him when on leave. I was too much of a coward to tell him about Robby, as I knew his feelings would be hurt. Oddly enough, I told Robby about Bill.

One of our favourite outings was to walk to the wee village of Furnace, a distance of about five miles in the opposite direction to Inveraray. In a wee cottage, elderly Mrs. Campbell made a living by selling teas in her front room. For a mere shilling or two you could have bacon and eggs followed by home-made scones and pancakes spread with home-made jam. I wondered where she got the sugar to make the jam, but I found out from my mother that in small places people who didn't use much sugar or other rationed food would pass it on to others. As far as eggs were concerned, in Argyll they were never collected for distribution because the county was so sparsely populated and scattered.

We went to the pictures often. Not long after my arrival at *Quebec* a big cinema-cum-dance hall-cum church was erected in the camp. We could also go to the one in the village Naafi. There was a class difference rather than a price difference in the seating. The front seats consisted of a motley collection of old armchairs reserved for officers and their guests. Behind those were similar chairs for non-commissioned officers, and behind those an assortment of hard kitchen-type chairs for the other ranks.

We danced a lot, too, and as winter gave way to spring we went for long walks over the hills or through the lovely woods. Occasionally we fell out when Robby would turn up late for a date. He had a habit of getting ready too early, knowing my dislike of unpunctuality then, having consumed his daily tot of rum, he'd lie down on his bunk and promptly fall asleep. I paced up and down for an hour one day, frustrated as I could see his hut from where I stood fuming. It was only a few hundred feet away, but out of bounds to Wrens. When he did arrive we had a right royal row. Eventually I capitulated and went on seeing him.

Our little private war was insignificant compared to the real one, but in that conflict we were beginning to see the light at the end of the tunnel as the Allied forces pushed their way nearer and nearer to Berlin. Finally, on Tuesday, 8th May, the glad tidings came through that the war in Europe was over. Hitler was dead by his own hand, and we could all sleep peacefully as there would be no more air raids. It was a wonderful day. There was talk of nothing else and everybody went around laughing out of sheer relief and happiness.

That night we at *Quebec* celebrated with a firework display. We wanted to light up the world after six years of darkness and hooded torches. Robby and I sat on the little wooded hill above the generating station, watching the fireworks in silence. Somehow words seemed out of place. I don't know how long we went on sitting there holding hands long after the fireworks had died down, looking out across the peaceful loch to where the Cowal hills were darkly outlined against the sky. Lights twinkled in every window on the opposite side of the loch, reminding us that the news wasn't just a dream. The war was really over. That night the curtains in the cabin were left open and I fell asleep looking at the stars for the first time in years.

Our joy in victory wasn't entirely complete as fighting was still going on in the Far East against the Japanese, but it is not in the young to worry overmuch about distant happenings. That summer was happy. The officers must have wondered how to keep us busy, we were all a bit too relaxed. One of their projects was a squad drill competition for Wrens. We were drilled by a burly sergeant of marines. The poor man must have suffered, as the one concession to our womanhood was that he mustn't swear at us. We weren't even placed in the eventual competition, but it was a great day out. We set off in a hired bus on the long trip to Greenock. I hadn't been on a bus trip since before the war. The weather was perfect and the scenery breathtaking. We stopped at Luss for a cup of tea. Bowling down the other side of the Clyde those in charge realised we were far too early so we stopped the bus for a final practice session on the road.

The weather that summer was, or seemed to be, better than usual, maybe I remember only the sunny days because I was so happy what with the war being over and enjoying the company of a nice young man. I spent one particularly memorable day on Loch Fyne with Robby and a group of our friends. Someone had managed to get the use of a now almost obsolete landing craft in which we puttered aimlessly down the calm waters of the loch for an hour or two. I lay, basking in the sun, on the ultra broad gunwale of the craft, putting at the back of my mind the true use of the boat and simply enjoying the sensation of being afloat once more.

Coming eventually to the small inlet of Lochgair, we landed and walked up towards the hotel which was the mainstay of the tiny hamlet and where we hoped to find refreshment. As we rounded a bend, chattering and not looking where we were going, I bumped into a portly figure. I apologised and was astonished to find I had nearly knocked over the Reverend Donald Johnston, our minister, whose sermons I had listened to for many years with varying degrees of interest in Carntyne St. Michael's Church in Shettleston. I introduced Robby to him, none of us aware that in a few month's time he would be performing our wedding ceremony.

We re-embarked for the equally pleasant journey home. Aware that not everyone of my acquaintance had been privileged to travel in such unusual transport I let my mind wander to all the other modes of conveyance I had used in my still short life. Apart from steamers, paddle boats, motor and rowing boats, which as a child I had taken for granted as being normal, I had sailed on a lobster boat, fishing boats and now a landing craft. On land I had enjoyed the dubious comfort of a jeep, and the canvas covered trucks of the shuttle. Once I hitched a lift to Glasgow in an army ambulance.

I thought the daddy of them all, though, was the pig swill lorry. As I hadn't been due any leave when my mother was in Glasgow one time, she had come to Inveraray for a day or two. I planned to show her a bit of the kind of life I led, including a visit to Mrs. Campbell's wee tearoom. Tough though my mother was, I had no intention of asking her to walk the five miles there and the same back. The bus as usual didn't pass at the right time. We would have to hitch-hike. That day there was a dearth of vehicles on the road. We were getting desperate and it had just started to drizzle when a canvas covered lorry drew up. "Climb up at the back," said the driver, "and I hope you don't mind the smell!" Puzzled, we clambered up, and found ourselves confronted by a dozen or so large open bins reeking to high heaven.

Holding my nose, I peered gingerly into the barrels and found they contained the leftovers from many meals. I remembered then that all the scrapings and unused food was sent to Lochgilphead to feed pigs. Nothing was wasted in those lean times. My mother asked if this was the way I always travelled. She took a bit of reassuring while we tried to keep on the lee side of the stench. The aroma hung about us for some time and we had to walk around Furnace before we ventured into Mrs. Campbell's pleasant wee tearoom.

I travelled one day early on in my time at Inveraray in more opulent style. Walking back from the village in the pouring rain with two friends, we were offered a lift in a gleaming black car. We jumped in gratefully, not taking time to look properly at the car or its occupant. We were only aware that he was an officer. My two friends sat in the back beside him with yours truly in the front seat next the chauffeur. As the car purred along one of my more outspoken friends gave the officer her views on life in the Wrens, including several faults she found with the regulations and the food. In the front I suddenly became aware of a pennant fluttering wetly on the car bonnet, signifying that we were in the presence of a high-ranking officer. I was powerless to give m friend a warning signal. When we were deposited at the camp gate, I scuttled off quickly followed by my two mystified companions. As the talkative one said, when I put her in the picture, "Well, at least he has no idea who we are." I waited several days for the summons to the regulating office that could have followed, but the gallant gentleman kept his own counsel. We heard no more.

When I returned to camp from that last leave at Barrahead at the beginning of August, I was just in time to be caught up in the rumour that the end of the war in the Far East might not be far off. I wrote home saying how wonderful it would be if it ended on the 15th, my mother's birthday. With remarkable suddenness the war did indeed end on that day. We wondered why the apparently suicidal Japanese should suddenly capitulate. Then we heard that a new type of bomb had been dropped on Hiroshima and Nagasaki, completely devastating those cities and killing great numbers of the inhabitants, with only two bombs. These fantastic, unbelievably horrific weapons were atomic bombs. In the space of a few days the world had entered the Atomic Age and would never be the same again.

Peace and a Wedding

*A*t that moment most people were blissfully unaware of the far-reaching effects of the new bomb. It was enough that the entire world was at peace. We had been happy and relaxed since V-E Day, but now everything was perfect and we could all look forward to being demobbed in the near future. All, that is, but Robby and the other regular servicemen who had joined before the war for at least a twelve year stint. The full implication of that didn't penetrate my bliss just then. I just enjoyed every day as it came.

Not many days after V-J Day, I was on duty when I was called to the office to take a personal telephone call. This had never happened before so I rushed there full of alarm. It was Bill. He had been given leave and wanted me to put in a request for some, too. At that exact moment I discovered I was in love, not with poor Bill, but with Robby. I was astonished. Bill thought the phone had been disconnected and had to repeat his question. When I found my voice I blurted out that I wouldn't be able to come as I hoped to spend my next leave and hopefully the rest of my life with somebody else. It was Bill's turn to be silent; then he simply hung up.

I floated back to the gen. in a daze. In the evening I told Robby it was all off between me and Bill. That was all. Nothing more was said. A week later, Robby and I set off on leave to Arbroath so that I could meet the family he had spoken of so much. He liked to spend as much time with his mother as he could so we didn't go far afield, but the weather was lovely and I was still in a state of euphoria. Towards the end of the week I 'phoned the camp, hopeful of being allowed an extension of leave as Robby had several days more than I had, but my request wasn't granted and I had to return alone to camp, to be greeted by my cabin mates with cries of, "Well, where's your ring?" How disappointed they were to find my left hand still bare.

When Robby arrived back a long lonely three days later, on 4th September, I was happy again. That evening we went for one of our favourite walks down by the little river nearby, where we sat under a tree in the serene quiet of the autumn evening. Robby was not his usual self. I knew a proposal was in the air. He was shy and a bit tongue-tied and I found myself incapable of helping him out. However, that night I went back to the cabin wearing the ring my friends had been expecting to see days earlier. I said nothing, but the ring seemed to burn on my finger and my left hand refused to stay still. It didn't take long for some eagle-eyed girl to notice, and I was surrounded by an enthusiastic crowd congratulating me. There was nothing they liked more than a touch of romance. Everyone tried the ring on for luck and we celebrated with cups of cocoa and biscuits from somebody's hoard.

We made no firm plans for a wedding. Everything was still so unsettled, no one knowing when demobilisation would start, that it seemed unwise to plan too far ahead. A couple of weeks later I was informed that my services were no longer required by king and country. I left *Quebec* on 29th September, exactly three years and one day from my arrival. I was somewhat older and a great deal wiser than on that day when as a rookie I tentatively made my debut as a Wren. I found I didn't want to leave as I had come to like the life, but I had no option.

The camp was deep in slumber as I left Woodpecker cabin for the last time and humped my worldly goods to where a truck waited. I had been offered a lift to Glasgow by one of the marine drivers who had to deliver something in the city. Robby came to see me off, his hair tousled, his eyes full of sleep and his pyjama collar sticking up untidily from under the greatcoat he had hurriedly thrown on. When the truck reached Glasgow the driver made an unauthorised detour, taking me right to Granny's close and carrying my cases up the stairs for me.

I had a month's leave before I was officially free of the forces, and after the first few days time began to hang heavily. I loved my granny, but I missed the companionship of my friends at *Quebec*. I missed the dances and other social occasions and most of all I missed Robby. Ten days passed and I could stand it no longer. I had to do something. I 'phoned the camp and asked permission to go back for a week of my leave. To my surprise my rather impertinent request was granted. It was strange to return to the place I thought I had left for ever such a short time ago, but I was made welcome and even given my old bunk in Woodpecker cabin. I took great delight in having a "long lie" when everyone else had gone to work and on the Sunday I enjoyed saying "no" to attending

Divisions, which has always been compulsory except in the case of illness.

All too soon it was time to say good-bye again, finally breaking the bond with the W.R.N.S. I felt I had spent my whole life leaving people and places I had grown attached to, and I began to wonder when and where I'd ever be able to put down roots.

Back in Glasgow, it was time to think about earning some money. I was entitled to be reinstated in my old job in Smith's if I wanted it. I had no immediate plans for marriage, so I took advantage of that rule and took up where I left off in the needlework department. My boss, like many another, was not enamoured of having to reinstate old employees, as he had taken on staff to replace those lost to the services, but rules are rules.

I had only been back at work for a couple of rather boring weeks when Robby dropped the bombshell which suddenly removed all traces of boredom. He had been drafted from *Quebec* back to his home port of Portsmouth with the possibility of being sent abroad in the near future. It all depended on what ship he was drafted to. A few days later a telegram arrived. It read, "Have twenty-eight days leave. Be prepared for anything. Signed Robby." My thoughts ran wild. Was he going abroad? Was he being discharged after all on account of his bad leg? I waited impatiently for his arrival next day, to be greeted with the news that he thought we should get married very soon in case he was sent abroad at the end of his leave. I wasn't long in making up my mind that there was no time like the present.

Next morning I went to work quaking a little as I would have to tell my boss I needed time off to get married after only two weeks back. As it transpired I had no need to worry. As soon as I mentioned the magic word "marriage," he, without preamble and with an expression almost of relief, said, "Oh well, you'll want to leave." I found myself saying, "Yes," and walked out of his office in a daze. He didn't even offer his congratulations on my impending marriage. When I had time to realise what had happened, I found I was elated at the thought of being free of the monotonous nine-to-five routine.

The following couple of days went by in a whirl of activity. Robby notified his parents of our intention; how I don't know, as none of us had access to a telephone. We saw the minister and the session clerk of my church, arranging to have the banns posted on the church door, there being no time to have them called in the normal way from the pulpit. We saw the registrar and the date was fixed for 17th December, only a week away. One important item on the agenda was to inform my long-suffering parents at Barrahead that their beloved daughter was about to be married to a man they had never set eyes on. When I had written and told them of our engagement their reply had been full of guarded cliches like, "We are sure you have made a wise choice," and "We hope to meet Robby in the near future." The news of the wedding plans had to go by telegram to

Earraid and from there broadcast over the radio at the usual daily call time. As usual they rose to the occasion and by some means were granted leave to come to the wedding. My father had to sacrifice his summer holiday in the middle of winter. They were to arrive on the Thursday before the wedding, weather permitting of course. I had neither the time nor the will to think about the turmoil in their minds. Uppermost in their thoughts must have been, was this a shotgun wedding. They couldn't know that it was more financial than anything else. Once married I'd have an allotment from the navy which would keep me comfortably while Robby was away and give him peace of mind.

We booked the reception at the Angus Hotel in Argyll Street, Glasgow. The reception room was called Glenesk, the name of the glen where Robby and his family had spent most of their annual holidays. I felt sure it was a good omen.

For a long time wedding cakes had been mostly cardboard ones placed over a small plain cake to give the impression of the good old-fashioned elaborate ones. Despite rationing Granny and Aunt Jean were determined mine was not going to be like that; scrounging a few sultanas here and some sugar there until they had all the ingredients necessary for a two-tier cake. Icing sugar was scrounged from friends and neighbours and I found a shop that, by some miracle, still had some favours and a decoration for the top. Granny baked the cake in two different-sized biscuit tins in her coal-fired oven. The two tiers were held apart by empty meat paste jars covered in silver paper so that nobody guessed their humble origin. It was a masterpiece of a cake, not only to look at but to eat.

The biggest question was what I was going to wear. It was next to impossible to buy a real wedding dress. Then I remembered Margo, a Wren friend, who had recently married a Canadian sailor. He had brought over a beautiful dress in white figured satin with matching shoes. I had said, "I'd love to be married in a dress like that." "O.K.," she said. "You can borrow it any time." I sent her a telegram and she arrived a couple of days later with my wedding outfit. Veil and headdress were borrowed from Robby's sister Peg and my two bridesmaids, Jean and Robby's other sister, Isobel, were to wear blue evening dresses.

My going away outfit was the only disaster. My father had acquired some extremely hairy Harris tweed, from whoever wove it, without having to give coupons for it. Aunt Jean knew a "wee wumman" who would run it up for me. I was so bemused by the hustle and bustle that I paid scant attention to the design and a day or two later I was in possession of a skirt and jacket in a style completely unsuited to the coarse sweet-smelling tweed.

The taxis were ordered and a photographer booked, and all that remained to be done was to introduce Robby to his new in-laws, who were arriving on the Thursday evening. That afternoon Robby and I went into town to buy the wedding ring before meeting the Oban train at Buchanan Street Station. Robby was unhappy because the only rings we were offered were "utility" ones, absolutely plain narrow nine carat gold, costing about £1.10/- (£1.50). He was highly indignant that his bride should have to wear such a cheap and in his opinion, tawdry ring. Having convinced him I'd be happy to wear a Woolworth's ring if necessary, we purchased one of the offending rings and set off to meet the train.

We hadn't gone more than a few hundred yards when Robby suddenly doubled up in pain, grabbing the nearest lamppost for support. He recovered in a minute or two, much to my relief, as I had visions of him being carted off to hospital with appendicitis. A couple of lampposts further on it happened again and so on all the way up the street. I was worried sick, but Robby insisted he was all right and we duly met the Oban train. Introductions over, we took a taxi back to Granny's with no recurrence of the mystery pains. It was only later I suspected it had all been caused by nervousness at meeting his future in-laws. He confessed he was afraid they wouldn't like him and would talk me out of the wedding. He little knew that nothing would have changed my mind, and in any case both my parents took to him right away.

On the Friday we banished the bridegroom to Arbroath while the ladies got on with the final arrangements. I had no show of presents for the simple reason that I didn't have enough presents to show. The guests at my wedding were given only a few days notice, and everything was either on coupons or units (used for furnishings). The few I received were items people already had in the house surplus to requirements, and other people promised presents when rationing ended.

The night before the wedding Margo and I spent hours talking about old times and it was the wee small hours before either of us closed an eye. After a hearty breakfast we had some hours to put in before getting ready at Granny's, we spent them searching the shops for Scottish shortbread for Margo to take back to England.

Only when I was dressed in my finery did butterflies appear in my stomach. Left alone in the house except for my father, my nerves disappeared when I realised he was in a worse state than I was.

It was all go in Arbroath, too. Robby's mother, much to our disappointment, was unable to come to her only son's wedding as she didn't enjoy robust good health. It must have been a sad day for her. The taxi that was to take the rest of the family to the station was late. They just caught the train by the skin of their teeth, my husband-to-be frantic in case I was left standing at the altar thinking I'd been jilted. I remember very little of the ceremony or the reception. We stayed a bit longer than we should as I wanted to enjoy wearing my glamorous dress as long as possible before changing into my hairy tweeds. We missed the train and had to wait an hour before boarding a freezing train.

The Wedding Day.

We had chosen to go to Edinburgh on honeymoon, it had a lot of hotels and a number of cinemas and theatres which would make the weather less important. Having browsed through *Murray's Diary*, a handy-sized railway timetable-cum-advertising booklet, we had made a reservation in a Temperance Hotel off Princes Street as it would be quiet and unlikely to be fully booked. Our lateness caused us to miss dinner at the hotel, and the manageress apologetically said the best she could do was to send up tea and sandwiches. So the new Mr. and Mrs. Robertson dined off doorstep corned beef sandwiches in a room full of venerable residents of the hotel.

Our room was enormous and as cold as the inside of a fridge. Fuel was scarce. The big fireplace stared at us coldly and my heart sank. We cut our honeymoon short to go back to Glasgow only five days later to spend a wee while with my parents before they set off home to Barrahead. Then we set off to spend Christmas with Robby's mother. By Hogmanay I had caught a terrible cold and Robby's mother dosed me with hot toddy. I carried my cold with me when Robby and I set off for Portsmouth, where he had to report to await a draft.

Travel and Travail

On arrival at Portsmouth the first thing that struck me was the evidence of how much that city had suffered in the war. Every street held ugly bomb sites, great gaping holes in the ground where once had stood terraces of houses and shops.

We found a room in a terrace of bomb-scarred houses, once quite well-to-do, but now bristling with "Room To Let" signs. Our ground floor room was a fair size, but so full of furniture we had to weave our way carefully between an ancient brass bed, two old armchairs and a big table. There was an ugly gas fire and a rusty gas ring on which I was to cook the traditional first meal for my husband. Unromantically it was beans on toast. We went out for most of our meals after that. While Robby was at work, I spent the long, boring and often cold days at home. In spite of all though, I was happy to be with Robby. We went to the pictures a lot, hopeful of finding some warmth there and we began to frequent the pubs, which would have horrified my strict Presbyterian forebears, but most pubs had big roaring coal fires near which I could drink my inoffensive orange juice.

Three weeks after our arrival, Robby came home with the news that he had been pronounced fit to go back to sea and subsequently been drafted to a minesweeper, *H.M.S. Onyx*. He had been given leave so we went back to Arbroath, saying goodbye to the dull room and unfriendly landlady.

At the end of Robby's leave we had to part company again as he had no idea where his ship would be going. As the seas around our coasts were still dotted with dangerous mines, minesweepers like the *Onyx* were being kept as busy as though the war was still on, moving from one area to another as the need arose. I went back to Granny's with a sad heart and my rotten cold. I hoped Granny's cosseting would cure it and so it might, given half a chance. It wasn't long before I was off on my travels again, this time to Dovercourt, where Robby's ship was to be based for an unspecified time. He especially wanted me to see that town as he had been born there while his mother was following *her* husband around in the R.N.

The address we were to stay at sounded romantic. "Myrtle Cottage, Manor Lane." The thatched cottage I expected turned out to be a small two storey house of raw red brick in an untidy neglected wintry garden. In spite of my now hacking cough, I enjoyed my spell there. The folk who owned the house were kindly and made us welcome. We had been there only a week and were just settling down when Robby brought home news that the ship was leaving for Plymouth the next day. I was shattered! As he was steaming down the English Channel, I was packing my bags and coughing my heart out.

By some miracle I negotiated the journey across London to catch the Cornish Riviera train to Plymouth. It was a lovely journey through some of the finest scenery I'd seen in some time. At my destination I headed for the station exit where I was to wait to be picked up by Robby. As time passed and Robby hadn't arrived, my feet grew colder and colder. An hour later I began to worry. Had his ship been delayed? Had I mixed up the arrangements? Snuffling and coughing from my cold, and frozen to the marrow, I was beginning to wish I had never come, when who should saunter past the entrance but Robby, looking as cold and worried as I felt. I threw myself on him and after a few minutes we solved the mystery. There were two exits and we had both been waiting at different ones. What a lot of wasted time and worry!

We were booked into the Continental Hotel for a week. It probably cost a lot more than we could afford. Robby had chosen it for the excellent reason that it was one of the few big buildings left standing in what was a city of rubble even worse than Portsmouth as far as I could see. The hotel had miraculously escaped with only minor damage. The staff carried on as though nothing had happened. We were ushered to our room with as much deference as though we were royalty. From my bird's-eye view on the third floor I saw the devastation all around, gaping craters and the jagged remnants of what had been fine old buildings and big department stores. Rebuilding had started, but only the skeletons of new stores could be seen bearing the legend "Re-opening shortly." Meantime, as in Portsmouth, the various departments were scattered in small shops which had escaped complete destruction.

We visited all the places that tourists would visit, Plymouth Hoe for instance, and ventured further afield by bus into Cornwall to a lovely wee village called

Whitsands. I wanted to go down to the sandy beach, but we were prevented by a lot of barbed wire and notices marked "M.O.D. Warning. Mines."

One evening as a special treat Robby took me for a meal in a small hotel possessing a real live Palm Court orchestra. Two gentlemen in tails played the violin and piano, and a sedate lady, resplendent in an evening gown and feather boa, played the cello. It was wonderful. I didn't know such things still existed, and I could imagine them playing on as the bombs dropped all around. I felt as though I had wandered on to a film set as they rendered "Toselli's Serenade" and other old favourites.

The week over, we had to vacate our room as we couldn't afford to stay there any longer. As Robby's ship was still there I was reluctant to leave. I spent the last forenoon hunting for some cheaper place to stay, valiantly tramping the streets until I found a vacant room in a tall uninviting building. The room wasn't only deathly cold, but deathly silent, so I quickly unpacked my trusty alarm clock and I was grateful for its friendly tick. Still fully clad, I huddled down, the bed was like an icebox. After a while I decided I'd be warmer outside where at least I could walk. At five o'clock I stood at the pre-arranged meeting place, and stood, and stood, until my feet became numb. Then I began to worry.

Darkness had fallen when one of Robby's shipmates appeared with the news that Robby was going to be very late. I went to the station cafe to wait until he appeared. When I poured out my tale of woe, he simply said, "You can stop worrying. I've got a week's leave and we're going home tonight." My coldness forgotten, we rushed back to the fridge of a room, where I threw my alarm clock into my case and left that house forever.

Robby's leave over, he journeyed south to rejoin his ship. I went back to Shettleston. It was summer before I saw Robby again, I spent a much warmer week with him at the Continental, before returning once again to Glasgow.

Jean was no longer at Granny's. Before the end of the war she had succumbed like many others to the effects of constant long hours in a factory doing work she wasn't really cut out to do. Eventually she was diagnosed as suffering from nervous debility, a vague term covering a lot of vague symptoms. She had gone home to Barrahead to rest and enjoy plenty of fresh air. My mother was happy to have her company in the long wearying days. Jean soon had roses in her cheeks again, but stayed on until something better would turn up.

Coming up for Christmas that year, Robby wrote that he was to be in Portsmouth for some time, so the day before our first wedding anniversary I packed my now battered suitcase and set off yet again into the cold. That very day snow began to fall, so I arrived at a Christmas card city. We were to stay in a boarding house with the hopefully pleasant name of *Seaview*.

Our room was clean and well-furnished. It was equipped with a gas fire and water. The fire gave only the tiniest peep of flame. The windows rattled and let in a draught resembling "a step-mother's breath." I spent a lot of time huddling over the peep of gas. I seemed destined to be forever cold!

That was the winter the snow turned to ice on the streets and stayed there, immovable, for months. We suffered from power cuts, too, which came without warning. Things were so bad in Portsmouth, that submarines were used to provide some power for the town at times. One afternoon I decided to treat myself to a visit to the hairdressers for a shampoo and set. I felt like a lady as the girl worked away. What a luxurious warmth came from the drier. For a few minutes that is, until click, the lights went out and the hum of the driers faded away. I was sent home wearing a towel round my head, with instructions to come back to have the job finished once the power cut was over.

At that time of year the boarding house had few transient guests, so my fellow boarders were all permanent residents, mostly old people who, sadly, either had no relatives or those they had cared little about them. I felt sorry for these abandoned hopeless souls as they sat in the chilly lounge waiting patiently for the end.

Three important events marked the early part of that year. My father was shifted from Barrahead to yet another island. The new station was only three miles from Campbeltown on the Kintyre peninsula, so my mother was to be nearer civilisation than she had been for a number of years.

At the same time our spell in Portsmouth came to an end as Robby's ship was setting off on its travels again. I was settling into Granny's when I discovered I was going to have a baby. It was something we hadn't given a great deal of thought to as we were so engrossed in travelling about that it came as something of a surprise to me. I was delighted and wrote immediately to break the glad tidings to Robby. My great discovery was going to present at least one big problem. Where was I going to stay now? Although we had put our names on the council housing list in Arbroath, there was a long waiting list. Council houses were as hard to come by as diamonds. We couldn't afford to buy one. As for Wee Granny's house, it was far too small and not suitable for a young baby.

My mother and father rose to the occasion, insisting that I should go home to stay with them as soon as they settled in the new station. My mother looked on that shift as a Godsend, as I couldn't, by the wildest stretch of imagination, have spent my pregnancy at that last outpost, Barrahead. So I packed my belongings, such as they were, in May of 1947 and set off to take up residence in the bosom of my family at Devaar.

Devaar

*T*here was a choice of routes to Campbeltown. The bus from Glasgow was the simplest if not the most direct. The scenic journey took about six hours. The alternative method, which was the one I chose, was first by train to Fairlie on the Ayrshire coast, where I boarded the steamer *Duchess of Hamilton* to take me the rest of the way through the waters of the Firth of Clyde, past Arran and finally into Campbeltown Loch. We had to pass Devaar to reach the pier. The island was like a hump-backed whale. Perched on a little cliff was the brilliant white tower with the two granite houses surrounded by the old familiar high white-washed wall. A lump came to my throat as I remembered the good days we had before the war separated the family, and excitement rose in me as I realised that, for a time at least, the original family was going to be together again.

I could see one or two people waving towels in greeting. They couldn't pick me out. They waved just because they knew I was on board. I waved a big white hankie in return. My mother and father were in town with Jean to meet me, looking up and waving as I waited impatiently for the gangway to be lowered. The journey wasn't quite over. We had to retrace the last three miles or so of the steamer's route, in a motor boat. The boatman, Duncan Newlands, was also the occasional lightkeeper, coxswain of the Campbeltown lifeboat and conveyor of tourists on boat trips to "see round the lighthouse."

Suddenly we were at the slipway. The road to the station was as usual rough, stony and uphill, but at least it wasn't long. We turned a corner and there was the familiar type of gate with its big white notice board informing the public

that there was "No admittance except at the discretion of the Principal Keeper."
I knew as I walked in that the kitchen would be on the right, the parlour on the
left and there would be two bedrooms at the end of the long lobby. After one of
my mother's meals I felt as though I was truly home.

I soon fell into the old routine, feeding the hens and helping with the
housework. I was forbidden, however, on account of my "condition," to carry
water from the spring down by the pier. My mother was visibly happier. She
was able to go shopping again, albeit by motor boat. It made her life much
easier. She was, as she said, "getting on a bit." She was still very fit, as she
seldom stopped working and still had no labour-saving appliances to help her
in the house. Electricity had not yet come to Devaar nor had plumbing. Washing
day still involved lighting the big boiler and though there were sinks in the
wash-house, water still had to be transferred from boiler to sink by means of
hard work and a bailer.

I had come to Devaar at the best time of year. The weather seemed set for a
lovely spring and summer. My father had planted the fertile garden with a variety
of vegetables, the hens were laying well and the island looked very attractive. As
I hadn't yet reached the ungainly stage of my pregnancy I was able to explore

Devaar lighthouse with the white pillar of the sundial visible.

My parents on Campbeltown pier. Devaar Island can just be seen in the background (to the right) while the funnel of the steamer is clear.

the place. There wasn't a lot of it but there was one part of it of great interest. My father lost no time in showing it off to me as though he was personally responsible. At the back of the island are a number of caves which can only be reached at low tide by clambering for some distance over the rocky shore. They were so difficult to reach that they were usually ignored by the local populace, until one day early this century some local men had gone to explore the caves. To their utter astonishment, they found in the biggest one a life size painting of the Crucifixion, on the rough wet stone wall. The discovery caused great consternation in the little town and soon the painting became renowned. It was many years before the artist was traced and eventually persuaded to return to Campbeltown to repaint his work, which was deteriorating because of the dampness in the cave.

It transpired that he had dreamed one night about the Crucifixion and, unknown to anyone, had made his way to the cave to put his dream on permanent though secret record. Since it was found, thousands of visitors have made the pilgrimage across the rocky shore to look at the Picture Cave. When my father took me to see it, I had to stand for a minute or two until my eyes became accustomed to the gloom, before the picture emerged. Painted straight on to the rock face, it is extraordinarily realistic. Where the gash in the side of Christ's body is painted, there is actually a gash in the rock which seems to fit all the contours of the body perfectly.

We visited this place often, taking friends to view the wonder of it. Droves of holiday-makers on their return from the cave made a day of it by visiting the lighthouse and being shown up the tower. My father revelled in this part of his job, not only because the tips were handy, but because he loved meeting people.

My father, below on the balcony at Devaar and right, with some wood found on the beach in which he saw some fun. One of our small amusements at Devaar!

He had often to be called away by my mother who could see that the visitors were having difficulty in getting away from him in order not to miss their evening meal in their boarding houses.

My first priority was to arrange where my baby was to be born. On my mother's first shopping trip ashore I accompanied her in Duncan's boat, registered with her doctor and walked round to the posh end of town to where a large villa had been converted into a small maternity home. This was before the days of the National Health Service, so I'd have to pay. In the event my bill was only £5.5/-, but it was more than one week's Navy allowance.

The weather was exceptionally good. I spent the waiting months knitting

How my mother went shopping at Devaar.

Sitting outside at Devaar.

and sewing a layette, sitting outside most of the time, getting as brown as a berry in the process. My mother and Jean, fired with the same enthusiasm, helped, and soon a suitcase was full of everything from bootees to nightgowns, all hand made. My father found an old wicker travelling basket, left over, no doubt, from some Victorian household. It was just the right size for a first cot. I lined the basket with cotton wadding and contrived a frilly cover from some old material my mother had stowed away at some time "in case it came in handy."

Coupons and furniture "units" were still curtailing purchasing power, but I found I was entitled to some to enable me to buy a dropside cot, a pram and a chest of drawers. Clothes were also in short supply. I was able to purchase one maternity dress, a clumsy tent-like thing in turquoise with a pattern of large dark blue spots. When it was in the wash I wore an old skirt and a smock. I looked and felt hideous and by the time my baby arrived I was sick of the sight of that frock.

Devaar was a tidal island, joined to the mainland by a mile long causeway of rocks and smaller stones which from a distance resembled an umbilical cord. It was handy if anyone wanted to go into town on a non-boat day. The usual routine was to 'phone for a taxi to meet us at the landward end of the Dhorrlinn. By the time we had walked over a mile of rough stones we were too tired to walk a further couple of miles into Campbeltown. I couldn't do this trip in the later months of my waiting time so had to be content with going ashore with Duncan's boat twice a week. I was happy with my little lot, except that I only saw Robby a couple of times before the birth. I baked and cooked and washed clothes and knitted and sewed. We had the wireless to listen to and plenty of reading material in the evenings, and we played cards or ludo.

The island was alive with rabbits, mice, moles and rats besides birds, so our cats were sleek and healthy. One of them would perhaps disappear for a couple of days, reappearing looking bloated and contented, with wisps of bluish fur clinging to the parts of its body it couldn't quite reach to clean. Sometimes one would be seen waddling slowly and awkwardly up the road, dragging between

The author and Robby before Sheila's birth.

its front paws a rabbit bigger than itself. Gasping for breath, it would deposit its prey at my mother's feet and purr frantically round her, until she skinned the rabbit. Some of the bits would be given to the cats, but most of it was made into a delicious casserole for our next day's dinner. Yet again we had a source of good free food as we had found at other stations.

My baby was due on 17th October, by which time the glorious summer would have become less predictable. My mother was a natural born nurse, but she drew the line at having to deliver her first grandchild in the middle of a storm. Although it was easy enough to walk ashore via the Dhorrlinn there was no way I could see myself staggering across it in October, stopping at intervals to cope with a contraction. More than likely the birth certificate would have read "Place of birth…middle of the Dhorrlinn." So it was arranged that three weeks before the due date I would go into lodgings in town. Jean and my mother took turns in staying with me.

With still a week to go, my mother and I went to the pictures. The film was a famous one about the Battle of Arnhem, in the middle of which I realised that all the excitement wasn't in the film. I was having "funny sensations" in my back. I went into the home early next morning although it was to be a couple of days of hard work before I was able to hold my baby daughter in my arms.

Sheila Margaret Robertson made her entrance into the world at 3.20 in the afternoon of Monday, 13th October, 1947, weighing in at a solid nine pounds. Once back in the ward I listened to the wireless playing the hit song of the day, "Oh! What a beautiful morning. Oh! What a beautiful day." "So it is. So it is," I thought as I drifted into a well-earned sleep.

The weather, at cross purposes with the season, was indeed beautiful. During the two days of my incarceration in the labour room I had watched from my high hard bed the comings and goings of fishing boats and other small craft, cutting a white swathe in the otherwise glassy blue water on their way in and out of Campbeltown Loch. I could easily have stayed on the island until the time was ripe after all.

While all this was going on, Robby, whose ship was in Portsmouth, was slowly going round the bend as he waited for news. He had to go ashore by boat every so often to 'phone for a progress report. At first he felt only the natural excitement of a first-time father, but as time passed and the message was always, "nothing to report," he began to feel anxious. By the end of forty-eight hours he was a nervous wreck and according to friends smoked literally hundreds of cigarettes. The tension eventually over, he celebrated in true naval fashion with a crowd of his shipmates.

Once I left the nursing home I stayed a few days in town to finish some treatment I needed. Sheila was more than a fortnight old before Robby was granted leave to meet his new daughter. He had just been with us an hour when it was time to set off to take Sheila on her first sea trip to Devaar where she was to stay until just before her first birthday. The calm spell of weather had broken when we set off on the rather choppy crossing to the island. On the way over I was struck by the fact that history was repeating itself. My mother had taken me home to Inchkeith on the same kind of day all those years ago.

It was quite a thrill, though unnerving, to find myself in charge of a strange, constantly hungry, active wee bundle and I was grateful for having my practical experienced mother on hand for help and advice. I was over-anxious about my responsibilities, so much so that I constantly had words with poor Robby who somehow always seemed to make more noise than usual just as Sheila was falling asleep. He banged doors, called from one room to another and generally disturbed her. I think he was quite relieved when his short leave was over and he could go back to living normally. Needless to say, I was then overcome with remorse. My mother sensibly maintained a policy of non-intervention. Robby didn't see Sheila again until Christmas.

Robby's sole aim was to reach the house in time to fill Sheila's very first Christmas stocking. It was a clear but windy night when he reached Campbeltown and there was no way he could come over by boat. He'd have to face the Dhorrlinn in the dark. My father, although now in his fifties, excelled himself that night. It became clear that if Robby waited until the causeway was dry it would be past midnight before he reached the house, so my father waded across and, like St. Christopher, carried Robby on his back, suitcase and all. At five minutes to midnight we heard the crunching of feet on the gravel, and Sheila's first real toy, a pink and white woolly rabbit, was placed at the side of her cot as midnight struck.

We had arranged for Sheila to be christened while Robby was home. It was a somewhat unusual ceremony, as, to save subjecting a three-month-old baby to the rigours of a double sea trip in midwinter, we asked the minister to come over and christen her in the house. He duly came along with a boatload of friends, and the ceremony was performed in my mother's parlour, a crystal sugar bowl being substituted for a font. I remember I warmed up the water to room temperature, so that my wee girl wouldn't have to put up with freezing cold water being sprinkled on her head. Sheila lay peacefully in the minister's arms throughout and later the minister commented that he wondered why nobody had thought of warming the water before.

That night, with Sheila tucked in her wee home-made cot, we adults had a bit of a party. The young keeper next door, a single man, had an empty spare bedroom so we set up trestle tables there for a celebratory meal. We took turns nipping into our house to see that the wee guest of honour was safe and sound. It was a day to remember, but tinged a little with the thought that two days later her father would have to leave us, with little chance of seeing his daughter again before Easter.

So history seemed about to repeat itself again. Sheila, as I had been in my tender years, was the only child on the island. While she was tiny, the arrangement worked well. The baby thrived. I made sure she got plenty of fresh air, by taking her for walks in her collapsible pram. It was neither easy nor interesting as the route could never be varied. The first quarter of a mile was over the rough road full of jagged lumps of the inevitable granite and thereafter I had to push the protesting pram over rough grass to the corner of the island where the Dhorrlinn began. There were days when even that was impossible because of high winds blowing round the side of the hill. Sometimes when the weather was less inclement we ventured to town. The pram had to be folded up to get it in the boat, while I sheltered Sheila from the spray by wrapping a travelling rug round my shoulders to form a sort of tent.

Spring came, followed by better weather as summer approached. Sheila blossomed and gained a lovely tan in the clear sunshine. Everything was fine except that she was not a good sleeper. Perhaps the environment was partly to blame because most of the time, apart from the gentle clucking of hens and the bleating of sheep, there was little in the way of noise. The result was that any unexpected sound such as a plane passing overhead woke her up.

One noise was unavoidable at certain times of the year. Devaar, though only a two-man station, had a fog signal. It was neither a horn, as at the Rhinns of Islay, nor a radio signal as at Barrahead. It was worked by acetylene gas. Water dripped on to the chemical at a steady rate, so that every thirty seconds or so, the resulting gas exploded in its container with a sound like a rifle shot. The hut that held the "gun" as we called it was only a few yards from the house. The house walls were so thick the sound was muffled, but once outside it was loud enough to blast your eardrums. We became clever at avoiding the worst of it.

The Crucifixion painting on the Picture Cave wall.

When, for example, during a spell of fog it became necessary to go and feed the hens, the person whose turn it was for that job, waited by the closed door until the blast went off, before dashing round the corner of the house to reach the shelter of the henhouse before the next "shot." As at other stations our ears became so accustomed to the explosions that we often didn't hear them. Fortunately, Sheila seemed to adapt like the rest of us and slept peacefully until she woke up hungry. She was perpetually hungry!

The same tactics had to be adopted in foggy weather when someone had to visit the toilet. It was still in an outhouse, but facilities had improved greatly over the years. There was now an Elsan chemical toilet. The inevitable bucket had to be partially filled with a hygienic fluid with dissolving properties, thus supposedly lessening the chance of infection. This innovation was situated in a storeroom next to the house and had the advantage of having a big window which let in a great deal of sunshine. Thus we no longer spoke of the "shunky". The apartment was henceforth known as "the Sun Parlour."

At Devaar we had two sources of free nourishing food. One was the rabbits kindly brought home by the cats. The other, which only happened once, was

Other aspects of Devaar – below, the kitchen with my father and sister Jean's fiancé (the only interior view I have of a lighthouse house!) and left, Wee Granny on a visit to the island.

the result of the stupidity of the sheep which were grazed by a local farmer on the island. Sheep always face into the wind, they also follow each other no matter what. Now and again the wind blew directly off the Dhorrlinn and occasionally this coincided with a low tide. One windy day my father spotted the sheep heading blindly for the Dhorrlinn just as the tide was coming in. He 'phoned the farmer and set off to help, but it was too late. Several sheep had walked straight into the incoming tide and were drowned, dragged down by the weight of their wool. The farmer and my father dragged the dead sheep ashore. "You can keep one of them," said the disgruntled farmer.

We were delighted, as rationing was still in force and meat in short supply. The farmer instructed my father on the niceties of preparing and cutting up the sheep. It was hung in a store down by the pier and was subsequently skinned and cut into joints and chops. With neither fridge nor freezer, we ate almost gluttonously for days before it went off. After five days of a solid diet of mutton we never wanted to see mutton again. It was too much for our meat-deprived palates.

Sheila cut her first tooth and took her first steps at Devaar. Shortly afterwards Robby was drafted to a shore base in Portsmouth, *H.M.S. Hornet*, where he was likely to stay for some considerable time. It was an opportunity of being together as a family for the first time. There was no chance of married quarters so Robby found a furnished flat in Southsea, near Portsmouth. The elderly landlord had no qualms about having a baby in the house. Once more I embarked on a new phase of my life, but this time with the added responsibility of an eleven-month-old daughter.

Portsmouth

My father took a week of his holidays to enable him and my mother to accompany me down south. They were anxious about me travelling "all that way" with Sheila, but I think they really wanted to see for themselves what kind of house I'd be living in and what kind of people I'd be consorting with in that foreign country. Sheila was scared of the noise of trains and crowds of people so I was only too pleased, as I wasn't sure how I'd cope with the long train journey and having to change stations in London.

Our new abode, Duncan Road, was a typical English street of red brick terraced houses. We were welcomed by a shy, balding little man in his sixties. He was to prove no ordinary landlord, starting off by immediately offering my mother and father the use of his spare upstairs bedroom for as long as they stayed. We had the use of the entire ground floor, consisting of a parlour, a bedroom, a kitchen-cum-dining room and a wee scullery, with an outside toilet in the back yard. The house was clean and comfortable and I knew we were going to be happy there.

The next day I registered with the local shops for our rations. The white-coated grocer smiled at me and said "Ah! You're from bonny Scotland," adding, "That customer over there is from Scotland, too." The lady in question came from Shettleston and in fact had lived just down the road from Wee Granny's, had like me attended Eastbank Academy, and actually knew my Aunt Jean. We had lived all those years a few hundred yards apart only to meet in a shop in Southsea. We remained good friends for the rest of our stay there.

The day my mother and father left I sallied forth to do the first real family shopping of my life. In some ways it was simple, as the first word was always simply "Rations." Everything that wasn't rationed was either unavailable or in very short supply, so the rest of my list was liberally embellished with question marks. Streaky bacon wasn't rationed, when I was offered some I was delighted. On one occasion the grocer let me have a whole pound of lentils. I carried them home along with a few streaky rashers and some carrots to make a pot of soup. That, to me, was the first sign that things were beginning to improve at last.

It took me a while to get to know our landlord. Sheila was the one who broke the ice by crawling upstairs to the wee box-room he had converted into a kitchen. I found the two of them happily sharing lemonade and biscuits. From then on we drank cups of tea together and we soon came to call him "Uncle." He became as attached to Sheila as a grandfather and we stayed two and a half years.

We had only been in Southsea a few weeks when Sheila celebrated her first birthday. I baked a sponge cake in the miniscule oven of my tiny cooker and took pleasure in putting the single candle on it. Just the three of us shared the wee party. I wished my mother and father could have been there after having devoted a whole year to helping to bring up their first granddaughter.

I found it difficult if not almost impossible to make friends with the local people. I was still shy and most of the inhabitants still retained the reticence that had been the hallmark of the English before the war. Our next door neighbour had a little girl Sheila's age, and the two wee ones played together happily in the garden, but it was many months before she asked me into her house.

Sheila and me at our front door in Portsmouth where was our home for 2½ years.

Apart from this small difficulty with the local people, some of which was no doubt due to my own shyness, I liked living in the south. Summer lasted from April until October, and winter seemed to pass much more quickly. Being near the sea we took Sheila for walks almost every day along the prom. Sheila loved the colour and music of the fun fair and South Parade pier and we were content with our life.

Our wee house soon became a home as we became familiar with all its quirks and deficiencies and in spite of being filled with someone else's furniture. The bed held a huge, down-filled mattress which had to be turned daily. This was more like a wrestling match than bed-making as I pummelled the unruly feathers into submission.

The kitchen was small, with a tiny fireplace right in a corner. The furniture was much too big for such a small space. Even smaller was the scullery, home to a small cooker and an enormous cumbersome mangle which was too heavy for me to handle. In the opposite corner was a shallow sink. Here I had to cope not only with dishwashing, but also nappies and all the rest of the laundry. Nappies had to be boiled in a zinc bucket on one of the gas rings on my wee cooker. The other problem was the water; it was hard and I couldn't raise a decent lather no matter how much soap I used.

The back yard was completely surrounded by a high wall, shutting us off from neighbours and passers-by. It provided a safe place for Sheila to play, but I felt imprisoned there. Our toilet was out there, too and next to it was the coal cellar. One dark winter's morning I got the fright of my life there as I leaned over the boards that prevented the coal from falling out. Suddenly I became aware of something wriggling and squeaking and I was horrified to find I had trapped a big rat between my leg and the boards.

That first Christmas I encountered a custom I was unacquainted with. As there was no back gate tradesmen could only come to the front door. No matter how old and infirm it was the householder's job to carry the dustbin through the house. Shortly before Christmas I was surprised when the bin man knocked on the door and asked kindly if he could carry my empty bin back through the house. I thanked him and went back to the living room. A minute later he knocked on the living room door and called out, "Merry Christmas, lady." I answered, and went on with my knitting. He called again, more insistently. The penny didn't drop until the man called bluntly, "It's customary to give us a Christmas box!" Only then did I realise why he had been so unusually helpful. Robby and I had a good laugh, and I made sure I had the money ready the next year.

We looked forward to that first Christmas down south, with Sheila just beginning to be aware of the excitement. We bought a Christmas tree. Tree decorations were scarce, but I found a couple of sheets of cardboard cutouts of lanterns, Santas, and stars which we threaded with lengths of cotton. Rationing meant there wasn't much scope for a feast. My father had promised he'd send a chicken, so I collected the other ingredients for a meal. When the chicken hadn't arrived by Christmas Eve I began to panic. In those days mail was delivered up until lunch time on Christmas Day. The parcel arrived at midday. To my delight, my mother had cooked the chicken to prevent it going off, so we celebrated in style and on time.

Although several years had passed since the war ended, winter still brought hardships, inevitable power cuts, low gas pressure and unreliable coal deliveries. We had to order coal in bulk, half a ton at a time. On our second winter in Southsea my stock of coal diminished rapidly as the frost and ice remained for months. No coal was reaching us because of the frozen roads. Eventually we were left with only a few shovelfuls of dross.

Robby decided we'd heat only the wee kitchen and camp out there as long as possible. We filled some old shoes with dross, dampened so they would burn longer, an old tip of Granny's, and with Uncle's permission we broke up an old chair. Just as we were about to put the last boot on the fire, the coalman arrived. Black as he was, I could have kissed him. He told us that as the roads were still impassable, some coal had been brought in by sea.

Robby was working on a new experimental project for the R.N. to discover if jet propulsion worked as well on boats as it did in the air. Trials were being conducted on a motor torpedo boat of which Robby was a crew member. After a time the boat set off on a tour of European ports to demonstrate the new concept to other nations. Robby brought back photographs of every place he visited. I never did hear the full outcome of the exercise, but as far as I know, it wasn't a great success.

Robby and I still had to make the kind of adjustments that normally would have been made after the honeymoon. We argued quite a lot, but only once in Portsmouth did we have a real quarrel. Sheila disturbed me at least twice a night. I was constantly tired and, though ordered by the doctor to rest, found it impossible to follow his advice. Robby worked hard six days a week and on Sundays automatically stayed in bed to recover from his week-day efforts. He didn't realise how much I longed for even one hour extra in bed without having full care of Sheila. On one particularly tiring Sunday, I rebelled. At midday I ordered Robby out of bed, telling him he was a lazy good-for-nothing. Taken aback, he protested. "But I work hard all week. I deserve a bit of a rest." "Do you think I loaf about all week?" I shouted. "I work twenty-four hours every day seven days a week!" The poor man hadn't even thought about it, and I didn't speak to him for three days. After that we took it in turns to have a long lie. It made all the difference to my well-being and we have never had such a bad quarrel since.

On one other occasion Robby and I were separated when he developed an uncomfortable form of dermatitis and was admitted to the naval hospital at Haslar on the other side of the Gosport Ferry. That evening Sheila and I went to visit him. Swathed from head to foot in bandages, each finger and toe wrapped separately, he looked more like a mummy than a daddy! It was a couple of weeks before he was literally released from bondage and allowed home.

Every so often we sallied forth northwards alternating Robby's leave periods between his folks and mine, Sheila becoming a seasoned traveller. During this period, Robby had to make a decision about his future. Having almost completed twelve years in the navy he had to make up his mind whether to come out without a pension and look for a good civilian job while he was still young, or sign on for a further ten years, at the end of which he could retire with a pension. At last he decided he'd like to follow my father into the lighthouse service. He had an interview in Edinburgh, followed by a medical, and he was all set to take up a new life when fate stepped in, in the shape of the Korean War. The order was issued that all those who had signed on for twelve years should be retained in the service until further notice. We gathered it would be for at least eighteen months thereafter, depending on how the war went. For all the time that would be left to serve after that, Robby would be just as well to sign on for his pension. He signed on the dotted line, cancelled the arrangement with the lighthouse service and we continued to live in Southsea. We waited for a draft to a ship, but as it turned out the war made no difference to us. Robby remained at the shore base.

In the spring of 1950 Robby was eventually drafted to *H.M.S. Coquette*, a fishery protection vessel, thus bringing our pleasant spell together to an end. There was no alternative but to give up the flat and go back to Devaar. I was not unwilling to go home. Poor old Uncle. He was shattered when we broke the news. We had grown fond of the old chap and he had come to look on us as part of the family. He doted on Sheila, spoiling her terribly. For the last two weeks of our stay he went about looking as though the world was coming to an end. I noticed he had suddenly become unsteady on his feet. One day he confessed he was having trouble with his eyes, seeing blank spaces where objects ought to be. We parted tearfully, my last words being that he really should see the doctor. I never saw the old chap again.

Devaar to Arbroath

*R*obby, having been granted the customary draft leave, travelled north with us to Devaar, where we soon settled down, and two weeks later he bade us all a sad farewell to go back to Portsmouth to join his new ship, the minesweeper *H.M.S. Coquette.*

Sheila was quite happy to be back with her beloved grandpa. The two were great friends. He'd sit and play hymns on the piano, Sheila standing by his side gradually learning the words of such favourites as "Rock of Ages," "Jesus Loves Me," "Jesus of Nazareth Passeth By," and the lightkeepers' hymn, "Let the Lower Lights be Burning". My father would sit there, tears running down his face, enjoying having a "good greet" as he played. Sheila showed signs of having a good ear for music, and a clear singing voice.

My mother took it all in her stride, carrying on with her multitude of chores. There was no improvement in amenities although it was 1951, but at least she had me to help. The washing was still done by the old-fashioned boiler and wringer system, after which we all bathed in the last of the hot water. We now possessed a full length zinc bath which seemed quite luxurious after our cramping wee one. It took two people to empty the thing afterwards.

All rubbish that couldn't be burned or fed to the hens was tipped down a chute just opposite the houses. This chute constituted the only real danger to Sheila as it was completely unprotected. If her inquisitiveness had led her to investigate it, one slip would have sent her flying to land amongst the rubbish, rocks and rats below.

Summer at Devaar.

One of the local men told my father a hair-raising tale about rats. It seemed that once a basking shark had become stranded on the rocky shore at the back of the island and had subsequently died unnoticed. One night, the keeper on duty in the tower heard a kind of rustling squeaking noise, getting louder by the minute. Curious, the man went out on the lightroom balcony, from where he saw beneath him a huge dark moving shape, undulating through the gate, past the houses and out through the far side of the gardens. As his eyes became accustomed to the dark he realised with horror that it was a line of marching rats. They had apparently crossed the Dhorrlinn at low tide to search out the decaying carcass of the shark. A few nights later, the now replete army of rodents

Father's 9-hole putting green at Devaar.

marched back the same way, to disappear forever across the Dhorrlinn, leaving behind only the bare bones of the shark.

My father, though now on the wrong side of fifty-five, was still full of new ideas. At Devaar the drying green was in front of the houses on a sloping grassy area full of humps and hollows. It was anything but flat, but it gave my father the notion of constructing a putting green among the clothes poles. He rolled and mowed until the grass was as smooth as possible. The holes were lined with old syrup tins and the flags were made from scrap metal. Some of the holes were very tricky. One, though only about six yards, had the hazard of a clothes pole to be negotiated, not to mention a steep bumpy slope. We all became adept at the game. Visitors to the lighthouse invariably asked if they could have a go too. The putters had to be stowed away as the weather became colder and windier.

My mother began to worry about Sheila being confined to the island just at the age when she was liable to catch some childish ailment on a trip to town, with the possibility of being unable to summon a doctor. Eventually I found a middle-aged widow whose flat was at the top of a three-storey tenement. She kept it very clean and it was comfortable, if a bit old-fashioned. The rent was within my means and to my relief the widow would still be occupying part of the flat. I was to have full use of the kitchen and toilet. The house was lit by gas, with the old style pull cord for turning it on and off. The light was much dimmer than that given by the Tilley lamps at the island and the house gave off an atmosphere of depression not entirely due to the bad lighting.

I had heard of houses that gave off an aura of either happiness or misery, depending on events that took place in them. The theory was proved right in this case. As I got to know our quiet landlady I gleaned bits of information about her life. She had married late in life, had no children and her husband had died. I formed the impression she was simply waiting for time to pass until she could join her husband.

While we stayed in Campbeltown, Sheila did become ill with a sore throat and raised temperature, so the doctor had to call. I knew him well as he had delivered Sheila. When I opened the door of the flat that day, however, he looked astonished, and said, "Good God! What on earth are you doing in this menage?" Somewhat taken aback I ushered him in to see the young sufferer. As he left he said quietly, "This is no place for you. Get back to the island as soon as you can." He wouldn't explain further.

Devaar, at long last, had plumbing installed. The old kitchen range was replaced by a modern Rayburn coal-burning stove, and my mother was able to throw away her old black lead brushes. The new stove required only a quick wipe with a damp cloth. To her further delight, a section of one bedroom was walled off and converted into a neat bathroom with hot and cold water and a

My mother and father at Devaar Lighthouse, about 1950.

W.C. No longer did we have to don wellies and raincoat in bad weather or time the blasts of the fog signal in order to spend a penny. The two men still had to pump water up from the pier to the supply tank on the roof, but my mother felt it was like a miracle.

Robby and I had been married nearly six years with no sign of a home of our own. I knew, however, that I was putting an extra strain on my mother and father. Sheila was fast approaching school age, she was almost five. It wasn't as though we had made no attempt to find a home. Our name had been on the Arbroath council list since we were married. Every time we visited Arbroath we asked at the housing office how far up the list we had moved. Every time the official shook his head and said, "You don't have enough points."

In summer 1952 an official-looking letter with an Arbroath postmark arrived. It was from the housing office. I had to read it twice before the news sank in. We were to be allocated a house in the near future. When Robby 'phoned I babbled out the news and could talk of nothing else.

With my mother's help I gathered together an assortment of items which might come in useful. I was to take the piano. There was a nursing chair. My inventive father converted an obsolete hair mattress with matching spring mattress into a strong bed by fixing a block of wood to each corner. Then there was my wee collection of wedding presents that had spent seven years in my mother's cupboard. The chest of drawers I had been allocated units for when Sheila was born, and there was Sheila's high chair and some spare dishes and pots. I had made a couple of rugs during my time at Devaar, so those and some old curtains completed my furnishings.

During Robby's summer leave we went to have a look at the housing scheme where we were to live in Arbroath. We had no idea which house would be ours, but we peered in every window of the still uncompleted houses. Later we went back to Arbroath armed with our new address and an entry date in September.

Robby's mother was in hospital and the news wasn't good. It was with great reluctance that Robby said goodbye to her when he had to go back to his ship. He had scarcely arrived there when his mother died and he was immediately granted compassionate leave. I had stayed on in Arbroath, knowing he would soon be back needing my support. The funeral over, Robby rejoined his ship and Sheila and I went back to Devaar to pack. I sadly took leave of my mother and father, realising I'd know no-one in Arbroath except my in-laws.

September 15th, 1952 was the day of the flitting. Sunny and calm, it was a good day for moving in. I had the welcome assistance of Robby's sister Peg and her husband Wat. I remember little of that day; Wat lighting the fire to check that smoke didn't blow back into the room, and Peg saying to me, "Well! Aren't you going to sit down and see what it feels like to be in your own house?"

After Peg and Wat had gone home, I sat down again in that strangely silent house, Sheila sitting contentedly on the rug playing with her toys and singing to herself. The house was redolent of new wood, plaster, distemper, paint, linoleum and new furniture. Suddenly I felt lonely. There was only one thing to do. I cooked a meal on my new gas cooker and within minutes the smell of bacon and egg dispelled the others. This was more like home.

Winter brought the discovery of the biggest snag. The houses in our scheme were poorly insulated. The only room which could be heated was the living room, and I soon found that the two bedrooms, in the depths of winter, resembled the inside of a fridge. When making the beds I had to don a coat and gloves, my fingers were so cold. How we survived I don't know, but survive we did.

Sheila and I were free to do as we pleased. As one of the "Bulge" babies, born in the years after the war when husbands were demobbed and thinking of starting a family in peacetime, there was no room for Sheila at school for another year.

It took time to get to know my neighbours who all had friends and relatives living in town. I felt left out and lonely but Sheila soon made friends. Children have less inhibitions than their elders. I remember the warm feeling when a wee lass knocked on the door only a few days after we moved in saying, "Is your wee girl coming out to play?" At night time I couldn't come to grips with my fear of being alone. I dreaded the moment when I had to draw the curtains, knowing I'd see no-one until sometime next morning. I stuck it out as long as I could but there were times when I felt I would have welcomed a burglar just to have somebody to talk to. One day I spilled it all out to a neighbour and she suggested that her teenage daughter might be willing to sleep in my house for a wee bit of pocket money. What a difference it made to my well-being. I was immediately more relaxed.

Robby was drafted to Malta and was given leave. My mother looked after Sheila so that Robby and I could have a week on our own in Portsmouth before we had to part. We thoroughly enjoyed renewing acquaintances with old haunts and old friends. All too soon it was over and Sheila and I reluctantly went back to Arbroath and the silent house awaiting us there.

I settled down to bringing up Sheila on my own and we were quite happy with each other's company. Only one thing really bothered me. We had mice. When the old farmland was dug up to make way for our housing scheme, the resourseful field mice took residence in with the new tenants. In the quiet evenings I could hear them scuttling around, but as long as they stayed inside the wall I didn't bother them. It was a different matter when the braver ones let themselves be seen. One fine morning I woke very early to the sound of scuffling under my bed. I leaned over and peered below to see two mice playing hide and seek on the dusty lino. I leapt up and gave chase, launching myself angrily on the pair until to my later regret, I committed "mouseocide" with a shovel. I remember the incident well, because that same day it dawned on me that I might be expecting my second child.

My doctor confirmed my suspicion, calculating my baby would probably arrive on New Year's Day. My first reaction was, "How am I going to cope alone with this big event, with Robby so far away and my mother and father at the other side of the country?" I gradually came to the conclusion that the only thing to do was make sensible preparations to welcome Sheila's wee brother or sister, initially by booking a bed in the local maternity ward, writing to tell Robby and giving my mother and father something else to worry about during the remainder of their time at Devaar.

In August Sheila finally started school. She was almost six and would be the oldest child in her class, but she still seemed to me to be too young to be thrown into the big wide world. A brand new school was being built just a few hundred yards away, until it was ready she attended one of the oldest schools in the town, quite a walk from where we lived. I had a wee bit of freedom to rest while Sheila was at school.

In November my mother came to stay, well aware of the possibility of a less than nine month pregnancy. It was a wonderful relief to have that capable lady with me. She was wrong, however, about an early arrival. On Hogmanay, the two of us sat up to bring in the New Year before going to bed. At four in the morning I woke to the knowledge that my baby was going to be a New Year's Day baby. My mother went hunting for the kind neighbour who had volunteered to escort me to the hospital as Sheila couldn't be left alone. Eventually she arrived breathlessly, towing a somewhat inebriated volunteer, who had been doing her own bit of first-footing. I travelled to hospital with my neighbour breathing fumes all over me. It was deathly quiet as my tipsy friend and I made our way to the maternity ward. The silence didn't last long, as my friend began to wonder, aloud, where the nurse was. When the nurse arrived she found two giggling women, both wearing swagger coats, so that it was difficult to tell which was the expectant mother. My friend was dispatched homewards and I settled down to producing a New Year's Day baby.

James Scott Robertson entered the world at ten to ten that morning, deprived of the status of first baby in Arbroath of 1954 by half an hour. Jimmy weighed in at nine pounds two ounces, and he had red hair, taking after the Petries, half of whom were dark and half red-headed.

I stayed in hospital for about ten days, during which time my father got some time off. Sheila came with my mother to meet me. She remained silent when she saw her wee brother but announced, "Well, Mum, you certainly have slimmed since you went in there." When I said Jimmy wasn't to get a bottle, Sheila became worried. I told her not to worry, I'd let her see how he was to be fed when he woke up. My mother was scandalised! She needn't have worried, after watching solemnly Sheila announced "Is that what those are for? I've often wondered!" and my mother saw the funny side of it.

Jean married a couple of months later to a quiet young man, Eric Nathan. Sheila was a flower girl. That excitement over, I tried to settle down, but didn't feel at all well. Jimmy was a poor sleeper and I can see now that I was suffering from post-natal depression, aggravated by lack of sleep. For some months I suffered in silence, feeling unable to either go out or stay in alone. One day I cried out for help to a young neighbour and she, good soul, helped me in every way she could despite being the mother of five, one of whom had spina bifida. With Amy's help I lived through that illness. It turned out to be a blessing in disguise, as it was the beginning of a friendship that has withstood the test of time.

Thanks to our new Queen Elizabeth, Robby and I were not separated for as long as we first thought. As it turned out *H.M.S. Saintes* was chosen as escort from Malta back to Britain on the last leg of the Queen's journey after a tour of the Commonwealth. A neighbour invited me to watch the news on television as the *Britannia* and escort steamed up the English Channel. Sheila and I watched intently, but we couldn't pick out Robby's ship.

All the time Robby was away I had tried to keep his image clear in Sheila's mind by means of a big photograph in her bedroom, which she kissed goodnight at bedtime. So it was that when Robby returned, Sheila greeted him with great joy and proudly introduced him to her wee brother. Jimmy was a cherubic baby by day, so Robby soon fell for his wide smile and acted the proud father for the rest of his leave.

Soon after Sheila's new school was completed, just along the road, good news arrived. Robby was drafted to, of all places, Arbroath, to be an instructor there at *H.M.S. Condor*. Nothing is ever perfect, Robby had to put up with Jimmy's reluctance to sleep for more than an hour at a time. During his time at *Condor*, too, both Sheila and Jimmy took measles, chicken pox and other tiresome childhood ailments which involved a lot of sitting up at night. I was grateful for not having to do that on my own.

One year was all Robby had with us before he was sent back to sea. A lot of events took place in that year. Jean and Eric settled in a wee tenement not a stone's throw from Wee Granny's where Jean could keep an eye on that apparently indestructible old lady. My mother and father, after a long search, found a wee flat for their retirement. At that time the N.L.B. made no provision towards assisting keepers to find accommodation. The flat in Campbeltown was badly in need of repair and decoration, but they considered themselves fortunate in being able to rent it. Eventually the dingy flat took on a warmer cheerier aspect with several coats of paint. From then on my mother spent a lot of time there, putting the finishing touches to it and enjoying going to the shops without regard to the weather and the timetable of the lighthouse boatmen. I suspect my father had mixed feelings, the lighthouse service had been his whole life through childhood and marriage.

We had one last nostalgic holiday at Devaar that summer. It was to be Jimmy's first and last at a lighthouse station. I felt that the wee lad was missing out on something the rest of us could share. It wouldn't bother him. It did bother me.

Later that year, my mother spent more and more time in the flat. The bedroom had a dormer window, through which the beam from the lighthouse flashed every few seconds as the lens revolved. This gave my mother a comfortable feeling of nearness to my father as she settled down to sleep. One night she became aware that the beam of light was no longer flashing, it shone steadily on the patch of wallpaper. There could be only one reason. The keeper on duty hadn't wound up the mechanism that kept the light turning. He must have fallen asleep, the most heinous crime in the lighthouse book. It wasn't my father's watch, but as principal keeper he was responsible. My mother shoved on her slippers, threw a coat over her nightie and made her way to the nearest phone box to alert him. My father swore, banged down the 'phone and rushed off to sort it out. By the time she reached her bedroom the light was once more serenely turning and silently flashing. My father, of course, should have reported it, but for once in his life he chose to remain silent. The keeper on duty would have been sacked and my father, close to retirement, could have lost his pension. From that night on, my mother's only wish was for the time to pass quickly until my father would be forever free of responsibility.

It was on 17th December, our ninth wedding anniversary, that my father extinguished the light for the last time, dressed himself in civilian clothes and turned his back on the old life to take up residence in Campbeltown. For many years he had signed letters to head office "Your obedient servant," and that is exactly what he had been for thirty-four years. He deserved a long and happy retirement. My mother deserved a medal, having served uncomplainingly in spite of all the hardships and loneliness she had to put up with.

Robby was drafted again. This time to the Far East, his ship, the cruiser *H.M.S. Newfoundland*, was already out in the China Seas and would be gone for anything up to two years. As luck would have it, he had been gone a little over a year when it was announced that the navy was to cut back on personnel. Those who only had a year or two to serve were to be offered early retirement. Robby jumped at the chance. It was wonderful news. He was only forty-two and fit. Employment wasn't easy to find. After some time on the "Buroo," he was offered the seasonal job of helping deliver the heavy Christmas mail. In January, a 'flu epidemic gave him more work delivering mail . After the epidemic he was asked to stay on permanently. He was to stay there for eighteen years.

When Jimmy was five and Sheila eleven we exchanged our two bedroomed house for one a mere hundred yards away with three bedrooms. I was content. I knew that here at last I was going to put down roots. Not so my mother and father. They were so used to flitting that after a few years in Campbeltown my mother became restless. She wanted to be nearer her family. They moved to Shettleston and eventually to the flat opposite Jean's at "Ten-nine-eight." It gave us great pleasure and peace of mind to know that my mother had her wish granted. She couldn't have been nearer her family than that. She died in the winter of 1969, when she was seventy-five. My father remarried and moved to Dundee and lived until his ninetieth year. That leaves Robby and me, "the old folks."

In my middle forties I went back to school as a mature student and achieved at last one of my childhood ambitions. I became a teacher. I thoroughly enjoyed working with the little ones for thirteen years before I retired. Robby had retired a few years earlier. Now we are enjoying a quiet life in which we can do what we want, and come and go as we please.

I still hanker after the lighthouse days, and have several times revisited old haunts: Earraid, the Rhinns of Islay, and the Isle of Man. They say you should never go back, but I'm glad I took Robby and my family to see where I spent my childhood. It was sad, of course, almost like seeing ghosts. What saddens me even more is the knowledge that lighthouse-keeping is almost a thing of the past, with automation taking the place of the good men who faithfully watched over shipping and kept an eye open for folk in distress. That, of course, is my romantic view, rose-coloured by happy memories. My mother would probably have thought it a good thing that lighthouse wives no longer have to live in isolation as she did at all my father's stations, or part from their children at an early age.

I often think of the hardships my mother so uncomplainingly put up with: black-leading the big kitchen range, scrubbing the washing on an old scrubbing board and washing dishes in a basin of water, which then had to be poured into one of the ubiquitous buckets. I live in centrally heated double-glazed comfort now. I come down my fully carpeted stairs on cold winter mornings knowing my kitchen will be warm. I press a few switches and the room becomes filled with light, the kettle sings until it boils and switches itself off, and my little transistor radio soothes me with soft music. I only have to turn a tap to get piping hot water, and the toast makes itself while I stuff my washing into an automatic machine. It's a wonderful world in spite of all its hazards, and I appreciate having had the privilege of knowing both the old and the new.